CLASSICS ILLUSTRATED DICTIONARY

CLASSICS ILLUSTRATED DICTIONARY

by Dr J. W. FUCHS

Translated from the Dutch by
Livia Visser-Fuchs

General English editing and
adaptations by
Kathleen Bolton,
M.A., M.Litt.(Cantab)

KAYE & WARD - LONDON
in association with
HICKS SMITH & SONS,
Australia and New Zealand

First published in Great Britain by
Kaye & Ward Ltd 1974

ISBN 0 7182 0943 5

All enquiries and requests relevant to this title should
be sent to the publisher, Kaye & Ward Ltd, 21 New Street,
London EC2M 4NT, and not to the printer.

Printed Photolitho in England by Ebenezer Baylis & Sons Ltd
The Trinity Press - Worcester - London

Preface to the English Edition

Classics Illustrated Dictionary is a translation of the Dutch *Klassiek Vademecum*, now in its fifth edition in Holland.

To some extent the text has been emended and adapted to make it more relevant for English-speaking readers; for example, some entries about Roman Britain have been included and strictly Dutch references removed. However, the book is intended for general rather than specific use, and a short list of recommended books for further reading has been included. Translations of Greek and Roman names are those most currently used, and the stress given on the entries indicates the English pronunciation.

Cross-referencing of the entries is denoted by the symbol °, and the Dutch symbols used in the 'family trees' have also been retained (∞ = married; † = died).

Suggested book-list for further reading and reference

Oxford Classical Dictionary (2nd ed.) (Clarendon Press)
A History of Greece, J. B. Bury (Macmillan)
A History of Rome, M. Cary (Macmillan)
Greek and Roman Architecture, D. S. Robertson (Cambridge University Press)
Greek and Roman Sculpture, A. W. Lawrence (Jonathan Cape)
An Introduction to Ancient Philosophy, A. H. Armstrong (Methuen)
Greek Painted Pottery (2nd ed.), R. M. Cook (Methuen)
Prehistoric Greece, F. H. Stubbings (Rupert Hart-Davis)
Greek Myths, R. Graves (Cassell)
Handbook of Greek Literature, H. J. Rose (Methuen)
Handbook of Latin Literature, H. J. Rose (Methuen)
Roman Britain (rev. ed.), R. G. Collingwood (Oxford University Press)

A

Ábacus. **1.** The uppermost member of a °capital beneath the °architrave; °Doric order. **2.** Counting-board. The photograph shows a bronze pocket abacus from the Bibliothèque Nationale, Paris; pegs moving in the slots indicated the required number. From left to right the slots were used for calculating (at the minimum): 1,000,000; 100,000; 10,000; 1,000; 100; 10; 1; $\frac{1}{12}$; on the extreme right the values were for $\frac{1}{24}$; $\frac{1}{36}$; $\frac{1}{48}$. In the drawing the calculation is for $5,367,408\frac{5}{8}$. (The slots at the top held the pegs with a value of five times that of the pegs at the bottom); °Counting systems; °ill. 1.

Ábdera (Ἄβδηρα,-ων). Greek city on the Thracian coast, east of the river Nestos, member of the °Delan Confederacy, birthplace of °Democritus and °Protagoras; the stupidity of its inhabitants was proverbial.

Absýrtos. °Apsyrtus (Ἄψυρτος).

'Ab urbe cóndita'. A Roman system of dating, 'from the foundation of the city'. °Livy 2.

Abu Símbel. Site of cliff-temple built by °Ramses II on the western bank of the Nile in Upper Egypt. At the entrance are four statues of the Pharaoh, 20m high.

Abýdos (Ἄβυδος). **1.** City of Mysia on the °Hellespont, the home of °Leander. °Xerxes built his bridge there (480 BC); °Alcibiades, °Hero. **2.** Egyptian necropolis of the Middle Kingdom where an important inscription showing lists of kings was discovered.

Acádemy (Ἀκαδήμεια). A park to the north-west of Athens, where °Plato held his lectures. He bequeathed the property to his successors, whence the name of his philosophical school. Plato's successors of the first period, the Old Academy, were chiefly interested in ethics: Speusippus, Plato's nephew (347-339 BC) and Xenocrates (339-314 BC). In the second period the tendency was towards °Scepticism (Arcesilaus of Pitane, 315-240 BC) and the third, the New Academy, was founded by Carneades of Cyrene (214-124), who propounded the theory of probability, and taught in Rome.

acánthus (ἄκανθος). The elaborate, deeply-serrated leaf ornament used on °Corinthian °capitals, based on the foliage of the Mediterranean plant (Acanthus spinosa).

Acástus (Ἄκαστος). Son of °Pelias, took part in the °Calydonian hunt and the expedition of the °Argonauts.

acatalectic. Non °catalectic; is a line of poetry that is complete in its syllables.

Acca Lárentia. °Faustulus.

accents. Greek accents were first used by °Aristophanes of Byzantium early in the 2nd century BC, to preserve the correct pronunciation which was in danger of being corrupted by the expansion of the Greek language.

Áccius, *L. Accius* (170-c. 86 BC), Latin poet. Besides 'fabulae °praetextatae', he wrote many tragedies which were adapted from the Greek with great freedom and realism, also other works.

Achaéa (Ἀχαία). **1.** Region of the northern coast of the Peloponnese. **2.** After 146 BC the whole of Greece, as a Roman province, was called 'Achaea'. **3.** *Achaéa Phthiótis* region of south-eastern Thessaly.

Achaéans (Ἀχαιοί). **1.** In °Homer, the name, used together with Danáans (Δαναοί), for the Greeks generally. **2.** A tribe which possibly invaded Greece from Central Europe (?) 1000 BC. **3.** The inhabitants of °Achaéa.

1

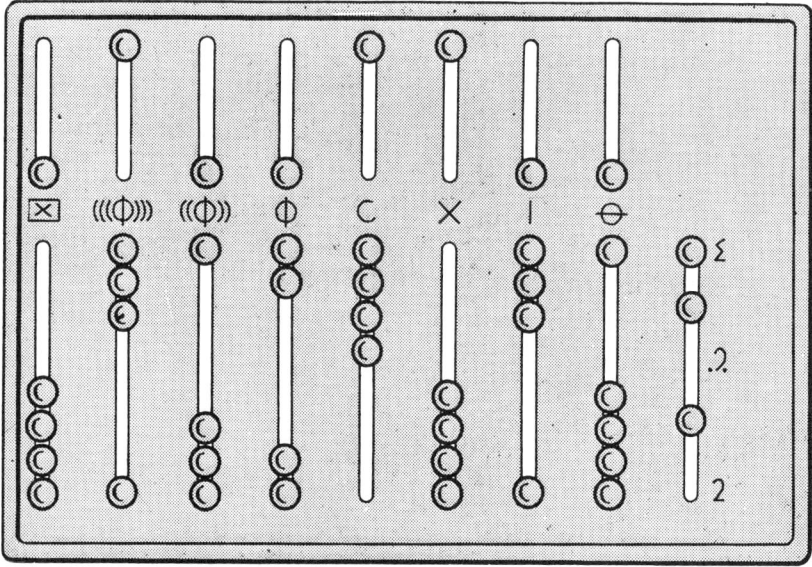

1. An °abacus.

Achaéan League or **Confederacy**. The league of twelve cities under democratic rule in Achaéa. It disintegrated in the time of °Alexander the Great, but in 280 BC ten cities united again, under the leadership of °Aratus of Sicyon, °Philopoemen and others. The league gained great influence but it was dissolved by the Romans in 146 BC.

Achaémenids. First royal house of Persia. The first king who ruled all Persia was °Cyrus, the last °Darius III.

Acheloüs (᾿Αχελῷος). River dividing Aetolia from Acarnania (the modern Astropótamos); also the god of the river who was lord over all rivers, and fought with °Heracles for °Deïaneira, but was defeated (Ovid *Met*. 9, 1-97).

Acheron (᾿Αχέρων). One of the rivers of the Underworld, also said to be a lake.

Achílles (᾿Αχιλλεύς). Son of °Peleus and °Thetis, grandson of °Aeacus (°Aeácides), the bravest of the Greek heroes at Troy. According to later legend he was invulnerable, except in his heel by which his mother held him when she plunged him into the °Styx as an infant; °Aeácidae, °Deïdameia, °Lycomedes, °Neoptolemus; °Patroclus.

Achílles Tátius (end of the 3rd cent. AD). Writer of a novel called *The adventures of Leucippe and Cleitophon*.

Acílius, *C. Acílius*. °Annalist who wrote a history of Rome (c. 155 BC).

Ácis (῎Ακις). A shepherd of Sicily who was loved by °Galatea and killed by his rival Polyphemus (Ovid. *Met*. 13, 750-897).

Acóntius (᾿Ακόντιος), of Keos, fell in love with Cydippe. When she was in the temple of °Athena on Delos, he dropped a golden apple with the inscription: 'I swear to marry Acontius'. She picked it up, read the words aloud and thus had sworn the oath. °reading; (Ovid *Her*. 20 and 21).

Acrísius (᾿Ακρίσιος). King of Argos, father of °Danaë.

Acrópolis (᾿ακρόπολις), Citadel of Athens. In general, a fortress built on high ground to protect a city. The Acropolis of Athens is the most famous.

Its entrance was at the western end (°Propylaea) and on it (among other buildings) were the °Parthenon and the °Erechtheum with its °Caryatids; °ill. 2; °Capitol.

acrotérion (᾿ακρωτήριον). Ornament placed on top of a °stele and on the apex or lower angles of a °pediment; °Doric order.

Actaéon (᾿Ακταίων). Grandson of °Cadmus, who saw °Artemis bathing. She changed him into a stag and he was torn to pieces by his own hunting dogs (Ovid *Met*. 3, 131-252).

Áctium (῎Ακτιον). Promontory and town on the coast of Acarnania, where the fleets of °Antony and °Cleopatra were defeated by °Octavian (31 BC).

áctus. °weights and measures 2a.

Acusiláüs (᾿Ακουσίλαος). °Logographer (end of the 6th cent. BC). He wrote *Genealogies*, of which fragments are extant.

Ádherbal. Son of Micipsa, the king of Numidia; with his brother Hiempsal, he was killed by °Jugurtha (Sall. *Jug*. 26).

Adméte (᾿Αδμήτη). °Hippolyta.

Admétus (῎Αδμητος). **1**. King of Pherae in Thessaly, husband of °Alcestis. He took part in the °Calydonian hunt and the expedition of the °Argonauts. **2**. King of the Molossians, to whom °Themistocles fled for protection.

adnominátio. °Paronomasia.

Adónic verse. In metre a °dactyl followed by a °trochee: (‿ ∨ ∨ ‿ ∨) or a °spondee; °Sapphic verse.

Adónis (῎Αδωνις). A beautiful youth, loved by °Aphrodite. He was killed by a wild boar sent by °Ares (Ovid *Met*. 10, 288-739).

Adrástus (῎Αδραστος). Legendary king of Argos, father-in-law of °Polyneices. He led the army of the °'Seven against Thebes', to put Polyneices on the throne, but he was the only survivor. In his old age he led a second expedition with the °Epigoni. He captured Thebes but died on his way home, after his son's death.

ádyton. Innermost sanctuary of a temple,

4

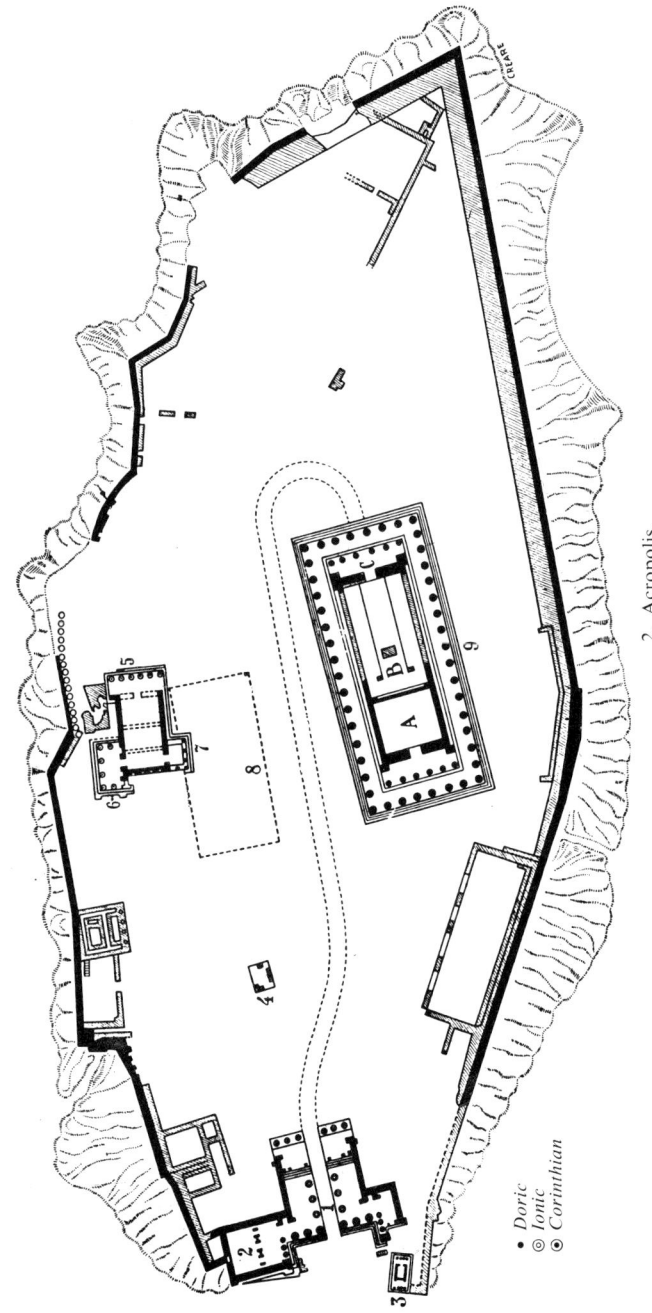

2. Acropolis.

1 Propylaea
2 pinacotheca
3 temple of Nike
4 site of the statue of Athena ° Promachos
5, 6, 7 Erechtheum
6 cella of Poseidon-Erechtheus
7 Caryatids
8 foundations of the old temple of Athena Polias
9 Parthenon (A: opisthodomos; B: statue of Athena Parthenos; C: pronaos).

• Doric
◎ Ionic
◉ Corinthian

behind the °cella, only to be entered by the priests.

Aeácidae

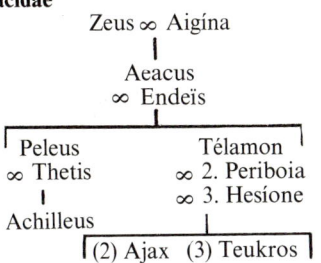

Zeus ∞ Aigína
|
Aeacus
∞ Endeïs
|

Peleus	Télamon
∞ Thetis	∞ 2. Periboia
|	∞ 3. Hesíone
Achilleus	
	(2) Ajax (3) Teukros

Aeácides (᾿Αιακίδης). Descendant of °Aeacus: °Achilles; °Peleus; °Pyrrhus, etc. °Aeácidae p. 3.

Aéacus (᾿Αιακός). Legendary king of the Myrmidons in °Aegina, father of °Peleus. After his death he became one of the three judges in the Underworld; °Minos; °Rhadamanthus; °Aeácidae p. 3.

aédes Antoníni et Faustínae. A temple next to the °basilica Aemilia, built by °Antoninus Pius in honour of °Faustina, 141 AD; °plan p. 81.

aédes Castóris. A temple in the forum, built to commemorate the help of the °Dioscuri in the battle of Lake Regillus, near Tusculum (490 BC), where the Romans defeated the Latins. It was often used as an assembly hall by the Senate; °plan p. 81.

aédes Concórdiae. °Concordia.

aédes Dívi Iúlii. A temple built by °Augustus in 29 BC in front of the °regia on the spot where °Caesar's body had been cremated; °plan p. 81.

aédes Satúrni. A temple on the western side of the forum, where the °aerarium was kept; °plan p. 81.

aédes Vespasiáni. A temple next to that of °Concordia, built in 80 AD in honour of °Vespasian and °Titus; °plan p. 165.

aédilis. **1.** *aédilis plébis.* After the °secessio plebis in 494 BC, the aediles, two in number, were in charge of the temple of Ceres, where they had their office and kept the archives of the plebeians; they assisted the °consuls and °tribuni plebis and supervised the police,

the markets, the corn-supply and the public games. **2.** *aédilis curúlis.* In 367 two 'aediles curules', who could be patricians, were added. Their tasks were the same as those of the plebeian aediles and they were chosen in the °comitia tributa.

Aeétes (Αἰήτης). King of Colchis, father of °Medea. By murdering °Phrixus he obtained the °Golden Fleece and had it guarded by a venomous dragon; °Jason.

Aegaéon (᾿Αιγαίων). °Centimani.

Aegéan civilisation. The period of civilisation of Greece, Crete and the islands in the Aegean between c. 3000 and 1000 BC. The °Minoan, the °Cycladic and the °Helladic civilisations come under this heading.

Aegátes Insulae. The islands west of Sicily, where the Romans defeated the fleet of the Carthaginians and ended the first °Punic War, 241 BC.

Aégeus (Αἰγεύς). King of Athens. When his son °Theseus, returning from Crete after killing the °Minotaur, forgot to hoist white sails to signal his success as he had promised, Aegeus threw himself into the sea (hence the name 'Aegéan'); °Androgeos.

Aegína (Αἰγίνα). **1.** Mother of °Aéacus; °Aeácidae p. 3. **2.** Island between Attica and Argolis, inhabited, according to legend, by the °Myrmidons. Excavations of an archaic temple (probably of °Athena, perhaps of °Aphaea) started in 1810. The war of °Heracles and Telamon against Troy was depicted (probably in the west pediment). Both pediments were filled with sculpture, °Athena being the central figure in both; °ills. 3, 4. After a period of commercial prosperity, rivalling that of Athens, Aegina did not play a prominent part in Greek history. In 1811, a joint expedition took eleven days to excavate the ruins. They found seventeen statues and many fragments. These were sold and today, partially restored by Thorwaldsen, they constitute the core of the 'Antikensammlung' in Munich.

aégis (αἰγίς). The shield of Zeus,

3. Hypothetical reconstruction of the west side of the temple in °Aegina. The °pediment shows battle scenes and in the middle °Athena (°aegis). Below the pediment the metopes, triglyphs and the °Doric capitals.

4. °Heracles from the west pediment of the Aegina temple (79 cm. high); left hand, left arm, nose and part of the °chiton have been restored.

which caused thunderstorms when it was shaken. It was represented as a goat-skin, thrown over the shoulders and covering the breast. The goddess °Athena often carried it; ill. 5.

5. Statue of °Athena from the west pediment of the temple of °Aègina. She wears the stylized °aegis (1.68 m. high).

Aegísthus (Αἴγισθος). Son of °Thyestes. With °Clytaemnestra's help, he killed his nephew °Agamemnon, on the latter's return from Troy. He was killed by °Orestes (°Eur. 'Electra'); °Tantalidae p. 182.

Aegospótami (Αἰγὸς ποταμοί). River and town on the east coast of the Thracian Chersonese, where °Lysander defeated the fleet of Athens, 405 BC.

Aegýptus (Αἴγυπτος). Son of °Belus, brother of °Danaus; °Danaids.

Aélia Capitolína. The name the emperor °Hadrian gave to Jerusalem.

Aélia Paetína. Second wife of the emperor °Claudius, mother of °Antonia; °Julio-Claudian dynasty p. 101.

Aelián, *Claudius Aeliánus* (end of the 2nd cent. AD). Greek °sophist, writer of (Ποικίλη Ἱστορία) *Poikile Historia* (a collection of anecdotes) and a textbook on zoology.

Aélius. 1. *Aelius Aristeides.* Rhetorician (129-189 AD), pupil of °Herodes Atticus. Two textbooks and fifty-five speeches are extant. His speech on the earthquake at Smyrna persuaded the emperor °Marcus Aurelius to rebuild the city. **2.** °Hadrian. **3.** °Paetus. **4.** Aelius Túbero, °Annalists.

basilíca Aemília. °basilica.

via Aemília. °Lepidus 1.

Aemília Lépida. Daughter of M. Aemílius °Lépidus, consul 6 AD, who restored the °basilica Aemilia in 22 AD. She was married to °Drusus, son of °Germanicus; °Julio-Claudian dynasty °Lepidi pp. 101-103.

Aemílius. 1. Lepidus. **2.** *L. Aemílius Paúlus,* consul 219 and 216, subjugated the Illyrian coast (219). He was defeated and killed by Hannibal at °Cannae (216). His colleague °Varro began battle against his advice. **3.** *L. Aemílius Paúlus Macedónicus,* Roman general and statesman; consul for the second time in 168 BC. He ended the third Macedonian War by defeating °Perseus at Pydna. He was the father of °Scipio 3. **4.** *L. Aemílius Paúlus,* husband of °Julia, grand-daughter of Augustus, consul 1 AD, died 13 or 14 AD; °Julio-Claudian dynasty p. 101.

Aenéas (Αἰνείας). Son of °Anchises and °Aphrodite (°Dardanidae p. 60), who fled from burning Troy with his father, his wife °Creüsa and his son °Ascanius (or °Iulus). His wanderings ended in Italy where he became the ancestor of the Roman people (Virg. *Aen.*).

Aenéas Sílvius. °Dardanidae p. 60.

Aenéid. °Aeneas. Epic poem of °Virgil.

Aeólia (Αἰολίη). The floating island of °Aeolus.

Aeólians (Αἰολεῖς). One of the tribes of Greece. They lived in Boeotia, Thessaly and the northern part of western Asia Minor.

Aeólus (Αἴολος). Ruler of winds and

storms, appointed by °Zeus. He had the power to banish winds or keep them at home.

Aéqui. Tribe of Central Italy. The Aequi and the Volsci were at war with Rome for a long time; in 304 BC they were finally subjugated and Romanized.

aerárium. 1. The treasury of the Roman people, kept by the °*quaestores urbani* in the temple of °Saturn. **2.** *aerarium sanctius.* The reserve treasury.

Aésacus (Αἴσακος). Son of °Priam. Mourning the death of his beloved Hesperia, he threw himself into the sea and was changed into a bird by °Thetis (Ovid *Met.* 11, 749-795).

Aéschines (Αἰσχίνης). Athenian orator (390-314 BC), leader of the Macedonian party, adversary of °Demosthenes. Three of his speeches are extant.

Aéschylus (Αἰσχύλος). Oldest and greatest of the three Athenian tragic poets, 525-456 BC. Seven of his tragedies are extant: 1. *Prometheus Bound,* in which °Prometheus was punished for his theft of the fire from heaven but, in spite of cruel torture, would not ask for Zeus' mercy. 2. *Seven against Thebes,* the war between °Eteocles and °Polyneices. 3.-5. *Oresteía,* a trilogy consisting of 3. *Agamemnon;* 4. *Choéphoroi* (Libation Bearers), the murder of °Clytaemnestra by °Orestes and °Electra; 5. *Euménides* (Furies) in which Orestes was rescued from persecution by the °Erinyes. 6. *Persians,* the defeat of °Xerxes at °Salamis; 7. *Suppliant Women,* the flight of the daughters of Danaus (°Danaids) to Argos.

Aesculápius. °Asclepius.

Aéson (Αἴσων). Father of °Jason.

Aésop (Αἴσωπος). According to tradition, a slave in Samos in the 6th cent. BC. The body of native fable is generally ascribed to him ; °Phaedrus.

Aethéria. °Peregrinátio Aethériae.

Aétna. An anonymous poem (written before 79 AD) on volcanic activity, handed down among the works of °Virgil.

Africánus. °Scipio.

Agamémnon ('Αγαμέμνων). Son of °Atreus, king of °Mycenae, leader of the Greek army against Troy. On his return from the war, he was murdered by °Aegisthus and °Clytaemnestra; °Aeschylus; °Briseïs; °Iphigeneia; °Tantalidae p. 182.

Agáthocles ('Αγαθοκγῆς). °Tyrant of Syracuse 317-289 BC. He brought all Sicily under his power and after his defeat at Himera by the Carthaginians, carried the war into Africa. His son-in-law was °Pyrrhus of Epirus.

Ágathon ('Αγάθων). Tragic poet, friend of °Plato. His house was the scene of °Plato's *Symposium.*

Agáve ('Αγαυή). Mother of °Pentheus and daughter of °Cadmus and Harmonia.

Agénor ('Αγήνωρ). Legendary king of Phoenicia, father of °Cadmus and °Europa.

ager públicus. Land confiscated from Italian states conquered by Rome. Part of it was leased by the °censor. Its produce was set apart for the cult of the gods. Part of it was common pasture, for which a grazing fee (*scriptura*) was paid. A large part, for which a tax (*vectigal*) was paid, was intended for occupation (*occupatio*) by anyone who was able to cultivate it (*possessores*).

Agesiläüs ('Αγησίλαος). King of Sparta (401-360 BC), who fought the Persians in Asia Minor near the °Pactolus (395). When Athens, Thebes and Corinth after Persian scheming declared war with Sparta (the °Corinthian War), Agesilaus was recalled. He defeated them at °Coronea (394). In 369 and 362, he forced the Thebans to retreat but was defeated near °Mantinea (362). He died in 358.

Ágiads. The senior of the two royal houses of Sparta, to which °Cleomenes I, °Cleomenes III, °Leonidas and °Pausanias belonged; °Eurypontids.

Ágis ('Αγις). **1.** *Agis II*, king of Sparta (427-399 BC); °Mantinea. **2.** *Agis III*, king of Sparta (338-330), attempted to expel the Macedonians from the Peloponnese. **3.** *Agis IV*, king of Sparta (244-240), made an attempt at social reform at Sparta but without success; °Lycurgus.

Agláïa (Ἀγλαΐα). One of the three °Graces.

ágora. The Greek market-place, an open space either in the middle of the city or near the harbour, surrounded by public buildings and temples; °Athens.

Agram—Zagreb. In the museum of this town five bandages of a mummy (found 1892) are preserved, on which the longest known °Etruscan text (c. 1500 words) is written.

Agrícola. *Cn. Iulius Agrícola.* A governor of °Britain (76 AD), outstanding in his achievements. He was recalled by the emperor °Domitian in 85. His son-in-law °Tacitus wrote his biography.

Agríppa. °Menénius; °Vipsánius; °*Heródes Agríppa*, °*Julius Agríppa I, II*; °Julius 4.

Agrippína. **1.** *Vipsánia Agrippína*, daughter of M. °Vipsánius Agríppa, wife of °Tiberius, who was forced to divorce her to marry °Julia. She re-married C. °Asínius Gallus Salonínus; °Julio-Claudian dynasty p. 101. **2.** *Vipsánia Agrippína* (the Elder), (14 BC-33 AD), daughter of M.V. Agríppa and Julia, wife of °Germanicus. She died in exile in Pandatéria; °Julio-Claudian dynasty p. 101. **3.** *Julia Agrippína* (the Younger), daughter of Germanicus and °Agrippína **2.**, born 15 AD. Married, first (28 AD) to Cn. °Domitius Ahenobarbus, secondly (c. 44 AD) to C. Sallústius Passiénus °Crispus, whom she murdered, and thirdly 49 AD to the Emperor °Claudius; her death was attributed to her son, °Nero. °Domitii p. 68; °Julio-Claudian dynasty p. 101.

Ájax (Αἴας). **1.** Legendary son of °Telamon and Periboea, king of Salamis, the bravest of all the Greeks (after °Achilles) in the °Trojan War. When after the death of Achilles, the latter's arms were given to °Odysseus, Ájax was so enraged that he lost his reason and killed himself (Ovid *Met.* 13, 1-383; Soph. *Ájax*); °Aeacidae p. 4. **2.** Son of Oïleus, one of the Greek warriors at Troy.

Akkad. First Semitic empire in Mesopotamia (c. 2350-2150 BC), founded by °Sargon; °Sumer.

ála. Two alcoves behind the °atrium (later on either side of it) were called *alae*. Their use is not known.

alabástron (ἀλάβαστρον). Small perfume jar without handles; °ill. 6.

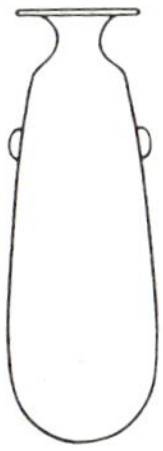

6. Alabastron.

Álba Longa. The town traditionally founded by °Ascanius, to the south-east of Rome. It was destroyed by the Romans under °Tullus Hostilius (c. 600 BC); °Horatii.

Álbius. °Tibullus.

Álbula. Old name for the Tiber, on which °Rome was situated.

Alcaíc stanza,

⏓ –́ ⏑ –́ ⏓ –́ ⏑ ⏑ –́ ⏑ ⏓
⏓ –́ ⏑ –́ ⏓ –́ ⏑ ⏑ –́ ⏑ ⏓
⏓ –́ ⏑ –́ ⏓ –́ ⏑ –́ ⏓
–́ ⏑ ⏑ –́ ⏑ ⏑ –́ ⏑ –́ ⏑.

Used by °Alcaeus and °Horace.

Alcaéus (Ἀλκαῖος). **1.** Legendary father of °Amphitryon and son of °Perseus. **2.** Lyric poet from Mitylene in Lesbos (c. 600 BC). Only fragments of his work survive.

Alcéstis (Ἄλκηστις). Daughter of °Pelias, married to °Admetus. She was the only one willing to die instead of her husband (°Euripides' 'Alcestis').

Alcibíades (Ἀλκιβιάδης). Nephew of °Pericles, Athenian nobleman and histrionic politician (c. 450-404 BC). He suggested the Sicilian expedition in the Peloponnesian War (415 BC, °Nicias), but took little part in it. One night, shortly before the departure of the fleet, the °Herms in the streets of Athens were mutilated and Alcibiades was accused of sacrilege, and was condemned to death in his absence. At Sparta, he agitated against Athens, but his influence grew so great that king °Agis became jealous. He fled to Persia where he set °Tissaphernes against Sparta, returned home after the °oligarchy of the °Four Hundred, and defeated the Spartans at °Abydos (411) and °Cyzicus (410). Again, however, he fell into disgrace and fled to Persia, where he was murdered (404). He was brought up by °Pericles and was the pupil of °Socrates.

Alcídamas ('Αλκιδάμας). Orator and °sophis (4th cent. BC), pupil of °Gorgias.

Alcídes. Descendant of °Alcaeus (Heracles).

Alcínoüs ('Αλκίνοος). Legendary king of the Phaeacians, father of °Nausicaä, according to °Homer (°Odyssey).

Alcmaeónids. Noble family of Athens, opponents of °Peisistratus and exiled by him. With the support of °Delphi, they brought about the expulsion of °Hippias by °Cleisthenes (510 BC).

Álcman ('Αλκμάν). Choral poet of Sparta (c. 650 BC). Only fragments of his poems survive.

Alcména ('Αλκμήνη). Legendary wife of °Amphitryon and mother of °Heracles, who was the son of °Zeus.

Alcýone ('Αλκυόνη). **1.** Daughter of °Aeolus, married to Ceyx. When she heard that her husband had been shipwrecked, she threw herself into the sea and both were changed into halcyons (Ovid *Met.* 11, 410-748). **2.** °Pleiades.

Alexánder ('Αλέξανδρος). **1.** °Paris. **2.** *Alexander III, 'the Great'*, king of Macedon, born 356 BC (°Ephesus), son of °Philip, whom he succeeded in 336, and °Olympias. He was a pupil of °Aristotle from the age of thirteen. After subjugating Greece, he crossed the Hellespont in 334 and defeated the Persians near the °Granicus and at °Issus (333). He freed Syria and Egypt, where he visited the oracle of °Ammon, from the Persians. Returning to Persia, he was victorious at °Arbela and °Gaugamela. At last he reached India, but on the banks of the river °Hyphasis his troops forced him to turn back. He returned reluctantly and died from fever at Babylon (323). His empire disintegrated because he had no heir (°Diadochi) and died young. Though Alexander failed in his attempt to create one vast Greek empire embracing Asia, his conquests led to the period of civilisation which we call °Hellenistic; °ill. 7; °Bucephalus.

7. Alexander the Great shown with rams-horns on a stater of Lysimachus.

Alexánder Severus, *M. Aurélius Alexánder Sevérus* (290-235 AD). He was adopted by Elagabalus, whom he succeeded as emperor (222) under the guardianship of his mother, °Julia Mammaea, and the jurist °Ulpian. He was murdered in 235; °Sevéri p. 173.

Alexándria ('Αλεξανδρεία). Name of many cities founded by °Alexander the Great. Most famous is Alexandria in the Nile delta, the cultural centre of the known world at the time of the °Ptolemies; °Alexandrian library.

Alexandrian library. Contained some 700,000 books in the first century ‑BC. Famous librarians were: °Zenodotus (285 BC), °Eratosthenes (234 BC), Aristophanes of Byzantium (195 BC), °Aristarchus (180 BC); °Apollonius, °libraries.

Allécto (Ἀλλήκτω). One of the °Erinyes.

allegory. The presentation of a subject under the guise of another suggestively similar (in narrative or other form).

Állia. A stream flowing into the Tiber, near which the Romans were defeated by the Gauls, led by °Brennus (18th July ('dies Alliensis') 387 BC).

alliteration. The repetition of the same sound, usually the first letter of words: 'libera lingua loquemur ludis Liberalibus'.

alphabet. The Latin alphabet had 21 characters in °Cicero's day: A B C D E F G H I K L M N O P Q R S T V X. Under the empire Y and Z were added with a view to Greek loan words. V could be used both as a vowel [u] and as a consonant [v]. In order to distinguish between these the emperor °Claudius invented a new character for V: Ⅎ. Moreover he wanted to introduce Ɔ for 'ps' and Ⱶ for the sound midway between [u] and [i] (lubet, maxumus) and for Greek υ. His reforms did not meet with approval and fell into disuse after his death. An example of Roman script, °ill. 8.

The Greek alphabet taken from the Phoenicians consisted of 22 letters; A B Γ Δ E F Z H Θ I K Λ M (another s-sound, afterwards the same as Σ)N Ξ O Π M Ϙ Ρ Σ T. At a later date Y Φ X Ψ Ω

were added, F fell into disuse and Ϙ was only used as a numeral. An example of Greek script; °ill. 9.

Alphéüs (Ἀλφειός). River of ‑ Elis; °Arethusa.

Althaéa (Ἀλθαία). Mother of °Meleager.

Áltis (Ἄλτις). °Olympia.

Alyáttes. King of Lydia (c. 610-560 BC), fought against the Medes. When they were about to begin the battle of the Halys, there was an eclipse of the sun (28th May, 585 BC), which had been predicted by °Thales.

Amálthea (Ἀμάλθεια). The goat (or nymph), which suckled °Zeus in Crete. As a reward one of its horns became the Horn of Plenty ('cornu copiae'), symbol of wealth and abundance, often seen on Roman coins.

Amárna. Modern site of the city of °Amenhotep IV (= Akhenaten), on the east bank of the Nile. In 1887, a deposit of 337 clay tablets was found: the correspondence of Amenhotep III and Amenhotep IV in Babylonian cuneïform writing.

Amásis (Ἄμασις). King of Egypt, who (570-526 BC) encouraged Greek settlement and trade and brought prosperity to his country.

Amazons (Ἀμαζόνες). Daughters of °Ares. A legendary tribe of warlike women from Scythia (so named from their habit of cutting off the right breast, in order to use the bow more easily). They are represented wearing Oriental dress, armed with bow and arrows, °bipennis and °pelta, and often on horseback; °Hippolyta; °ill. 10.

Ambarvália. A rural festival of the

8. Roman script (pre-79 AD) found on a wall in °Pompeii. It reads: 'Quid pote tan. durum saxso aut. quid mollius unda dum tamen molli saxsa cauantur aqua', a careless rendering from a poem by Ovid.

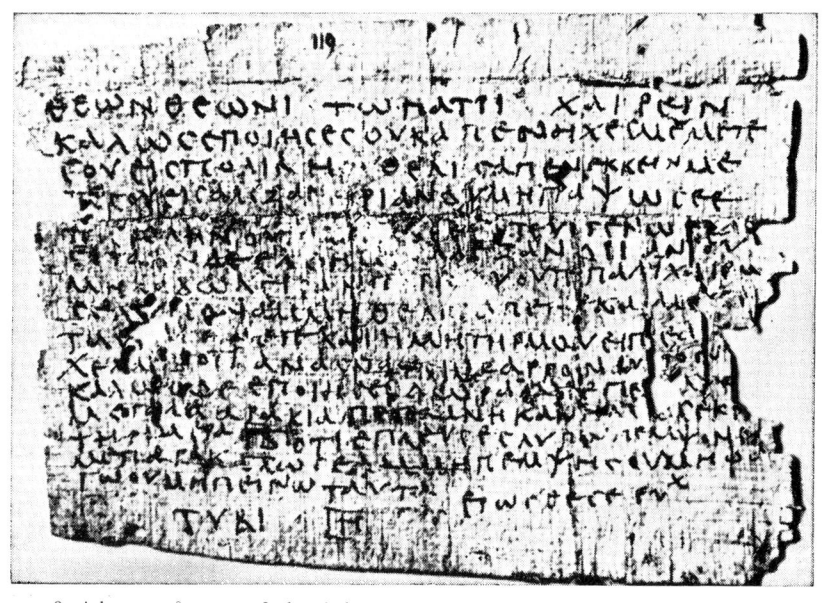

9. A letter on °papyrus, 2nd or 3rd cent. AD, written in Greek script, found in Egypt.

θεων θεωνι τω πατρι χαιρειν.
καλως εποιησες. ουκ απενηχες με μετε
σου εις πολιν. η ‹ου› θελις απενεκκειν με
‹τε› σου εις αλεξανδριαν ου μη γραψω σε ε-
5 πιστολην ουτε λαλω σε ουτε υιγενω σε.
ειτα αν δε ελθης εις αλεξανδριαν ου
μη λαβω χειραν παρα ‹σ›ου ουτε παλι χαιρω
σε λυπον. αμ μη θελης απενεκαι μ‹ε›
ταυτα γενετε. και η μητηρ μου ειπε αρ-
10 χελαω οτι αναστατοι με αρρον αυτον.
καλως δε εποιησες. δωρα μοι επεμψε‹ς›
μεγαλα αρακια. πεπλανηκαν ημιν εκε (?)
τη ημερα ΙΒ οτι επλευσες. λυρον πεμψον ει‹ς›
με παρακαλω σε. αμ μη πεμψης ου μη φα-
15 γω ου μη πεινω. ταυτα
                                    ερωσθε σε ευχ
         Τυβι ΙΗ

Romans in May, celebrated with a procession and offerings to °Ceres, led by the fratres °Arvales.

Ambíorix. Leader of the Eburónes in Gaul against °Caesar (55 BC), finally defeated after initial successes.

10. Greeks fighting Amazons (on a red-figured volute °krater, about 445 BC).

Ambrósius. Governor (c. 340-397 AD) of north Italy. In 379 he was elected bishop of Milan by the people, although he had not been baptized. He defended the orthodox religion against the doctrines of °Arius and left many writings.

Amenémhet III. King of Egypt (1842-1797 BC), who erected many important monuments; °labyrinth.

Amenhótep. 1. *Amenhótep III* (1410-1372 BC), king of Egypt (18th dynasty). He married a commoner, Tiyi. Under his rule Egypt reached the height of her power; °Memnon. **2.** *Amenhótep IV* (1372-1356), king of Egypt (18th dynasty), the son of Amenhótep III and Tiyi, well-known because of his introduction of the worship of Aton (the Sun). He changed his name to Akhenáten and made Akhetáten his capital (°Amarna).

Amenóphis = °Amenhotep.

Ammiánus Marcellínus. Officer in the army of the emperor °Constantius. He wrote a history of Rome from 96 to 378 AD; the last part from 353 to 378 is extant.

Ámmon (Amun). Egyptian god, identified with °Zeus by the Greeks. His greatest temple (with an oracle) was in the oasis of Siwah. Here °Alexander the Great had himself declared son of Zeus-Ammon, and was represented with the horns of a ram; °ill. 7.

Ammónius Sáccas. °Neo-Platonism.

Ámor (Cupído, "Ερως). The god of love, son of °Aphrodite. Represented as a small boy, armed with bow and arrows; *Amor and Psyche*, °Apuleius.

Amphiaráüs ('Αμφιάραος). Son of Oicles, hero and soothsayer from Argos. He took part in the °Calydonian Hunt and the expedition of the °Argonauts. Foreseeing his own death, he would not march against Thebes with °Adrastus, but his wife °Eriphyle, bribed with the necklace of °Harmonia from °Polyneices, betrayed his hiding-place. In later times, he had an oracle at Oropus, where one could consult him in one's dreams.

ámphibrach. A metrical foot, ⌣ _ ⌣.

Amphíctyones ('Αμφικτύονες). The united tribes living around a sanctuary to protect it, e.g. °Delphi.

Ámphion ('Αμφίων). Son of °Zeus and °Antiope, twin-brother of Zethus and husband of °Niobe. He was a

13

11. The amphitheatre in Nîmes.

famous citharist; to the sound of his instrument the stones gathered of their own accord and formed the walls of Thebes; °cithara.

ámphitheatre. °theatre; °ill. 11.

Amphitríte (᾽Αμφιτρίτη). One of the °Nereids, wife of °Poseidon. Their son was °Triton.

Amphítryon (᾽Αμφιτρύων). Legendary son of °Alcaeus, king of °Tiryns, afterwards of Thebes, husband of °Alcmena. Zeus took the shape of Amphitryon and by Alcmena became the father of °Heracles (comedy by °Plautus).

ámphora (᾽αμφορεύς). **1.** Large vessel with two vertical handles, with variants; sometimes with neck off-set, called neck-amphora. It served as a container for wine and other supplies; °pelike; °Panathenaic amphora; °ill. 12. **2.** °weights and measures 2c.

Amúlius. Brother of °Numitor, the king of °Alba Longa; °Dardanidae p. 60.

Anábasis. °Arrian; °Xenophon.

anacolúthon. A change of construction in the course of a sentence.

Anácreon (᾽Ανακρέων). Lyric poet from Teos in Ionia. He lived at the courts of °Polycrates, the °tyrant of Samos, and of °Hipparchus of Athens.

Anacreóntea (᾽Ανακρεόντεια). Imitations of °Anacreon, written in later periods.

Anacreóntic metre. A metrical line: ⌣ ⌣ ‿ ⌣ ‿ ⌣ ‿ ‿.

ánapaest. A metrical foot ⌣ ⌣ ‿ (reversed °dactyl).

anáphora. Repitition of the same word at the beginning of successive clauses.

anástrophe. Inversion of the natural order of words or clauses.

Anaxágoras (᾽Αναξαγόρας). Ionian philosopher of Clazomenae (c. 500-428 BC), teacher of °Euripides and °Thucydides. He taught that mind (νοῦς) caused the dissolution (διάκρισις) of qualitatively distinct matter and the condensation (σύγκρισις) of similar matter. The condensation and dissolution were not perfect, hence everything contained particles of strange matter. In 430 he

12. Attic amphora early 5th cent. BC: probably Dionysus dining on °Olympus.

was banished for impiety (ἀσέβεια).

Anaxaréte (᾽Αναξαρέτη). °Iphis.

Anaximánder (᾽Αναξίμανδρος). Early philosopher of Miletus (610-c. 536 BC), pupil of °Thales. He lived at the court of °Polycrates of Samos. In his works he taught that the origin of all things was the Infinite (τὸ ἄπειρον). He is said to have invented the sun-dial.

Anaxímenes (᾽Αναξιμένης). Philosopher from Miletus (c. 585-525 BC), who held that everything originated from air, out of which by condensation (πύκνωσις) and rarefaction (μάνωσις, ἀραίωσις) all things came to be.

ánceps sýllaba. Syllable which may be either long or short in a certain line of verse.

Anchíses (᾽Αγχίσης). Father of °Aeneas. He boasted of °Aphrodite's love for him and Zeus punished him with paralysis; °Dardanidae p. 60.

ancíle. The sacred shield which, according to legend, fell from heaven in the reign of °Numa Pompilius. The fate of Rome was said to depend on its preservation, so Numa caused eleven others, exactly like it, to be forged and thus made theft impossible. The *ancilia* were guarded by the °Salii.

Áncus Március. Fourth king of Rome. He built the °pons sublicius and the port of °Ostia.

Andócides (᾽Ανδοκίδης). Born c. 440 BC at Athens, politician and orator. Three speeches of his have been preserved.

Ándria. °Terence.

Andrógeüs (᾽Ανδρόγεως). Son of °Minos and °Pasiphaë. Because he won all prizes at the first °Panathenaic Games, °Aegeus killed him; °Minos punished Aegeus by making him send seven girls and seven boys annually to Crete, as a sacrifice to the °Minotaur; °Theseus.

Andrómache (᾽Ανδρομάχη). Daughter of Eëtion, wife of °Hector. After the fall of Troy she became °Neoptolemus' slave; °Euripides.

Andrómeda (᾽Ανδρομέδα). Daughter of °Cepheus and Cassiopeia. Her mother boasted of being fairer than the °Nereids. °Poseidon punished her by sending a monster to devastate the land. When Cepheus could only save his country by offering to sacrifice Andromeda, he did so, but °Perseus killed the monster and married Andromeda (Ovid *Met.* 4, 663-803).

Annáles. 1. *annáles máximi* (*pontíficum*). Notes the °pontifex maximus made of important events. They have been lost. **2.** Title of an annalist's work; °Ennius; °Tacitus.

Ánnalists. The first Roman historians who, in imitation of the °*annales maximi*, recorded events year by year. The most important are: Q. °Fábius Píctor (c. 225 BC), L. °Cíncius Aliméntus (c. 210 BC), C. °Acílius (c. 155 BC), A. Postúmius Albínus (c. 150). They all wrote in Greek.

15

Ánnius. °Florus.

Antaéus (᾽Ανταῖος). Son of Poseidon and °Gaea, a giant who received new strength every time he came into contact with his mother the Earth. °Heracles lifted him and thus killed him.

Antálcidas (᾽Ανταλκίδας). Politician of Sparta, who made Artaxerxes promise to help the Spartans and who saw to it that the Athenians and their allies were forced to make peace (387 BC). By the terms of this peace the Greek cities remained autonomous and those in Asia Minor were abandoned to the Persians; °Corinthian War.

ántefix. °tiles; °pediment.

Anténor (᾽Αντήνωρ). **1.** Brother-in-law of °Priam, urged to send °Helen home. He was married to the priestess °Theano. **2.** Athenian sculptor (c. 540-500 BC), who made the statues of °Harmodius and Aristogeiton, which stood in the marketplace of Athens.

Anthestéria. °Dionysia.

Anthólogy, *Greek Anthology*, a collection of °epigrams, started by °Meleager (c. 100 BC). In 925 AD, Constantinus Cephalas composed the present *Palatine Anthology*, which was enlarged for the last time by Planudes in the 14th century.

Antígone (᾽Αντιγόνη). Daughter of °Oedipus. She accompanied her father when he was banished. After his death she returned to Thebes and buried her brother °Polyneices, though this had been forbidden by King °Creon. She was punished by being buried alive. °Haemon, her betrothed, died with her (°Sophocles).

Antígonus (᾽Αντίγονος). **1.** *Antígonus I Monophthálmus*, general of °Alexander the Great, °satrap of Mysia. After many wars against the other °Diadochi, he was killed near °Ipsus in 301 BC; °Demetrius. **2.** *Antígonus II Gónatas* (c. 320-239). King of Macedon, grandson of **1.**, son of °Demetrius Poliorcetes. **3.** *Antígonus III Doson* (c. 263-221), unlawfully called himself king of Macedon in 227.

Antílochus (᾽Αντίλοχος). The swift-footed son of °Nestor, killed by °Memnon.

Antínoüs (᾽Αντίνοος). **1.** One of °Penelope's suitors. **2.** The favourite of the emperor °Hadrian, who was drowned in the Nile. After his death Hadrian erected many statues in his honour.

Ántioch (᾽Αντιόχεια). Name of several cities. The best-known is the capital of Syria, founded by °Seleucus I (c. 300 BC).

Antíochus III (᾽Αντίοχος). King of Syria (223-187 BC), defeated by M. Acílius Glábrio at Thermopylae (191) and by L. Cornélius °Scípio in a naval battle. Finally, defeated near °Magnesia in 190, he had to sue for peace: the peace of Apamea (188); °Hannibal.

Antíope (᾽Αντιόπη). **1.** Mother of °Amphion and Zethus. **2.** An °Amazon, wife of °Theseus (= °Hippolyta).

Ántipas (᾽Αντίπας). °Herod.

Antípater (᾽Αντίπατρος). **1.** General (397-314 BC) of Philip of Macedon, regent of Greece and Macedon during the absence of °Alexander the Great on his campaigns, after whose death he was made ruler in 320. He died in 319 having appointed Polyperchon his successor. **2.** °Caelius.

Ántiphon (᾽Αντιφῶν). Athenian politician and orator (c. 480-411 BC), who composed speeches for others (°logographer). He was the instigator of the °oligarchic conspiracy of 411 and so, after the fall of the °Four Hundred, he was executed.

antispástus. A metrical foot: ⌣ _ _ ⌣.

Antísthenes (᾽Αντισθένης). Athenian philosopher (c. 444-c. 366 BC), pupil of °Socrates, founder of the °Cynic sect. He rejected state-cults and advocated abstention from pleasure and limitation of one's needs in order to find happiness through virtue; °Cynosarges.

Antístius. °Labeo.

antístrophe. °strophe.

Antónia. 1. Daughter of the emperor °Claudius and °Aelia Paetina, married in 41 AD to °Pompey and 47 AD to

Faustus Cornelius Sulla Felix. She had one son, who was killed by °Nero in 62. She, too, was murdered at Nero's command; °Julio-Claudian dynasty p. 101. **2.** *Antonia Maior*, daughter of °Antony and °Octavia, born 39 BC, married to L. Domitius Ahenobarbus. Her children were Domitia Lepida and Cn. Domitius, the father of Nero; °Domitii p. 68. Tacitus erroneously calls her the younger daughter of Antony. **3.** *Antonia Minor*, daughter of Antony and Octavia, born 36 BC, married to °Drusus, °Augustus' stepson (16 AD). She was famous for her beauty. Her children were Germanicus, Livilla and °Claudius; °Domitii p. 68; °Julio-Claudian dynasty p. 101.

Ántonine Wall. Turf-built fortification running for 59 km. between the Firths of Forth and Clyde with nineteen forts, built for °Antoninus Pius about 145 AD; °Britain.

antoniniánus. A coin introduced by the emperor °Caracalla and named after him. Its value was two °denarii; °ill. p. 164.

Antonínus Píus. *T. Aelius Hadriánus Antonínus Píus*, Roman emperor (138-161 AD), born 86, adopted son of °Hadrian. He was gentle and just; °Aurelii p. 31.

Antónius. **1.** *M. Antónius* (143-87 BC). Orator, supporter of °Sulla, one of the' principal figures in Cicero's 'de Oratore'. He was the grand-father of Mark Antony. **2.** *M. Antónius*. The °triumvir (°Antony, 83-30 BC), friend of °Caesar, enemy of °Cicero. Defeated near Mutina by °Hirtius and Pansa (43). Afterwards triumvir with °Octavian and °Lepidus. In 41 he went to Egypt, where he met °Cleopatra. His second wife was °Octavia but eventually there was a breach between him and Octavian. After °Actium he killed himself (30); °Domitii p. 68.

Antoníni (= Antonines). °Antoninus Pius, °Marcus Aurelius, °Commodus.

Antony. °Antonius 2.

Anúbis. Egyptian god, son of °Ra, represented as a jackal.

Anýtus (Ἄνυτος). Leader of the democratic party at Athens; the principal accuser of °Socrates.

Apélla. The assembly of the people at Sparta.

Apélles (Ἀπελλής). Painter (356-308 BC), whose work was admired by °Alexander the Great. No extant work.

Ápex. Head-dress of the °flamen; °acroterion; °ill. p. 164.

Aphaéa (Ἀφαία). °Aegina.

Aphrodíte (Ἀφροδίτη). Goddess of love and beauty, daughter of °Zeus and Dione, wife of °Hephaestus, beloved of °Ares and °Adonis. °Cupid, Himeros and Hymenaeus were her sons. She had sanctuaries in Cyprus, Cnidus, Cythera and in many coastal towns. Toilet-requisites and flowers, the dove, hare, dolphin, rose, poppy, myrtle and apple were sacred to her. The famous statue of Aphrodite, the so-called Venus de Milo, was found in the island of Melos in 1820; ill. 13.

Apícius. A gourmet at the time of °Augustus and °Tiberius. A book of recipes which bears his name was compiled in the third century AD.

Ápis. The sacred bull of the Egyptians. He had a temple at Memphis.

apócope (ἀποκοπή). The omission of a vowel or a syllable at the end of a word (*e.g.* 'hunce' becomes 'hunc').

Apóllo (Ἀπόλλων). Son of °Zeus and °Leto, twin-brother of °Artemis, born in Delos. He was patron of the arts and leader of the °Muses. His principal sanctuaries were at °Delphi and °Delos. His attributes were a bow and arrows, a quiver, a °cithara and a °tripod. The laurel and the palm-tree were sacred to him. Famous statues are the 'Apollo Sauroctonus' by °Praxiteles (now in the Vatican Museum), the Apollo Belvedére (°ill. 14), and the Apollo of Véii, discovered in 1916; °ill. 15.

Apollodórus (Ἀπολλόδωρος). **1.** *Apollodórus of Carystus*. New °Comedy poet (c. 300 BC), from whose plays the 'Hecyra' and the 'Phormio' of °Terence were adapted. **2.** *Apollodórus of Athens* (c. 180-109 BC), °Stoic and scholar.

13. Aphrodite from Melos.

14. Apollo Belvedere.

15. Apollo of Veii, terra-cotta statue; a typical example of °Etruscan art.

A compilation of myths, written in the second century AD, bears his name. **3.** Athenian painter (c. 430-400 BC), who is said to have been the first to use shades and perspective in his painting. **4.** A famous architect in the time of °Trajan and °Hadrian.

Apollónius (Ἀπολλώνιος). **1.** *Apollónius of Rhodes* (c. 295-215 BC). Epic poet. His long poem (c. 5000 lines) 'Argonautica' contains many scholarly digressions, while relating the story of °Jason and the °Argonauts. He was librarian at °Alexandria. **2.** *Apollónius of Tyana* (in Cappadocia), °Pythagorean philosopher, prophet and mystic (1st cent. AD). **3.** *Apollónius of Perga* (in Pamphylia). Mathematician (c. 265-170 BC), pupil of °Euclid. His books about conics and irrational numbers have come down to us. **4.** *Apollónius Dýscolus*. Grammarian (2nd cent. AD). His book was still the leading work on syntax in the 19th century.

Apólogy. °Apuleius; °Xenophon; °Plato.

apóstrophe (ἀποστροφή). A rhetorical figure by which the speaker suddenly addresses an absent or deceased person.

Apoxyómenus. °Lysippus.

Appéndix Próbi. List of 227 spelling directions (probably 3rd cent. AD), *e.g.* 'aper non aprus' 'amycdala non amiddula'. It is an important source for our knowledge of Vulgar Latin.

Via Áppia. Road from Rome *via* Aricia, Anxur, Minturnae and Formiae to Capua; it was built by App. °Claudius Caecus (312 BC); later extended to Brundisium (via Áppia Nóva).

Áppius Claudius. °Claudius.

16. Pont du Gard (°aqueduct).

Apsýrtus. Younger brother of °Medea; °Jason.

Apuléius. 1. *L. Apuléius Saturnínus,* Roman demagogue, contemporary of °Sulla, tribune of the people 103 and 100 BC. **2.** *L. Apuleius,* born c. 125 AD at Medaura in north Africa. Philosopher and orator. The following works are extant: 1. *Apologia,* in which he defended himself against an accusation of poisoning and witchcraft; 2. *De Magia,* an elaboration of the former; 3. *Florida,* a collection of abstracts from his speeches; 4. *Metamorphoses,* a novel about one Lucius, who was turned into an ass and after many adventures was changed back again. An important episode is the story of *Amor and Psyche.* The last part of the work was devoted to the cult of °Isis. Apuleius' style is full of archaic, poetic and new words, extravagant and sometimes almost metrical.

Aquae Sextiae (Aix-en-Provence). The place where °Marius defeated the °Teutones (102 BC).

áqueduct (aquaeductus). In Rome the oldest aqueduct was the Aqua Claudia, built by App. °Claúdius Caécus in 312 BC. In southern France a short stretch of an aqueduct is still standing, the 'Pont du Gard', 49 m high, 275 m long. Originally its length was c. 50 km and it had a slope of 34 cm to every km. Daily it brought 3,300,000 gallons of water to Nîmes, enough for a city of 80,000 inhabitants; °ills. 16, 17.

Áquila, *Áquila Pónticus* (2nd cent. AD). Made a very literal Greek translation of the Old Testament; °hexapla.

Aquitánia. Part of Gaul, extending in °Caesar's time to the south-west of the river Garumna. After °Augustus' time, it stretched to the Loire and the Cevennes.

Aráchne ('Αράχνη). A Lydian girl who dared to challenge the goddess °Athena to a weaving contest; when she won

17. View through the watercourse of the Pont du Gard: 1.35m. wide, 1.66m. high. On both sides is a thick coating of lime.

the goddess tore up her work. Arachne hanged herself and Athena turned her into a spider (Ovid *Met*. 6, 5-145).

Ára Máxima. °Cacus.

Ára Pácis. An altar sacred to the °Manes of the imperial family, erected at Rome by °Augustus after the pacification of Gaul and Spain (13 BC). Fragments of the fine reliefs survive in museums all over Europe. In 1937 the building was reconstructed near the original spot; °ills. 18,19.

Áratus (῎Αρατος). **1.** Greek politician (271-213 BC), born at Sicyon, leader of the °Achaean League. **2.** of Soli (c. 271-245). Writer of a poem on astronomy 'Phaenomena'; °Avienus; °Germanicus.

Arbéla (τά ῎Αρβηλα). Town of Assyria, where °Alexander the Great defeated °Darius (331 BC).

Arcádia. Region in the centre of the Peloponnese. Because of its remoteness, the rustic simplicity of its inhabitants became proverbial.

Arcádius. Emperor of the Eastern Roman Empire (337-403 AD), son of °Theodosius the Great.

Árcas (᾿Αρκάς). Son of °Zeus and °Callisto.

Arcesiláüs (᾿Αρκεσίλαος). °Academy.

archaeology. Excavation, followed by the study of the material remains of antiquity, such as the products of art, industry, etc. found at excavated sites. The study is subdivided: *e.g.* epigraphy, relating to inscriptions.

Archaic. When our knowledge of a certain period of ancient civilization is chiefly based on archaeological research, not on written material, we call this period archaic. Particularly used when referring to the pre-Classical period in Greece.

Archidámian War. °Archidamus.

Archídamus (᾿Αρχίδαμος). The name of several Spartan kings. The most notable is *Archidamus II* (468-427 BC). The first part of the °Peloponnesian War was named after him: the Archidamian War.

Archílochus (᾿Αρχίλοχος) of Paros (c. 650 BC). Lyric poet, and supposed creator of iambic poetry. Some fragments of his work survive.

Archimédes (᾿Αρχιμήδης). Mathematician of Syracuse (287-212 BC), killed when the city was captured by °Marcellus. He was a pupil of °Euclid and wrote several works, which are partly extant. He discovered the relation between the volumes of sphere and cylinder and between the circumference of a circle and its diameter; he invented the compound pulley, the 'Screw of Archimedes' and formulated the hydrostatic principle which bears his name. On this last occasion, he is supposed to have left the bath-house, where he made his discovery, crying: 'Eureka' (= 'I have found it').

árchitrave (᾿επιστύλιον). The lowest

18. Reconstruction of the °Ara Pacis.

19. Part of a relief of the °Ara Pacis. Of the five principal figures the second from the left wears the °toga over the head, the fourth has the right arm inside the 'sinus'.

member of the °entablature, the main beam resting on the columns. In the °Doric order it consisted of one beam, in the °Ionic of three.

árchons (᾿αρχοντες). Title of several holders of office in Athens. In classical times there were nine, chosen (after the time of °Solon by ballot) for one year. The first archon (᾿επώνυμος), who gave his name to the year, presided over all law-suits concerning family rights. The second (βασιλεύς) was in charge of all religious cases; the third (πολέμαρχος), originally the commander-in-chief of the army, in later times had charge of private suits in which °metics were involved. The other archons were judges (θεσμοθέται).

Arctúrus (᾿Αρκτοῦρος). A star in the constellation of Boötes, also used for the whole constellation; °Callisto.

árcus. °Bow. Also a triumphal arch. **1.** *arcus Augústi*, in the Forum, next to the temple of Caesar, built in 19 BC to commemorate the victory over the Parthians; °plan p. 81. **2.** *arcus Severi*, in the north-western corner of the Forum, erected (203 AD) in honour of Septimius °Severus, °Caracalla and °Geta; °plan p. 81. **3.** *arcus Tiberii*, near the north-western corner of the °basilica Julia; erected to commemorate the recapture of the 'eagles' (= standards) which °Varus had lost; °plan p. 81.

Areópagus (῎Αρειος πάγος). **1.** A hill at Athens, sacred to °Ares. **2.** The name of the body which, sitting on this hill, judged cases of murder; °Solon. When the votes were evenly divided, the defendant was acquitted, because the goddess °Athena was then supposed to be in favour of acquittal, as she had been in the case of °Orestes; °Aeschylus.

Áres (῎Αρης). Greek god of war, son of °Zeus and °Hera, father of the °Amazons. Identified with °Mars by the Romans; °Aphrodite.

Aretaéus (᾿Αρεταῖος) of Cappadocia. Medical author at Rome (2nd cent. AD). Some of his works, on acute and chronic diseases, are partly extant.

Arethúsa (᾿Αρέθουσα). A fountain of Ortygia, an island near Syracuse. The nymph Arethusa was pursued by the river-god °Alpheüs and turned into a fountain by °Diana (Ovid *Met.* 5, 572-641).

Argilétum. An important thoroughfare in °Rome between the °curia and the °basilica Aemilia; °plan p. 81.

Arginúsae (᾿Αργινοῦσαι). Three small islands near Lesbos, where the Athenians defeated the Spartan fleet (406 BC). The Athenian admirals were afterwards condemned to death for their failure to salvage the bodies of the slain.

Árgonauts (᾿Αργοναῦται. The fifty heroes who, led by °Jason, sailed in the ship Argo to recover the °Golden Fleece.

Argonaútica. °Apollonius 1.

Árgus (῎Αργος). **1.** The hundred-eyed herdsman, set by °Hera to watch °Io, but killed by °Hermes (Ovid *Met.* 1, 625-667). **2.** The builder of the ship Argo; °Argonauts. **3.** The faithful dog of °Odysseus (Hom. *Od.* XVII, 300-327).

Ariádne (᾿Αριάδνη). Daughter of °Minos and °Pasiphaë, saved °Theseus from the °labyrinth. Theseus took her with him, but left her behind on °Naxos, where °Dionysus took pity on her.

Arianism. The doctrine of °Arius.

Árion (᾿Αρίων). Bard from Methymna in °Lesbos. He lived at the court of °Periander of Corinth (600 BC). He was thrown overboard by pirates but saved by a dolphin (Hdt. 1, 23-24). He developed the hymn to °Dionysus, the dithyramb, the precursor of Greek tragedy.

Ariovístus. Leader of the Germans. Defeated by °Caesar at Vesontio (Besançon) (58 BC).

Aristágoras (᾿Αρισταγόρας). Tyrant of Miletus in the absence of °Histiaeus, for whom he instigated the revolt of the °Ionian cities against Persia.

Aristaéus (᾿Αρισταῖος). Ancient Greek God of country life, patron of agriculture, cattle, hunting and beekeeping; °Virgil (*Georgics*).

Aristárchus (Ἀρίσταρχος), of Samothrace. Librarian at °Alexandria (180-145 BC), critic and interpreter of °Homer.

Aristeídes (Ἀριστείδης). **1.** Athenian °archon, famous for his incorruptability and righteousness, political adversary of the progressive °Themistocles. He was banished in 483 BC (°ostracism), but recalled after the battle of °Salamis (480). He was general of the Athenians at the battle of °Plataea and charged with the organisation of the Confederacy of °Delos. He died poor (467). **2.** °Aélius Aristeides.

Aristion. Stele of Aristion, famous tombstone at Athens with the figure of a soldier in relief; °ill. 20; °stele.

20. Stele of Ariston.

Aristíppus (Ἀρίστιππος), of Cyrene (c. 435-360 BC), pupil of °Socrates, founder of the °Cyrenaic school. According to him, pleasure was the greatest good provided one did not allow oneself to be ruled by it; °Epicurus.

Aristóbulus (Ἀριστόβουλος), of Cassandreia, followed °Alexander the Great on his campaigns and recorded his deeds. He was the chief source of °Arrian.

Aristogeíton (Ἀριστογείτων). °Harmodius.

Aristóphanes (Ἀριστοφάνης). **1.** Athenian comic poet (446-385 BC). Eleven comedies of his are extant: 1. *Acharnians*, depicted the advantages of peace; 2. *Knights*, criticized °Cleon; 3. *Wasps*, criticized the people's law-courts; 4. *Peace*; 5. *Birds*. Two Athenians, sick of war and quarrels, created a new country among the birds; 6. *Lysístrata*. Women on strike against war; 7. *Clouds*, ridiculed °Socrates as a sophist; 8. *Thesmophoriazusae*; 9. *Frogs*, criticized the tragic poets; 10. *Ecclesiazusae*; 11. *Ploutus*, a merry allegory in which the god of wealth was cured of his blindness. **2.** *Aristophanes of Byzantium*, head of the °Alexandrian library (c. 195 BC).

Áristotle (Ἀριστοτέλης), of Stageira in Chalcidice (384-322 BC), pupil of °Plato, after whose death in 347 he left Athens. In 343, he became tutor to the young °Alexander the Great. Later he returned to Athens and in 335 taught in a precinct (περίπατος) of the °Lyceum, from which the school got its name (Peripatetic). Because he thought philosophy should incorporate research into the first origins of all existing things, he aimed at attaining the widest knowledge possible, based on careful observation. Thus the greater part of his works consists of collections of scientific data, which he put into order and from which he tried to deduce general laws. He collected the constitutions of 158 cities, of which only the 'Athenaíon Politeía' is known to us, discovered on a °papyrus in 1891. Of his works on physics we have that on zoology (περὶ τὰ ζῷα ἱστορίαι), a course on physics (φυσικὴ ἀκρόασις), and on ethics, 'Éthica Nicomáchea'. His fourteen books on 'being *qua* being' (τὸ ὂν ἦ ὄν) and the first origins of being, called by him the 'first philosophy' were in later editions put after the 'physics' and so came to be called 'μετὰ τὰ φυσικά'= 'Metaphysics'. Of his 'Poetics' we have only the first book on tragedy and epos, and three books on rhetoric. Concerning the mind and soul, he also wrote 'περὶ ψυχῆς'.

Aristóxenus (᾽Αριστόξενος). Musician from Tarentum (4th cent. BC), whose writings are partly extant.

Árius (῎Αρειος). Presbyter at °Alexandria at the time of °Constantine the Great. He taught that Jesus was created from nothing and so was not eternal. His heresy was condemned and he was banished. He died in 336.

Arnóbius. Orator from Sicca in Numidia (born c. 260 AD). After his conversion (305) he wrote a defence of Christianity: 'Adversus Nationes', of which the last five books attacked paganism by recounting the immoralities in the ancient myths.

Arrecína Tertúlla. First wife of the emperor °Titus; °Flavii p. 79.

Árretine ware, °terra sigillata.

Árrian (Αρριανός). *Flávius Arriánus.* Philosopher and historian (2nd cent. AD). He wrote among other works Ανάβασις Αλεξάνδρου' (March of Alexander) and a small manual (᾽Εγχειρίδιον) on the teaching of °Epictetus.

Arringatóre ('orator'). Name of the statue of an Etruscan in the Florence museum (2nd cent. BC); °ill. 21; °toga.

arrow. °Homer's 'three-barbed arrows' in fact had three barbs; °ill. 22. °weapons.

Arsácidae. The royal dynasty of Parthia (250 BC-227 AD), descendants of Arsaces (᾽Αρσάκης), who founded his empire after a revolt against the °Seleucids. The Parthian Empire was overrun by the °Sassánidae.

Arsínoë (᾽Αρσινόη). °Lysimachus.

Ars Poética. °Horace.

21. The 'Arringatore'.

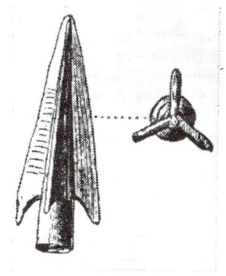

22. Type of arrow-head.

Artaxérxes (᾽Αρταξέρξης). The name of several Persian kings. **1.** *Artaxérxes I Mákrocheir* (Μακρόχειρ) (465-425 BC). Son of °Xerxes I. **2.** *Artaxérxes II Mnémon* (Μνήμων) (404-359). Son of Darius II Óchos. He defeated his brother °Cyrus near Cunaxa (401). **3.** *Artaxérxes III Óchos* (῏Ωχος) (358-337). Youngest son of **2.**, noted for his cruelty and finally poisoned.

Ártemis (῎Αρτεμις). Daughter of °Zeus and °Leto, twin-sister of °Apollo, protectress of women in childbirth. Represented as a huntress, with bow and arrows and a quiver. The deer, the dog and the goose were sacred to her. Her greatest temple was at °Ephesus, where she was worshipped as goddess of fertility; °Actaeon; °Iphigeneia.

Artemísia (Ἀρτεμισία). Queen of Caria. She erected a monumental tomb for her husband Mausolus at Halicarnassus: the °Mausoleum.

Artemísium (Ἀρτεμίσιον). Cape in Euboea, where the Greeks defeated the Persians on the same day as the battle of °Thermopylae.

Arváles, *fratres Arvales.* A Roman college of twelve priests. In May they had a festival in honour of the Dea Dia, at which they sang an old °hymn to pray for the fertility of the fields; °Ambarvalia.

Arvérni. Tribe in Gaul between the Liger (=Loire) and Garumna; °Vercingetorix.

arybállos (ἀρύβαλλος). Oil flask with short and narrow neck. Two forms are distinguished; °ill. 23.

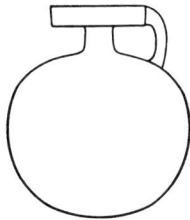

23. Corinthian aryballos.

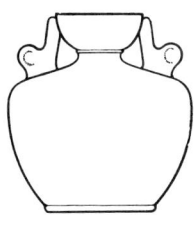

Attic aryballos.

Arx. The northern summit of the °Capitoline at °Rome; °plan p. 165.

as (or 'libélla'). Roman copper coin.. Its weight was originally 1 libra (=12 unciae), *i.e.* 11.5 oz. (the *as librális* or *aes gráve*). The value decreased continually:

200 BC—5 unciae
187 BC—2 unciae (*as sextális*)
c. 150 BC—1 uncia (*as unciális*)
89 BC—½ uncia (*as semiunciális*); °p. 164.

Ascánius. Son of °Aeneas (°Dardanidae p. 60), founder of °Alba Longa, legendary ancestor of the Julian family. His other name was Iulus.

Asclépiadae. Priests and descendants of °Asclepius, who were physicians.

Asclépiades (Ἀσκληπιάδης). **1.** Greek physician at Rome (c. 150 BC). **2.** Hellenistic poet (c. 300 BC).

Asclepiadéüs. A metrical foot. **1.** *A. minor*:

‿ ‿ ‿ ‿ ‿ ‿ ‿   ‿ ‿ ‿ ‿ ‿, *e.g.*:
"Maécénas atavís édite régibus";
2. *A. maior*:
‿ ‿ ‿ ‿ ‿ ‿   ‿ ‿ ‿ ‿   ‿ ‿ ‿ ‿ ‿, *e.g.*:
"Quís post vina gravém mílitiam aút paúperiém crepát?"

Asclépius (Ἀσκληπίος). Son of °Apollo and °Coronis, god of healing, educated by °Cheiron. He was worshipped especially at °Epidaurus, °Cos and °Pergamum, the ancient centres of healing.

Ascónius Lábeo Pediánus (c. 50 AD). Writer of a commentary on the speeches of °Cicero, partly extant, and grammarian.

Ashurbánipal. King of Assyria (668-626 BC), who collected a large library in Nineveh which has been discovered; °Sardanapalus.

Asia. After 133 BC a Roman °province; °Attalus III.

'Asianism'. After the fourth century BC oratory showed a tendency towards bombast, especially in Asia-Minor. The reaction against it was called °Atticism.

Asínius, *C. Asínius Póllio.* Writer of a history of the Civil Wars from the first °triumvirate until the battle of

°Philippi. His work is lost; °Virgil, 'Bucolics'.

áskos ('ασκός) (=wineskin). Asymmetric oil jug with convex top, mouth off-centre and one arched handle; °ill. 24.

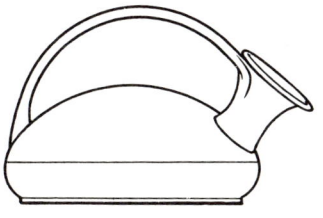

24. Askos.

Aspásia. Courtesan, beloved of °Pericles, who had great influence on him.

aspérgillum. Sprinkler, used by the priest for purification of sacrificial animals; °ill. p. 164, no 15.

ásphodel ('ασφοδελός). A plant which, according to °Homer, covered the Elysian Fields (*Od*. XI, 539); °ill. 25.

25. °Asphodel.

áspis ('ασπίς). The Homeric shield ('ασπίς 'αμφιβρότη') 'surrounded' the whole bearer and was carried on a strap around the neck and left shoulder. The illustrations (26 and 27) clearly show two shapes.

26. Imprint of a golden signet-ring (enlarged), found at Mycenae. It shows the form of the Homeric shield.

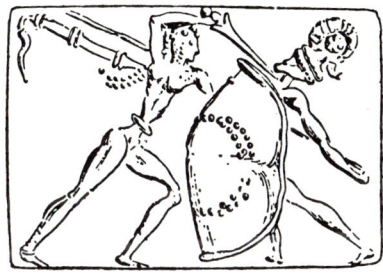

27. Seal from Mycenae (enlarged imprint).

Assáracus ('Ασσάρακος). °Dardanidae p. 60.

Assýria. The Assyrian empire flourished under °Sargon II (721-705 BC), °Sennacherib (705-681), Esarhaddon (681-669), and °Ashurbanipal II (668-626). It was conquered by the Persians.

Astárte ('Αστάρτη). A Syrio-Phoenician goddess, identified with °Aphrodite by the Greeks.

Astraéa ('Αστραία). Daughter of Zeus and Themis, goddess of Justice. In the 'Golden Age' she still lived among men.

ástragal (αστράγαλος). A small convex moulding placed round the top or bottom of columns; °ill. 28.

27

28. Astragal.

Astýages (Ἀστυάγης). Son of °Cyaxares, last king of the Medes (585-550 BC); °Mandane.

Astýanax (Ἀστυάναξ). Son of °Hector and °Andromache, killed by the Greeks after the capture of Troy. He was also called Σκαμάνδριος.

asýndeton (διάλυτον). The juxtaposition of nouns, adjectives or verbs without a conjunction ('oro obsecro').

Atalánta (Ἀταλάντη). Daughter of Schoineus, king of Scyros, or of Iasus and Clymene, from Arcadia. She was a great huntress and took part in the °Calydonian Hunt. Having refused at first, she eventually agreed to marry the man who would defeat her in a footrace; °Hippomenes succeeded (Ovid *Met.* 10, 560-708); °Meleager.

C. Ateíus Cápito. Consul 5 AD, famous jurist, adversary of °Labeo. Capito's adherents were called Sabiniani.

Atélla, Oscan town in Campania, which gave its name to the Fabulae °Atellanae.

Atellánae fábulae. Rustic comedies of the Romans; their stock characters were the Fool (Maccus), the Glutton (Manducus), the Hunchback (Dossenus), etc.

Áthamas (Ἀθάμας). °Phrixus.

Athanásius. Bishop of Alexandria, opponent of the doctrines of °Arius (died 373).

Athéna (Ἀθήνη). Daughter of °Zeus, who sprang from his head; goddess of the city of °Athens, patroness of urban arts, of wisdom and tactical warfare. Represented as a young woman, armed with helmet, spear, shield and the °aegis. The olive and the owl were sacred to her. Her principal temple was on the °Acropolis at Athens; °Parthenon; °Minerva; °ills. 5, 130, 136, 137.

Athenaéum (Ἀθηναῖον). A school of scientific and literary education in Rome, founded by °Hadrian.

Athenaéus (Ἀθήναιος). Scholar from Naucratis (c. 230 AD). His (Ἀειπνοσοφισταί) 'Sophists at dinner' was a collection of fictional dinner conversations on a wide range of subjects. It contains many quotations from lost writings.

Athenian Confederacy. 1. °Confederacy of Delos. **2.** Second Athenian Confederacy, between Athens and several former confederates against Sparta (378 BC).

Áthens (Ἀθῆναι). Capital of Attica, connected by the Long Walls with the port of °Piraeus.

Áthos (Ἄθως). Headland of the Chalcidian promontories (present 'Hagion Oros'), where the Persian fleet was wrecked (492 BC). In 480, °Xerxes dug a canal through the neck of the promontory. It is still famous for its twenty monasteries, which are said to contain treasures of ancient manuscripts.

Atlántis (Ἀτλαντίς). Until recently thought to be a legendary island at the entrance of the Mediterranean. Now thought to be Santorin (Thera), which erupted in the Late °Cycladic period.

Átlas (Ἄτλας). Son of °Iapetus. Zeus made him support the heavens on his shoulders. Also said to be an African prince turned to stone by °Perseus (Ovid *Met.* 4, 628-662). The °Pleiades (°Maea), the °Hyades and the °Hesperides were his daughters.

Átreus (Ἀτρεύς). Son of °Pelops and °Hippodameia, brother of Thyestes, father of °Agamemnon and °Menelaus (the Atreidae); °Tantalidae p. 182.

átrium. The centre of a Roman house (°domus). The ceiling had an opening (*compluvium*) in the centre, through which the rain fell into the basin (*impluvium*) beneath. When, in later times, houses became larger, the atrium was the reception hall; °ill. 29.

Átropos (Ἄτροπος). °Fates.

Áttalus III (Ἄτταλος Φιλομήτωρ). King of Pergamum, who bequeathed the whole of his empire and wealth to the Roman people. The Romans made his empire the province of Asia (133 BC).

29. Atrium of the Casa delle Nozze d'argento in Pompeii.

Attic dialect. The language of Athens in its great days, developed from the °Ionic dialect.

Attic orators. °Aeschines, °Andocides, °Antiphon, °Deinarchus, °Demosthenes, °Hyperides, °Isaeus, °Isocrates, °Lycrugus, °Lysias.

Attic stelae. In 415 BC, when in the streets of Athens the °Herms had been mutilated (°Alcibiades), the guilty were punished and their property confiscated and sold. Lists of the possessions were inscribed in stone and erected in Athens. These 'Attic stelae' record the amount of the tax, the proceeds and the nature of each lot of the sale. From the many fragments found during excavations (1953-56) an idea can be formed of the prices then prevailing and of the value of money at that time; °ill. 30.

'Atticism'. Reaction against '°Asianism' of the 2nd cent. BC, based on admiration

30. *(right)* Fragment of one of the °Attic stelae with a list of slaves of different nationalities.

for and consisting of a close imitation of the style of the °Attic orators of the 5th and 4th cent. BC.

Átticus, *T. Pompónius Átticus* (c. 109-32 BC). Friend of °Cicero, publisher and historian. Many of Cicero's letters were written to him.

Aúgeas (Αὐγείας). King of Elis, who had not cleaned his stables containing 3000 cattle for thirty years. °Heracles' task was to do this in one day. When he had finished the work by changing the course of the river Alpheus or Peneus, which carried away the dung from the stables, Augeas refused the promised reward of 300 cattle. Heracles killed him and laid waste his land.

aúgur. The college of augurs originally consisted of three, and later five members. After the lex Ogulnia (300 BC) was passed, there were nine priests (five were allowed to be plebeians), after °Sulla's time fifteen; °Caesar added a sixteenth. They had the knowledge necessary for taking the auspices; they interpreted the will of the gods from the behaviour of birds or the occurrence of thunder. They could interrupt the assembly of the people or an election by reporting an unfavourable omen.

Augústine, *Aurélius Augustínus* (354-430 AD), bishop of Hippo (396), one of the famous Fathers of the Church. After a turbulent youth, he was baptised in 387. His best-known writings are: *Confessiones*, stories about his youthful peccadilloes, his inner struggle and final conversion; *De Civitate Dei*, a defence of Christianity, in which this world was compared with the ideal state of God. He left hundreds of letters and sermons.

Augústus (63 BC-14 AD). The first Roman emperor. His original name was *C. Octávius*. When adopted by his uncle Julius °Caesar, he took the name of *C. Iulius Caesar Octaviánus*. After Caesar's death he marched against °Antony at the Senate's command. After his victory at °Mutina (43 BC) the second °triumvirate was formed (with °Antony and °Lepidus), which was dissolved in 33. In 31, he defeated Antony at Actium and became sole ruler. The Senate gave him the title of 'Augustus' and the power of a proconsul and of a tribune of the people. Eventually he became all-powerful. He tried to strengthen the empire not by military victories, but by internal measures: restoration of the state-cult, laws against childlessness. His own family caused him grave disappointments. His heirs (Marcellus, Lucius, Gaius, Drusus) died young. The licentiousness of his daughter Julia forced him to appoint °Tiberius his successor. He himself wrote a synopsis of the chief events of his reign, which he caused to be erected in many places (°Monumentum Ancyranum, °Monumentum Antiochenum). °Julio-Claudian dynasty p. 101.

Aúlis (Αὐλίς). Town and port in Boeotia, from where the Greek fleet sailed for Troy, after °Iphigeneia had been sacrificed. °Euripides.

aúlos (αὐλός, tíbia). Greek wind instrument similar in form to a double shawm, in sound to the clarinet; °ill. 31.

31. To the left a man ladles wine with a °kyathos, from a °kalyx krater in which a °psykter is placed. The other plays a double °aulos.

Aululária. °Plautus.
Aurélian. 1. *L. Domítius Aureliánus,*
Roman emperor (270-275 AD). He
evicted the Alemanni and the Mar-
comanni from Italy, surrounded Rome
with walls and defeated °Zenobia,
queen of °Palmyra. He was honoured
with the title of '*restitútor impérii*'.
2. °Caelius Aureliánus.
Aurélii (see below).
Aurélius. 1. °Caracalla, °Marcus
Aurelius, °Nemesianus, °Symmachus,
°Verus. **2.** *Sex. Aurélius Victor,* writer
of a history of Rome from °Augustus
to °Constantine (361 AD).
aúreus. Roman gold coin introduced
after 44 BC. The weight was originally
$\frac{1}{40}$ libra and was later reduced to $\frac{1}{70}$ libra;
°ill. 164.
Auróra. °Eos.
Aúsculum. Town of Apulia, where
°Pyrrhus of Epirus defeated the Romans
with great loss (279 BC), hence the term
'Pyrrhic victory'.
Ausónius, *D. Mágnus Ausónius* of
Burdigala (c. 310-c. 395 AD). Teacher
of grammar and rhetoric. After holding
high positions, he retired in 383 to his
estates. He wrote epigrams and other
poems. His most important poem is
'Mosella', a romantic description of
the river.

auspícium. Originally the taking of omens
from the behaviour of birds; later all
kinds of omens were meant by it;
°augur. The *Auspicia maxima* were
taken 'de caelo', from the flight of
birds; the *Auspicia minora* 'de extis',
from the entrails of sacrificed animals;
the *Auspicia pullaria* from the behaviour
of the sacred chickens (pulli) while
eating.
autóchthones (αὐτόχθονες; aborígines).
The inhabitants of a country who claim
that their ancestors have always dwelt
there, *e.g.* the Athenians.
Autómedon (Αὐτομέδων). The charioteer
of °Achilles.
Áventine. One of the °Seven Hills on
which Rome was built.
Aviánus. Latin writer of Aesopic (°Aesop)
fables (c. 400 AD).
Aviénus, Rúfius Féstus Aviénus (c. 400
AD). Translated the 'Phaenomena' of
°Arátus and the 'Periegésis' of °Diony-
sius. He wrote a description of the
south-west coast of Europe: 'Ora
Marítima'.
Avítus. 1. Emperor of the Western
Roman empire (455-456). **2.** *Alcimus
Avítus,* bishop of Vienna (died 518 AD),
opponent of °Arian, author of sermons
and letters.
Axíoche (Ἀξιόχη). °Tantalidae p. 182.

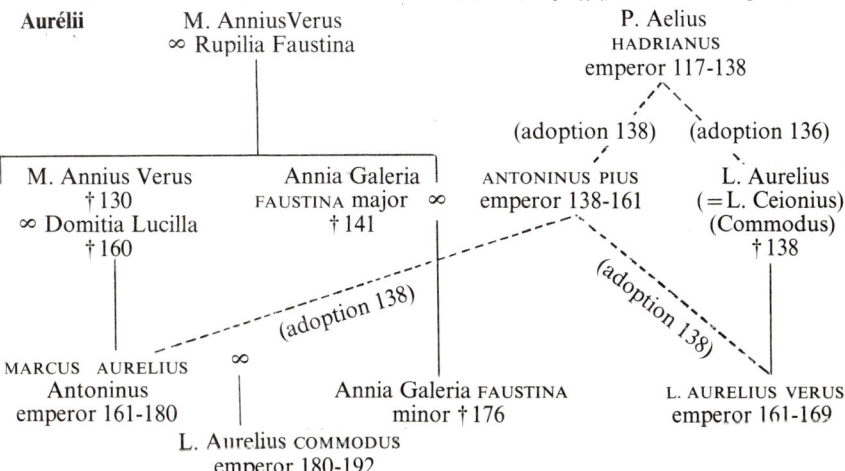

31

B

Baalbek (ancient Heliópolis). Town in Syria, which became a Roman colony at the time of °Caesar. The remains of some of its impressive monuments are still to be seen.

Bábrius (Βάβριος). Greek poet, who rendered °Phaedrus' fables into verse (possibly 2nd cent AD).

Bábylon (Βαβυλών). Capital of Babylonia on the river Euphrates. According to legend it was founded by Queen °Semíramis and enlarged by °Nebuchadnezzar. The Hanging Gardens were one of the °Seven wonders of the world. Captured by Cyrus (538); °Hammurabi. The remains were excavated 1899-1914.

Bacchanália. The orgiastic festival of °Bacchus (°Mysteries) which was prohibited (186 BC) by the 'senatus consultum de Bacchanálibus'. The text of this decree of the Senate is an important philological document, because it shows how much the Latin at that time differed from the literary language of the classical period. °Dionysus.

bácchius. A metrical foot: ⌣ _ _.

Bácchus (Βάκχος). °Dionysus. The Romans also gave this name to °Liber.

Bacchýlides (Βακχυλίδης). Lyric poet from Keos (c. 505-450 BC) at the court of °Hiero of Syracuse. Some of his songs commemorating victories (ἐπινίκια) were discovered in 1896 on °papyri in Egypt.

Bar-Cochba. Leader of the Jewish rising (132-135 AD) against the Romans (°Hadrian). Fifteen letters from his military correspondence were discovered in the desert of Judaea (1959).

base. The lowest member of a °column or wall.

basílica (βασιλική). A Roman rectangular building supported by rows of columns, which served as a social or commercial meeting-place. The *basílica Júlia* was built by °Caesar in 54 BC and after a fire rebuilt and enlarged by °Augustus. Of the 120 columns only the bases are left; °plan p. 81. The *basílica Aemília* in the °forum at °Rome was built by °Lepidus; °plan p. 81. The *basílica Pórcia,* built by °Cato Maior next to the °curia (184), was burned down in 52 BC.

Basílius the Great. Bishop of Caesarea (c. 331-379 AD), one of the greatest fathers of the church, famous for his letters and sermons.

Bassiánus. °Sevéri p. 172.

Batrachomyomáchia (Βατραχομυο-μαχία). A parody on an epic poem: 'The Battle of Frogs and Mice', attributed in antiquity to °Homer, but probably of a much later date.

Baúcis (Βαυκίς). °Philemon.

báxea. Plain sandal, mostly made of reeds or papyrus, worn by philosophers and in Roman comedy. Many were found in Egyptian graves; °ill. 32.

32. Baxea.

bed moulding. The moulding immediately under a projecting member such as a °cornice.

Bélides. Grand-daughters of °Belus, the °Danaids.

Belisárius (c. 505-565 AD), general of the Emperor °Justinian, who defeated the Vandals, 534; °Narses; °Procopius.
bell kráter. °Krater formed like an inverted bell; °ill. 33.

33. Bell krater from Spina c. 425 BC. Amazon and horse.

Bellérophon (Βελλεροφῶν). He left his country because of manslaughter and went to °Proetus of Argos, whose wife Stheneboea accused him of trying to seduce her. Proetus sent him to °Iobates of Lycia, carrying a letter asking to kill the bearer. Iobates made Bellerophon fight the °Chimaera, but with the aid of °Pegasus he killed the monster.
Bellóna. Ancient Italian goddess of war. A temple was consecrated to her in the °Campus Martius by App. °Claudius Caecus (296), which was sometimes used by the Senate.
Bellum Áfricum. Description of °Caesar's war against rebellious Pompeian troops in north Africa (47-46 BC). The author is unknown.
Bellum Alexandrínum. A. °Hirtius.
Bellum Hispaniénse. A book about °Caesar's war in Spain (45 BC). The

author is unknown.
Bélus (Βῆλος). Legendary son of Poseidon and Lybia, king of Egypt, father of °Aegyptus and °Danaus.
Bélvedere. °Apollo.
Bénedict. Founder of the order of Benedictines. He was born at Nursia c. 480 AD; in 528 he converted the people near Monte Cassino and afterwards wrote the 'Régula Monasteriórum'. He died in 543.
Benevéntum. Town of the Hirpini in Samnium; its original name was Maleventum, but after the Roman victory over °Pyrrhus (275 BC) it was changed into Beneventum 'boni ominis causa'.
Beraíce (Βερενίκη). **1.** Wife of °Ptolemy III (c. 273-221 BC). Grateful for the safe return of her husband, she sacrificed her hair to °Aphrodite. Next day it had disappeared and was said to have become a constellation ('cóma Berenícis'). **2.** Daughter of °Julius Agrippa I (born 28 AD), beloved of the emperor °Titus.
Bías (Βίας), of Priene. One of the °Seven Sages. His maxim was: 'the majority are evil': 'οτ πλείους κακοί'.
Bíon (Βίων). **1.** °Bucolic poet from Smyrna (200 BC). Eight of his poems are extant. **2.** *Bion of Borýsthenes.* °Cynic philosopher (c. 240 AD).
bipénnis. Double-edged axe; used by the °Amazons; °ill. 10.
biséllium. Seat for two persons, later used as seat of honour for one.
Bíton (Βίτων). °Cleobis.
Black-figured pottery had the design painted in black silhouette over the light red clay background. The scheme was reversed in the later red-figured pottery, where the background was painted in black. (Greek.)
Boadicéa. °Boudicca.
Boéthius, *Anícius Mánlius Torquátus Severínus Boéthius* (c. 480-524 AD). Philosopher and politician, adviser to °Theodoric the Great. Because he defended the rights of the Romans against the Gothic officials, he fell into disgrace. In prison he wrote 'De Consolatióne Philosóphiae'.

Bóna Déa. A Roman goddess whose festival in December was only attended by prominent women and the °Vestal Virgins; °Cybele; °Rhea; °Vesta.

books. The ancient book was a roll made of °papyrus (in Greek, βύβλος). Because too long a roll became impossible to handle, writings were later divided into separate 'books'. The text was written in columns. While reading, it was rolled up from left to right and afterwards rolled back. Sometimes a book of pages made of parchment was cheaper and was originally used in schools or on a journey, that is in cases when the less strong papyrus would break; °codex; °wax tablets.

Boótes (Βοώτης). °Callisto.

Bóreas (Βορέας). The north-west wind; °Oreithyia.

Bóudicca (Boadicéa). Queen of the Iceni in °Britain, who led a revolt against the Romans (61 AD). She was defeated and took poison (Bóudicca = Victoria).

Boúle (Βουλή) of Athens. The 'Council of Five Hundred' (originally 400), instituted by Cleisthenes. It had two functions: preparation of the work of the assembly of the people, and the execution of its decrees. Fifty members at a time were the executive council; they were called prytanes (πρυτάνεις) and met in the Prytaneum. The members of the Boule resigned after one year; °ecclesia.

boustrophédon (βουστροφηδόν). An inscription in Greek written alternately from right to left and from left to right, like the course of a plough; °ill. 34.

bow. The Homeric bow was made of wood, strengthened by strips of horn glued to it by a lengthy process. (A bow made of two horns fastened together in a direct line could not be bent). It was about 1 m long. The string was attached to one end of the bow and when bent fastened to the κορώνη; °ill. 35; °arcus.

brachýlogy. Condensed expression: 'facinus nulli tyranno comparandum'.

Brénnus. According to tradition the chief of the Gauls who defeated the Romans near the river °Allia in 387 AD

34. Illustration to show the direction of a 'boustrophedon' inscription.

35. Bow.

and captured Rome.

Briáreus (Βριάρεως). °Centimani.

Brisëïs (Βρισηΐς). Captive and slave of °Achilles, whom he was forced to hand over to °Agamemnon, when the latter had been commanded by °Apollo to give °Chrysëïs back to her father (Hom. *Il*. I, 8-347).

Britain (Británnia). Roman province, first explored by °Caesar, but no conquest was attempted until the reign of °Claudius. Many tribes were subdued by °Agricola (76-85 AD). °Hadrian; °Antonine wall.

Brittánnicus, *Ti. Caesar Claudius Britán-*

nicus, born 41 AD. Son of the emperor °Claudius and °Messalina, poisoned at the instigation of °Nero in 55 AD; °Julio-Claudian dynasty p. 101.

Bronze Age. The prehistoric period when tools were made chiefly of bronze, c. 3000-1000 BC in the Mediterranean area.

Brútus. 1. *L. Iúnius Brútus.* The first consul (510 BC) in Rome. He supposedly escaped the blood-lust of his uncle °Tarquinius Superbus by feigning feeble-mindedness. In 509, he had to condemn his son to death for high-treason. **2.** *M. Iúnius Brútus.* Tribune in 83 BC, supporter of °Marius, married to °Servilia. He wrote in dialogue-form 'De iure civili libri III'. **3.** *M. Iúnius Brútus.* Son of M. Iúnius Brútus and Servília, supporter of °Pompey, afterwards of °Caesar. In 45 he was governor of Gallia Cisalpina, in 44 °praetor urbanus. He was the best-known of Caesar's murderers; defeated at °Philippi (42) in Macedon, he killed himself.

búcchero. Native °Etruscan pottery with polished black surface, decorated with moulded ornament.

búccula. °helmet.

Bucéphalus (Βουκεφάλας). The horse of °Alexander the Great.

bucína. A bugle, short and curved, chiefly used in the Roman army for the changing of the guard.

bucólic. Poems which describe the ideal rural life of country-folk are called bucolic; °Theocritus; °Virgil; °Moschus; °Calpurnius.

Bucolica, — orum ('Eclogues'). Pastoral poems, title of a work by °Virgil; °Nemesianus; °bucolic.

Búrrhus, Sex. *Afránius Búrrhus.* °Praefectus praetorio under the emperor °Claudius. He and °Seneca had a brief salutary influence on young °Nero.

Busíris (Βούσιρις). Legendary king of Egypt, who sacrificed all foreigners who entered his country to the gods; killed by °Heracles.

Býrsa. The citadel of Carthage. In antiquity the name was connected with the hide (βύρσα) °Dido cut into strips to mark the area she had bought, but the name could have been derived from the Punic word 'basra' (=a fortification).

C

Ɔ. °Alphabet.

Cácus. Fire-breathing °giant, son of °Hephaestus who lived in a cave on the °Aventine. He was killed by °Heracles (Ovid *Fast.* 1, 543-584; Virg. *Aen.* 8, 185-272), who was honoured because of that at the Ara Maxima in °Rome; °plan p. 81.

Cádmus (Κάδμος). Son of Agenor, king of Phoenicia, and of Telephassa. Searching for his sister °Europa, who had been carried off by °Zeus, he was told by the °Delphic oracle to found a city. He founded Thebes in Boeotia, killed the dragon that guarded the fountain where he went to get water and sowed the dragon's teeth. From the teeth sprang armed men: the first Thebans (Ovid *Met.* 3, 1-130). Cadmus married °Harmonia. Both were turned into serpents after their death (Ovid *Met.* 4, 563-603).

cadúceus (κηρύκειον). The wand carried by °Hermes, the messenger of the gods. It was represented with two serpents twined around it; °ill. 97.

Caecílius, *Statius Caecílius* (c. 220-168 BC). Author of Roman comedies, free adaptations of °Menander.

Caélian. One of the °Seven Hills, on which °Rome was built.

L. Caélius Ántipater, c. 115 BC. Author of a history of the Punic Wars. He was the first non-°annalistic historian.

C. Caélius Aureliánus, of Sicca in Numidia (450 AD). Author of a book on acute and chronic diseases, translated from °Soranus.

Caésar 1. Surname (=cognomen) in the Júlian family; °Julius. **2.** *C. Caésar,* °Gaíus Caésar. **3.** *L. Caésar,* °Lúcius Caésar. **4.** After °Augustus' time the title of the princes of the imperial family. **5.** After °Nero's time the title of the emperor. **6.** *Imperátor Caésar Dívi Fílius.* The name °Augustus gave himself shortly after his adoption; °Julio-Claudian dynasty p. 101.

Caesónia, *Milónia Caesónia.* Wife of the emperor °Gaius (40 AD). Her daughter was Júlia Drusilla; °Julio-Claudian dynasty p. 101.

caéstus. A boxing-glove consisting of a leather strap wound around the hand and forearm; often weighted with pieces of iron and metal spikes placed over the knuckles; °ill. 36.

caesúra. A break in a line of verse, dividing it into two unequal parts in the middle of a foot. There are four kinds:

1. *semiquinária*: 'Spectatum veniunt, [veniunt spectentur ut ipsae'
2. *semiseptenária*: 'Inde toro pater [Aeneas sic orsus ab alto'
3. κατά τρίτον τροχαῖον (not often used in Latin):
"ἄνδρα μοι ἔννεπε Μοῦσα, πολύτροπον [ὃς μάλα πολλά"
4. °*bucolic*: 'Solstitium pecori [defendite; iam venit aestas'

Cálaïs and Zétes (Κάλαις; Ζήτης). The sons of °Boreas, took part in the expedition of the °Argonauts. They rescued °Phineus from· the °Harpies (Ovid *Met.* 6, 711-721).

cálceüs. Roman shoe of one of two kinds: **1.** *Cálceus patrícius,* worn by patrician senators. **2.** The more commonplace shoe of the ordinary Roman citizen; °ill. 37.

37. Cálceüs.

Cálchas (Κάλχας). The soothsayer who took part in the Greek expedition against Troy.

36. Caestus.

calendar. The Roman calendar had twelve months of 28-31 days each. Three days of each month had a name (°Kalends, °Ides, °Nones), the other days were numbered backwards from them. °Caesar, with the help of °Sosigenes, made the year consist of 365 days with an intercalary day every fourth year.

Calendar

	March May July October	January August December	April June September November	February
1	Kalendis	Kalendis	Kalendis	Kalendis
2	a.d. VI Nonas	a.d. IV Nonas	a.d. IV Nonas	a.d. IV Non.
3	,, V	,, III	,, III	,, III
4	,, IV	pridie Non.	pridie Non.	pridie Non.
5	, III	Nonis	Nonis	Nonis
6	pridie Non.	a.d. VIII Idus	a.d. VIII Idus	a.d. VIII Idus
7	Nonis	,, VII	,, VII	,, VII
8	a.d. VIII Idus	,, VI	,, VI	,, VI
9	,, VII	,, V	,, V	,, V
10	,, VI	,, IV	,, IV	,, IV
11	,, V	,, III	,, III	,, III
12	,, IV	pridie Idus	pridie Idus	pridie Idus
13	,, III	Idibus	Idibus	Idibus
14	pridie Idus	a.d. XIX Kal.	a.d. XVIII Kal.	a.d. XVI Kal.
15	Idibus	,, XVIII	,, XVII	,, XV
16	a.d. XVII Kal.	,, XVII	,, XVI	,, XIV
17	,, XVI	,, XVI	,, XV	,, XIII
18	,, XV	,, XV	,, XIV	,, XII
19	,, XIV	,, XIV	,, XIII	,, XI
20	,, XIII	,, XIII	,, XII	,, X
21	,, XII	,, XII	,, XI	,, IX
22	,, XI	,, XI	,, X	,, VIII
23	,, X	,, X	,, IX	,, VII
24	,, IX	,, IX	,, VIII	,, VI
25	,, VIII	,, VIII	,, VII	,, V (bis VI) ✣
26	,, VII	,, VII	,, VI	,, IV (V)
27	,, VI	,, VI	,, V	,, III (IV)
28	,, V	,, V	,, IV	pridie Kal. (a.d. III)
29	,, IV	,, IV	,, III	(prid. Kal.)
30	,, III	,, III	pridie Kal.	
31	pridie Kal.	pridie Kal.		
	Apr. Jun. Aug. Nov.	Febr. Sept. Jan.	May Jul. Oct. Dec.	March

✣ the words in brackets apply to leap years, when February has 29 days.

cáliga

cáliga. Shoe of soldiers and farmers; °ill. 38.

38. Cáliga.

Calígula. °Gaius.

Calléva Atrebátum. °Silchester; °Britain.

Cállias (Καλλίας). Son-in-law of °Cimon, head of the embassy which went to conclude peace with Persia in 449 BC: the 'peace of Callias'.

Callícrates (Καλλικράτης). Architect of the °Parthenon, together with °Ictinus.

Callicrátidas (Καλλικρατίδας). °Arginusae.

Callímachus (Καλλίμαχος), of Cyrene (c. 310-240), who lived at °Alexandria, where he was probably head of the library after °Zenodotus. From papyri discovered during the last few years, we know of six °hymns, sixty-three epigrams and fragments from other writings of his; °papyrus.

Callínus (Καλλῖνος), of Ephesus. The first Greek °elegiac poet (7th cent. BC).

Callíope (Καλλιόπη). °Muses.

Callísthenes (Καλλισθένης). Nephew of °Aristotle. He was an admirer of °Alexander the Great and accompanied him to Asia Minor, where he fell into disgrace and was executed. His book on Alexander is not extant.

Callísto (Καλλιστώ). Friend of °Artemis, beloved of °Zeus, changed into a she-bear by °Hera. °Zeus transformed her into a constellation with her son Arcas as the Great Bear and Arctophylax (or Boötes) (Ovid *Met.* 2, 401-530).

Calpúrnius. 1. °Piso. **2.** *T. Calpúrnius Sículus*, °bucolic poet in the time of °Nero, imitator of °Virgil. Seven of his poems are extant.

Cálvus. °Licinius.

Cálydon (Καλύδων). Town in Aetolia, where ruled king °Oeneus, who had angered °Artemis by sacrificing too little to her. She sent a wild boar which devastated the countryside. °Meleager called together the heroes of Greece to kill this beast. The first to wound it was °Atalanta, and Meleager finally killed it. He was rewarded with the hide (Ovid *Met.* 8, 267-444).

Calýpso (Καλυψώ). A nymph, who detained °Odysseus for many years on the island of Ogygia.

Cambýses (Καμβύσης). **1.** King of Persia (529-522 BC), son of °Cyrus. He conquered Egypt (527). Before his departure he had his brother °Smerdis murdered. When informed of a revolt in Persia he marched back, but died in Syria. **2.** The father of °Cyrus; he died in 558.

Caménae. Roman water-deities, later identified with the °Muses.

Camílla. A warlike maiden, who assisted °Turnus in his war against °Aeneas (Virg. *Aen.* 7, 803-917; her death 11, 648-835).

Camíllus, *M. Furius Camillus.* Roman general who captured °Veii (c. 396 BC). He was accused of appropriating some of the booty and exiled, but when Rome had been captured by the Gauls, he was recalled and succeeded in defeating the enemy. He suppressed defeatist attempts to abandon Rome (Liv. 5, 19 ff.).

Cámpus Mártius. An open space outside °Rome, on the bank of the river Tiber, used for public games, public meetings etc.; °plan p. 165.

Canal of Corinth. In antiquity, ships had

to be drawn across the °Isthmus; in the time of °Periander a slipway, about 4 m wide, was constructed. The present canal, 6 km long, was dug in 1882-1893; the first attempt (by Nero) had failed; °Corinth.

Cánnae. Village in Apulia on the bank of the river Aufidus, where Hannibal defeated the Romans commanded by L. °Aemílius Paúlus and C. Teréntius °Varro.

canópic jars, in which the Egyptians placed the viscera and brains of their dead; °Tutankhamun. Sometimes these were closed with lids bearing the heads of the four sons of Osiris: Hapi (baboon), Dive-metf (dog), Kebeh-senuf (falcon), and Emset (man). In Etruria, too, similar jars have been found.

cánticum. Part of a Roman comedy that was sung.

lex Canuleía. This granted '°conubium' (the right to marry legally by Roman law) to all citizens (445 BC).

Capáneus (Καπανεύς). One of the °Seven against Thebes. He was struck by lightning when he boasted of scaling the walls, even against the will of the gods.

cápital (capitulum, °ἐπίκρανον). The carved head of a column immediately above the shaft and beneath the enta-blature; °Doric, °Ionic, °Corinthian orders.

capital punishment. At Athens, in ancient times, the condemned were thrown into the 'βάραθρον', a chasm just outside the city. In later times they were forced to drink poison, an extract of hemlock; °Socrates. At Rome the condemned were thrown off the °Tarpeian rock or the 'scálae Gemóniae' or killed in the °carcer.

Cápito. °Ateius.

Cápitol (Capitolium). The south-western peak of the °Capitoline. The triple temple of °Jupiter Capitolinus, °Juno and °Minerva was here. The Capitol was the religious centre of Rome, where the consuls dedicated their first sacrifice.

Cápitoline (Mons Capitolínus). One of

the °Seven Hills on which Rome was built. It had two peaks: on the northern one was the °Arx and the temple of °Juno Moneta, on the south-western one the °Capitol; °plan p. 165.

Captíví. °Plautus.

Cápys (Κάπυς). °Dardanidae p. 60.

Caracálla, *M. Aurélius Sevérus Antonínus,* born 186 AD, emperor 211-217, son of °Septimius Severus and °Julia Domna. He murdered his brother °Geta and embarked on a series of wars until he was assassinated during an expedition against the Parthians (217). His chief reform was the *Constitútio Antoniána* (212), by which all freeborn inhabitants of the Empire were granted citizenship. On the Via °Appia the remains of the public baths (thermae) built by Caracalla are still to be seen. About 1600 people could congregate there and the building is now used for opera performances; °Sevéri p. 173.

cárcer. Prison. The Carcer Maximus in °Rome had three floors, of which the lowest had only an opening in the ceiling (Tullianum); °plan p. 80, 81.

Carínus. Emperor 283-285 AD, murdered by his soldiers when fighting °Diocletian.

Cármen Saeculáre. A poem by °Horace for the Secular Games commissioned by °Augustus (17 BC).

Carménta. Italian goddess of childbirth; her temple in Rome stood near the Porta Carmentalis (°plan p. 165); her festival, the Carmentalia, was cele-brated on the 11th and 15th of January.

Cármina Burána. Collection of chiefly 14th and 15th cent. Latin love- and drinking-songs, discovered on nineteen pages of parchment in the monastery of Benediktbeuern, Bavaria.

Carneádes (Καρνεάδης). °Academy.

Cárrhae. Town in Mesopotamia, in the vicinity of which °Crassus was defeated by the Parthians and afterwards mur-dered (53 BC).

Caryátids. Female figures used as pillars; °Erechtheum; °ill. 39.

Cassándra (Κασσάνδρα). Daughter of °Priam and °Hecuba. °Apollo gave her

39. The Caryatids of the Erechtheum.

the power of prophecy, but caused her never to be believed.

Cassánder (Κάσσανδρος). Son of °Antipater (355-296 BC), fought against his father's successor Polyperchon. He killed Olympias, °Roxana and her little son and was king of Macedon until his death.

Cassiodórus, *Flávius Mágnus Aurélius Cassiodórus* (c. 490-583 AD). Politician and scholar, author of a history of the Goths, which is lost, and several other works on theological and scientific subjects.

Cassiopeía. Mother of °Andromeda.

cássis. Metal °helmet.

Cássius. 1. *Cássius Dío.* °Dio Cassius. **2.** *Cássius Félix.* Physician, author of a manual 'De medicina'. **3.** *L. Cássius Hémina.* °Annalist (2nd cent. BC). **4.** *C. Cássius Longínus.* He was °quaestor of °Crassus at °Carrhae, and rallied the remnants of the Roman army. Supporter of °Pompey, he was afterwards reconciled to °Caesar. He was °praetor

peregrinus 44 BC; probably the chief instigator of Caesar's murder. After Caesar's death he went to Syria, raised an army, was defeated by °Antony at Philippi and committed suicide (42 BC). **5.** °Longinus.

Cástel Sant'Ángelo. Modern name given to the °Mausoleum of °Hadrian. In 590 AD. Pope Gregory the Great, during a procession, had a vision of St. Michael hovering over the monument.

Cástor and Póllux (Κάστωρ; Πολυδεύκης). Twin-brothers (= Dioscuri), sons of °Leda. Pollux was a boxer, Castor a horseman (Hom. *Il.* III, 237). They took part in the °Calydonian Hunt and the expedition of the °Argonauts. When Castor died, Pollux, who was immortal, asked Zeus to grant him death. Both were on °Olympus for six months and for the remaining six months in the Underworld: Zeus gave them the form of the constellation 'Gemini'. The brothers were especially honoured by seamen. Castor's temple was in the °Forum °plan p. 81.

cástra praetória. The barracks, in the north-east part of Rome, of the *cohortes praetoriae* (°praetorium).

catachrésis (κατάχρησις). A form of metonymy in which there is an inherent contradiction of terms: 'vindemia mellis'.

cátacombs. Subterranean cemeteries near Rome, where the early Christians held their services. The origin of the word is unknown.

cataléctic (καταληκτικός). A line of poetry lacking a syllable in the last foot, *e.g.* the dactylic °hexameter.

catalépton (κατὰ λεπτόν). 'In detail'; °hypostasis. Title of a collection of fourteen poems in different metres, supposed to be written partly by °Virgil.

cátapult. Siege-engine, which projected missiles upwards; °ill. 40.

Cátiline, *L. Sergius Catilína.* Instigator of the conspiracy against the Roman government which the consul °Cicero was instrumental in averting (63 BC). The plot was discovered and the leaders taken prisoner. Catiline left Rome and

40. Catapult.

was killed near Pistorium in 62 (°Cic. *Cat.*:°Sall. *Cat.*).

Cáto 1. *M. Pórcius Cáto* (Cato Maiór, Cato Censórius), 234-149 BC, consul in 195, °censor in 184 (°basilica Porcia). He was extremely conservative and patriotic and opposed the influence of Greece on Roman civilisation. Of his many writings only 'De agricultura' is left. **2.** *M. Pórcius Cáto* (Cáto Uticénsis), great-grandson of **1**. (95-46), supporter of °Pompey. He was a °Stoic and after the battle of °Thapsus he committed suicide, because he did not want to outlive the republic. Before his death he read °Plato's *Phaedo*. **3.** *M. Pórcius Cáto Liciniánus*. Eldest son of **1**., author of a manual on law which has been lost. **4.** *P. Valérius Cáto* (1st cent. BC). Poet and grammarian; of his writings none is extant.

Catúllus, *C. Valérius Catúllus*. Roman lyric and love poet (c. 87-54 BC), lover of°Clodia. The remains of his villa near Sirmio on Lake Garda are still to be seen.

Caúdium. Town in Samnium, in the proximity of which a Roman army was trapped in the 'Caudine Forks' by the Samnites led by Pontius Herennius, surrendered and was forced to pass under the yoke (321 BC).

caulículi. The fluted stalks of the conventional °acanthus on °Corinthian capitals.

Cécrops (Κέκροψ). King of Attica, founder of the Athenian citadel 'Cecropia'.

Celaéno (Κελαινώ). °Pleiades.

célla. That part of the temple where the statue of the deity was placed;°ill. 65.

Célsus, *A. Cornélius Célsus* (c. 30 AD). Author of an encyclopaedia on all branches of science, of which all but books 6-13 are lost. These deal with medicine. As he himself was a layman, he used Greek sources.

Celts (Κελτοί, Celtae). A tribe called Gauls by the Romans. Their civilisation is known mainly from archaeological researches.

cénsor. An important official in republican Rome. There were two, chosen every fifth year in the °comitia centuriata from among the ex-consuls. After 339 BC at least one of them had to be a °plebeian (lex °Publilia Philonis). Their period of office was eighteen months and they performed all functions together except the °lustrum. Their duties consisted of:

1. The *census*, the registration of all Roman citizens and their property, ending in a religious ceremony: the °lustrum.

2. The *régimen mórum*, the supervision of morals, whether every citizen had done his duty by the state. Punishment (*nóta censória*) consisted of removal from the senate (*senátu movére*) for senators, being struck from the list of °knights (*equúm adímere*) for *equites*, and for other citizens removal to another °tribus.

3. *léctio senátus*. The reading of the new list of senators. He whose name was read first was the 'princeps senatus'; he whose name was omitted, had been expelled (*praeteríre*).

4. *locationes censóriae*, the leasing of public areas and buildings (*aedifícia sárta técta tuénda locáre*), the farming out of tolls (*portória*) and taxes (*vectigália*).

An ex-censor was buried in °purple (*fúnus censórium*).

Censorínus. Grammarian, author of 'De die natali' (238 AD).

cénsus. °censor.

Céntaur(s) (Κένταυρος). **1.** Originally a wild tribe of Thessaly, exterminated by the °Lapiths. **2.** Later they were represented as half human, half horse; °Cheiron; °Nessus.

Centimáni (Ἑκατόλχειρες). Three °giants with a hundred hands: Cottus, Briáreus (or Aegaéon) and Gyas, son of °Uranus and °Gaea (Hes. *Theog.* 147-153). They helped °Zeus in his war against the °Titans.

centúria. In republican times the army of Rome was levied by dividing the citizens into 193 groups (*centúriae*) and taking a hundred men from each. There were eighteen *centúriae equítum equo publico*, five *centuriae* of *proletárii* and *libertíni* (freedmen), 170 *centúriae* of wealthy free citizens, divided into five classes of wealth. The lowest were the *velites*. This same division was also used at the election of a °consul, °praetor or °censor: the °*comítia centuríata*.

In °Marius' time, the °census was no longer used for the levy. Soldiers were recruited from all classes of citizens, and a *centuria* became part of the °maniple: two *centuriae* made up a *manipulus*.

centúrion (centúrio). Professional officer of the Roman army, two being in charge of a °maniple. Each legion had sixty, they had differing ranks, the chief centurion being called *primipulus*. Centurions were recruited from the ranks; °ill. 41.

41. Centurion from the end of the first century AD. He wears a Roman °helmet, coat of mail, °scutum, greaves sword (on his right) and a spear.

Céphalus (Κέφαλος). Husband of Procris. She followed her husband out of jealousy when he went hunting, and was killed accidentally by his spear (Ovid. *Met.* 7, 661-865).

Cépheus (Κηφεύς). King of Ethiopia, father of °Andromeda.

Cephisódotus (Κηφισόδοτος). Athenian sculptor (early 4th cent. BC), father of °Praxiteles.

Céphisus (Κηφισός). River to the west of Athens.

Cerameícus (Κεραμεικός). The 'Potters' Quarter', at Athens.

Cérberus (Κέρβερος). Three-headed dog, guarding the entrance to the Underworld, which allowed no-one to leave; °Heracles; °Orpheus.

Céres. Roman goddess of agriculture after the famine of 493 BC. Her festival, the 'Cerealia', was celebrated on the 19th April. She was represented with ears of corn and a basket of fruit. Later she was identified with °Demeter.

Ceriális, *Q. Petil(l)ius Ceriális Caésius Rúfus.* Legate (61 AD) of the 'Legio IX Hispana' in °Britain. Early in 70 AD he was sent to Germania Inferior to fight Julius Civilis. From 71-74 he was governor of Britain.

Cerýnea (Κερύνεια). Town and mountain in Achaea, where a stag lived which °Heracles had to catch.

Céto (Κητώ). °Gorgons.

Céyx (Κήυξ). Husband of °Alcyone.

Chaeronéa (Χαιρώνεια). Town in Boeotia notable for three battles: in 447 BC the Boeotians defeated the Athenians, in 338 °Philip of Macedon defeated the Athenians and Thebans, and in 86 BC °Sulla won a victory over °Mithridates.

chairs. The chairs of the Greeks were of three types: 1. *thrónos* (θρόνος). The stately chair used by gods, heroes, princes and other people of importance. It usually had a back, and sometimes arms, the legs were carved or turned. 2. *díphros* (δίφρος). A stool with four (turned) legs. 3. *klismos* (κλισμός). A light comfortable chair with curving back and legs. At about the height of the shoulders the back had a horizontal support. The seat might be plaited; ills. 42, 43, 44.

42. Diphros.

At dinner the Greeks did not sit on chairs but reclined on a κλίνη (couch) with one or two ends; °ill. 12.

43. Klismos.

44. Putting on a girdle.

Cháos (Χάος). The 'gaping void' out of which °Gaea was born (Ovid *Met.* 1, 5-88).

Cháres (Χάρης). °Rhodes.

Charísius. Author of a Latin grammar, 4th cent. AD.

Chárites (Χάριτες). The °Graces. °Homer mentioned one 'Cháris' as the wife of °Hephaestus (= °Αφροδίτη?).

Cháriton (Χαρίτων). Author of a novel, *Chaereas and Callirhoë* (1st or 2nd cent. AD).

Cháron (Χάρων). The old ferryman who conveyed the spirits of the dead across the °Styx. His charge was one °obol, which was put in the mouth of the dead before burial.

Charýbdis (Χάρυβδις). °Scylla.

Cheílon (Χείλων). Politician in Sparta, one of the °Seven Sages. His motto was 'know yourself' (γνῶθι σεαυτόν).

Cheíron (Χείρων). A centaur, who lived in a cave on Mt Pelion. He had been taught by Apollo and Artemis and was tutor to many heroes: Asclepius, °Jason, °Theseus, °Achilles. After his death he was changed into the constellation of the Archer.

Chéops. Greek form for °Khufu.

Chéphren. °Khafre.

Cherúsci. German tribe between the rivers Elbe and Weser. They defeated the Romans under °Varus in the 'Teutoburgian Forest' (9 AD), but never recovered their strength after their defeat by °Germanicus.

chiásmus. Crosswise arrangement of word groups, called after the Greek letter X (chi): 'ubi duxere impulsu vestro, vestro impulsu easdem exigunt'.

Chimaéra (Χίμαιρα). A fire-breathing monster which devastated the fields in Lycia; killed by °Bellerophon. It was 'lion before, serpent behind, she-goat in the middle' (Hom. *Il.* VI, 181).

chíton (χιτών). In °Homer, a linen dress for men; in later times, any

45. Statue of Artemis found at Gabii (after a Greek original from about 350 BC). She is wearing a large chiton with two girdles and she is about to pin a cloak over the chiton.

46. Relief on a tombstone in Athens. The lady sitting on a °klismos is wearing a fine linen chiton, with four fastenings on the shoulder and upper arm, a cloak over her legs. The maid-servant has a woollen °peplos with short bosom fold (*c.* 425 BC).

47. Funeral relief of Sosias and Kephisodoros (*c.* 425 BC). On the left is a priest in a long chiton without girdle and with short sleeves; on the right two soldiers in short chiton with girdle.

under-garment of wool or linen. The chiton was worn by women in the form of a °peplos which consisted of two pieces of linen ('pteruges') sewn together. However, the original form of the chiton was cylindrical. Its length varied from 1-2 m. Usually a girdle was worn round it (°ill. 44), occasionally two; °ill. 45; sometimes fastenings on the shoulder gave it the appearance of having sleeves (°ill. 46). For men the chiton was made of wool or linen, usually without a breast-fold and worn long or short; long by the Ionians (Hom. *Il.* XIII, 685) and by priests, short by others; °ills. 47, 48.

48. The Charioteer of °Delphi (*c.* 470 BC). He is wearing a long and ample °chiton sewn together on the arms and with a girdle.

chlaína (χλαῖνα). Woollen cloak with breast-fold, mostly worn by peasants and soldiers; similar to the °himation.

chlámys (χλαμύς). Cloak worn by young men, horsemen and soldiers, fastened by a °fibula on the right shoulder; °ill. 49.

Chlöe (Χλόη). **1.** Title of °Demeter at Athens as goddess of the young crops. **2.** *Daphnis and Chloë,* °Longus.

Chlóris (Χλῶρις). Goddess of flowers, wife of °Zephyrus; °Flora.

Choéphoroi. 'Libation-bearers', tragedy by °Aeschylus.

choliámbus (χωλίαμβος, also σκάζων). A 'limping' iambic verse, of which the last foot is a °trochee: ⌣ ⌣́ ⌣ ⌣́ ⌣ ⌣́ ⌣ ⌣́ ⌣ ⌣́ ⌣́ ⌣.

chorégia (χορηγία). One of the Athenian °liturgies: it consisted of defraying the expenses of equipment and rehearsals of the chorus in a theatrical performance.

chóreus = °trochee.

choriámbus (from χόριος, ἴαμβος). A metrical foot consisting of a °trochee and an °iamb; ⌣́ ⌣ ⌣ ⌣́.

'Chorizóntes' (Χωρίζοντες). Ancient scholars, who supposed the *Iliad* and the *Odyssey* to be the work of two different poets; °Homeric question.

Chryséïs (Χρυσηίς). Daughter of Chryses, priest of °Apollo at Chryse. She was in the Greek camp as a slave of °Agamemnon. When the latter refused to return her to her father, °Apollo sent a plague and thus forced him to obey (Hom. *Il.* I, 8-347); °Briseïs.

Chrysíppus (Χρύσιππος). **1.** Son of °Pelops and Axíoche, murdered by his step-brothers: °Tantalidae p. 182. **2.** °Stoic philosopher (281-208), pupil of °Cleanthes and third head of the Stoa. He was a prolific writer (fragments are left) and he greatly elaborated the Stoic system.

Chrýsostom (Χρυσόστομος). °Dio; °John.

Chrysóthemis (Χρυσόθεμις). Daughter of °Agamemnon and °Clytaemnestra; °Tantalidae p. 182.

Cícero, *M. Túllius Cícero* (106-43 BC). Born at Arpinum in Latium, Roman politician, orator and writer. From 79-77 he studied at Athens; after holding several other offices, he was °consul in 63 (°Catiline). Banished in 58, he returned in 57, was proconsul of Cilicia (51) and supporter of °Pompey. After °Pharsalus he was treated kindly by °Caesar, but after his death he fiercely attacked °Antony in his 'Orationes Philippicae'. He was outlawed by the °triumvirate (43) and murdered. By his first marriage, with

49. One of the reliefs of the °Parthenon still *in situ*. The horseman is wearing an °exomis and over it a fluttering chlamys.

Terentia, he had a son M. Tullius Cicero and a daughter °Tullia (Tulliola), whom he loved dearly. Many of Cicero's writings are left: 1. Rhetorical: *De inventione, Brutus, De claris oratoribus, Orator* (the perfect orator), *De oratore.* 2. Speeches: *Against °Verres, Against Catilina, In defence of Murena, In defence of °Sulla, Against Antony* (= 'Philippicae'). 3. Political: *De Republica (°Somnium Scipionis), De legibus.* 4. Moral treatises: *De officiis* (°Panaetius), *Cato maior, De senectute, Laelius, De amicitia.* 5. Philosophical works: *Academica, De fato, De finibus bonorum et malorum, Tusculanae disputationes.* 6. Religious: *De natura deorum, De divinatione.* 7. Letters.

'Cicerónianism'. The tendency to consider only the Latin of °Cicero correct.

Cílnius. °Maecenas.

Címbri. German race, who together with the Teutones invaded Roman territory, but were defeated at Vercellae in north Italy by °Marius, 101 BC.

Cimmérians (Κιμμέριοι). **1.** Legendary people of the West 'on whom the sun never looks' (Hom. *Od.* XI, 13-19). **2.** Tribe of the Crimea which invaded Lydia and were repelled (c. 650 BC).

Címon (Κίμων). Son of °Miltiades (born 504 BC). Athenian politician, who fought against the Persians and defeated them near the river Eurymedon in Pamphylia, 469. In 460, he was banished as leader of the conservatives (°ostracism). He defeated the Persians again off Salamis in Cyprus (449).

47

Cincinnátus, *L. Quínctius Cincinnátus.* Appointed °dictator in 458 BC; he was informed of his appointment while ploughing. Within sixteen days he defeated the enemy, the °Aequi, and resigned his dictatorship to return to his farm. He was often referred to as an example of Roman simplicity and loyalty to the state.

L. Cíncius Aliméntus. Roman °annalist, who wrote in Greek, c. 210 BC.

cínctus Gabínus. °toga.

cíngulum milítiae. The stomach armour of Roman soldiers, in use from the 1st c. AD, not meant to carry the sword, but in the form of an apron of metal; ill. 50.

50. Roman foot-soldier (1st cent. AD). He is wearing a leather cuirass, breeches made of strips of leather, a shield and a spear. His stomach is protected by an apron of metal ('cingulum').

Cíneas (Κινέας). Friend of °Pyrrhus of Epirus, who twice went on an embassy to Rome and advised Pyrrhus not to invade Italy.

Cínna, *L. Cornélius Cínna.* Consul 86 BC, supporter of °Marius. Together they terrorized Rome and massacred °Sulla's supporters. He was killed by his own soldiers (84). His daughter °Cornelia was °Caesar's first wife.

Círce (Κίρκη). Enchantress, sister of Pasiphaë, wife of °Minos, on the island of Aeaéa, who turned °Odysseus' companions into swine; °Picus.

circus. An enclosure for chariot races, divided down the middle by the *spína,* marked at each end by turning-posts (*métae*). The largest circus in Rome was the *Circus Maximus,* 600 m long, between the °Palatine and °Aventine. The *Circus Flaminius* was built in 221 BC by C. °Flaminius on the °Campus Martius; °ill. 51.

Círis. Poem by an unknown author, telling the legend of °Scylla who betrayed her father °Nisus.

cíthara (κιθάρα). Stringed instrument, with a sound-box of wood. It was played while standing, with the aid of a plectrum; °ill. 52; °Muses, °Amphion.

citizenship (= *civitas*). Roman citizenship, which originally only the freeborn inhabitants of Rome possessed, was first extended by granting limited citizenship (*cívitas sine suffrágio*) to the inhabitants of captured towns (the first being Caére in 353 BC), called *municipia.* This custom was about to be discontinued, when the °Social War made new extension necessary (*lex Iúlia* 90, *lex Plaútia Papíria* 89). After °Caesar's time several towns outside Italy were included, until finally the °*Constitútio Antoniniána* of the emperor °Caracalla granted citizenship to all free inhabitants of the empire. Complete citizenship comprised °*conubium,* °*commercium,* the right to hold offices (*iús honórum*), and voting rights (*iús suffrágii*).

Civil Wars. The first was fought between °Marius and °Sulla (88-82 BC), the second between °Caesar and °Pompey (49-45).

Cívilis. °Iulius Civilis.

Cívitas Déi. °Augustine.

Claúdia. 1. Daughter of the emperor °Claudius and Plautia °Urgulanilla (Suet. *Claud.* 27); °Julio-Claudian dynasty p. 101. **2.** *Claúdia Augústa.* Daughter of the emperor °Nero and °Poppaea, who died at four months (63 AD).

Claudiánus, *Claúdius Claudiánus* (died 404 AD). A Roman poet laureate. He eulogized °Stilicho and °Honorius. He wrote poetry of various kinds including the 'Ráptus Prosérpinae'.

51. Part of a reconstructed model of Rome. In the foreground is the Circus Maximus.

52. Playing the cithara.

Claúdius. **1.** *App. Claúdius.* One of the °decemviri; °Verginia. **2.** *App. Claúdius Caécus.* Censor in 312 BC. He built the via °Appia, the Aqua Appia, and was a political reformer. Of his writings, known to Cicero, only fragments are left. **3.** *Ti. Claúdius Caésar Augústus Germánicus.* The emperor Claudius (41-54), son of Nero Claúdius °Drúsus and °Antónia Minor, born 10 BC at Lugunum (Lyons). From childhood he suffered from bad health, but had a scholastic turn of mind (°alphabet). He remained in the background at court until the death of °Augustus. After °Gaius' death he was made emperor by the Praetorian Guard. During the last years of his reign, he was under the influence of his wife °Agrippina and freedmen. He invaded °Britain and pronounced it a Roman province; °Domitii p. 68; °Julio-Claudian dynasty p. 101.

4. *Claúdius Civílis*, °Július Civílis. **5.** °Galenus. **6.** °Marcéllus. **7.** *Ti. Claúdius Néro.* Married °Livia, father of the emperor °Tiberius. He was a supporter of °Antony and fled to Sicily (40 BC) with his wife and children. Afterwards he returned to Rome, where °Augustus met Livia and persuaded him to divorce her; °Julio-Claudian dynasty p. 101. **8.** *Q. Claúdius Quadrigárius,* °Annalists.

clávi figéndi cáusa. Once every hundred years a °*dictátor clávi figéndi cáusa* was appointed in Rome. He had to perform a religious ceremony, originally °Etruscan: to strike a nail into a temple wall to mark the passing of a century.

Cleánthes (Κλεάνθης). Successor to °Zeno as head of the °Stoa (258 BC). He is the author of an extant °hymn to °Zeus

Cleárchus (Κλέαρχος). Commander of °Cyrus' Greek army. After the battle of °Cunaxa (in 401 BC) he was treacherously murdered by °Tissaphernes.

Cleísthenes (Κλεισθένης). Leader of the Athenian popular party after the expulsion of Hippias (510 BC); founder of the Athenian democracy; °boule; °ostracism; °demos; °phyle.

Cleítus (Κλεῖτος). General of °Alexander the Great, who saved the king's life at the battle of the °Granicus (334 BC). Seven years later he was killed by Alexander in a brawl.

Clémens. **1.** Bishop of Rome, author of a 'Letter to the Corinthians' (c. 96 AD). **2.** *T. Flávius Clémens* (c. 200 AD). Teacher of °Origenes. In his chief work 'Strómateis' he tried to reconcile Greek philosophy with Christian faith.

Cléobis (Κλέοβις) **and Bíton.** Sons of a priestess of °Hera at Argos, who drew her chariot a long way to the temple. When their grateful mother begged the goddess to give them the greatest blessing possible, they died in their sleep (Hdt. 1, 31).

Cleóboulus (Κλεόβουλος). °Tyrant of Lindos, one of the °Seven Sages. His motto was: 'the best thing is moderation' (μέτρον ἄριστον).

Cleómenes (Κλεομένης). **1.** *Cleomenes I.* King of Sparta, who helped to expel °Hippias from Athens (510 BC). **2.** *Cleomenes III.* Son of Leonidas, king of Sparta (235-219), fought against °Aratus, the general of the °Achaean League. He reorganized the Spartan state by dismissing the °ephors and redistributing the land among the citizens.

Cléon (Κλέων). A tanner's son in Athens; after °Pericles' death 'leader of the people', and opponent of °Nicias. Historians of his time describe him as a demagogue.

Cleopátra (Κλεοπάτρα). Daughter of Ptolemy XI Auletes, married to her brother Ptolemy XII Dionysus. She was deposed because of her ambition, but succeeded in regaining the throne with the assistance of °Caesar (47 BC). She followed Caesar to Rome and, after his death, allied herself to °Antony. After the battle of °Actium she committed suicide; °ill. 53.

clépsydra (κλεψύδρα). Water-clock, used chiefly to mark the time allowed to a speaker at an assembly, its water running from one vessel into another in a set time; °ill. 54.

cléruchy (κληρουχία). A colony of Athenian farmers, originally in dangerous border regions, who retained their citizenship, and were not independent; °colonia.

clímax (κλῖμαξ). Rhetorical use of a number of ideas organised in a series to reach a crescendo: *e.g.* 'prope est a te deus, tecum est, intus est.'

Clio (Κλειώ). °Muses.

clipéus. Circular bronze shield, used by the Romans since the time of °Servius Tullius.

Clitías. Painter of the °François vase.

clivus Argentárius. A street in Rome which led past the °carcer to the °forum; °plan p. 81.

clívus Capitolínus. A street in Rome leading up the slope of the °Capitoline; °plan p. 81.

Cloáca Máxima. The great sewer of

53. Cleopatra.

54. Reconstruction of a clepsydra, found in 1933 in Athens. The cups are 23 cm. high and contain 6.5 l. of water ($\chi\chi = 2$ χόες), which runs away in 6 minutes. Then the cups are changed round, to be used again.

Rome, an underground vaulted stream, running into the Tiber; °plan p. 81.

Clódia. Sister of P. °Clódius Pulcher, beloved of °Catullus, in whose poems she is called 'Lesbia'.

Clódius, P. *Clódius Púlcher.* °Tribune of the people, enemy of °Cicero. In 62 BC, he forced his way into the house of the °Pontifex Maximus, dressed as a woman, where the festival of °Bona Dea was being celebrated. In 58, he had Cicero banished. He terrorized the city with armed gangs, but was killed (52) while fighting his rival T. Annius °Milo; °Clodia.

Cloélia. Roman maiden who fled from °Porsenna's camp where she was a hostage and swam across the Tiber (Liv. 2, 13).

Clótho (Κλωθώ). °Fates.

Clýmene (Κλυμένη). Wife of Iasus, mother of °Atalanta.

Clytaemnéstra (Κλυταιμνήστρα). Daughter of °Tyndareus and °Leda, wife of °Agamemnon. Helped by °Aegisthus, she killed her husband on his return from Troy and was herself killed by °Orestes, her son; °Aeschylus; °Eurpides; °Tantalidae p. 182.

Cnóssus (Κνωσός). °Knossos.

Cocýtus (Κώκυτος). One of the rivers in °Hades.

códex. Originally a block of wood, later a wooden writing-tablet (*tábula ceráta*) and eventually a book with pages as opposed to the book-roll: °books; °wax-tablet.

Códex Iustiniánus. °Corpus iuris.

Códex Theodosiánus. Collection of imperial laws (*constitutiones*) from the time of °Constantine the Great onwards, compiled in 438 AD, in the reign of °Theodosius II.

Códrus (Κόδρος). Legendary last king of Attica, who sacrificed himself for his country in the battle against the °Dorians.

Coélius. °Caelian.

cóhors (cohort). Military unit, consisting of six °*centuriae*. Ten cohorts made up a legion. In later times an auxiliary unit was also called cohort.

cóhors praetória. **1.** The body-guard of a general, consisting of °evocati and young men of established families who accompanied the commander voluntarily. **2.** *Cohórtes praetóriae*, °praetorium.

coins. Greek coins, °p. 85; Roman coins °p. 164.

Collatínus. °Lucretia.

colónia. The colonists who emigrated from Greek cities because of overpopulation, political quarrels etc., to found trading-posts, were politically independent when founding an 'ἀποικία' but relations with the mother-city remained. Roman colonies were meant to be military outposts. Many retained Roman citizenship especially the 'colóniae maritímae'; others were 'colóniae Latínae' and possessed Latin citizenship (°ius Látii).

colónia Agrippína. Cologne; °Germany.

Colónus (Κολωνός). A hill a mile north of Athens, where °Oedipus died; °Sophocles.

Colosséum. The name usually given to the *Amphitheátrum Flávium*, built by the emperor °Vespasian, opened by °Titus in 80 AD, and restored by °Domitian, °Trajan and °Hadrian. It was erected in the middle of °Rome, p. 49. Its height was 49 m., its length 188 m. Beside it was the enormous Colossus, statue of Nero as the sun-god, hence its name; °theatre.

Colóssi of Memnon. °Memnon 2.

Colóssus of Rhodes. °Rhodes; °ill. 55.

Columélla, *L. Iuńius Moderátus Columélla* from Gades (c. 60 AD), author of an extensive treatise on agriculture. The 10th book is written in hexameters as a supplement to °Virgil's Georgics.

cólumn kráter. °Krater with two handles, shaped as columns, between mouth and body; °ill. 56.

Colúmna Phócae. In the centre of the Forum, erected in 608 AD, probably on the spot of an earlier column.

Colúmna Rostráta. Column erected at Rome to commemorate the victory of °Duillius over the Carthaginians. It was decorated with the beaks of captured ships; °rostra; ill. 57.

Comedy. We divide Greek comedy into

55. The Colossus of Rhodes, as shown (theoretically) on a Greek stamp.

three periods: 1. The Old Comedy, in which °Aristophanes was the most important writer. Political and topical allusions were never absent from his plays. 2. The Middle Comedy, without political purport, in which the chorus no longer played a prominent part (after 400 BC). 3. The New Comedy (from c. 320 onwards), its greatest poet being °Menander.

comítia. Assembly of the people in Rome, in which a proposal was put to the vote. The name is derived from °Comitium. There were several different *comitia*: 1. *Comítia curiáta*. The oldest Roman popular assembly, voted by °curiae. It witnessed the choice of a king, the declaration of war, adoptions, the making of wills, etc. C. 240 BC the *comitia curiata* had lost all real authority; an assembly of thirty °lictors was considered sufficient. 2. *Comítia centuriáta*, voted by °centuriae. In this assembly, presided over by a °consul, the consuls, °praetors and °censors were elected. The *centuriae* of the °equites

56. A red-figured column krater of the 5th cent. BC, showing a battle of Amazons.

originally had the right to vote first (*praerogatíva*). After 240 BC this was decided by ballot. At the same time the *comitia centuriata* were re-organized in order to lessen the influence of the wealthy citizens. 3. *Comítia tribúta*, instituted in 449 BC (°secessio plebis), elected the less important officials (°quaestor; °aedilis curulis). It was presided over by a patrician, a °consul or the °praetor urbanus; °magistratus minores.

Comítium. 'Meeting-place' in Rome, a paved square on the north side of the °forum, where originally the *comítia curiáta* (°comítia 1.) were held; °plan p. 80.

commércium. The right of any Latin citizen to enter into contracts with a Roman according to the forms of Roman law; °citizenship.

Commodiánus. Christian poet (3rd cent.

57. The Columna Rostrata reconstructed.

AD?), author of 'Carmen Apologéticum' and 'Instructiónes', a collection of short poems. Much of his work was written in accented verse, without due regard for the quantity of the syllables.

Commódus, *L. Aélius Aurélius Commódus.* Roman Emperor (180-192 AD), son of °Marcus Aurelius and °Faustina, cruel and extravagant, °Aurélii p. 31.

concílium plébis. The °plebeian assembly, instituted in 494 BC after the first °secessio plebis. Laws that were passed here originally applied only to plebeians and were called *plebiscíta*. In later times the *plebiscita* were given equal validity with the laws. Consequently the difference between *concilium plebis* and °comitia tributa was no longer important.

Concórdia. Goddess of Concord; her principal temple at Rome near the °forum was built by °Camillus (367 BC). In this temple °Cicero delivered his fourth oration against °Catiline; °plan pp. 80, 81.

Confessiónes. °Augustine.

cóngius. °Weights and measures.

Cónon (Κόνων). Athenian admiral, who defeated the Spartans under Peisander at Cnidus (394 BC); °Timotheus.

Consolátio ad Líviam. A poem by an unknown author consoling °Augustus' wife on the death of her son °Drusus (9AD). Probably composed at a much later date.

Constantine the Great. *Flávius Valérius Constantínus.* Emperor 306-337 AD. He favoured Christianity and eventually made it the state cult (312). He reorganized the administration of the Empire and made Byzantium (= 'Constantinople') a new centre of government; °Constantius.

Constántius Chlórus, *Flávius Valérius Constántius Chlórus* (c. 250-306 AD. Appointed to rule by °Diocletian (293), co-emperor of the West (305), father of °Constantine the Great.

Constitútio Antoniniána. °Caracalla.

constitutiónes. The legislative enactments of a Roman emperor: 1. *Edícta.* General provisions of the emperor as an official. 2. *Decréta.* Judgments of the emperor as a judge. 3. *Rescrípta.* Answers to those who asked the emperor questions on points of law. 4. *Mandáta.* Instructions to officials; °Caracalla.

cónsul. After the expulsion of the kings (c. 510 BC) two consuls were the highest officials. They were elected annually in the °comitia centuriata (°Sextius). They presided at the sessions of the senate, received persons wanting to speak in the senate, maintained order and commanded the army. They were preceded by twelve °lictors. The year was named after them; °senatus.

Cónsus. Italian deity of the storing ('condere') of the harvest.

contaminátio. Blending of several Greek plays into one new Latin play, as done by °Naevius and °Terence.

cóntio. Assembly of the people; there were three kinds: 1. The *contio* which was summoned by an official or priest on occasions of political or religious moment (*in contióne* = publicly). 2. The *contio* in which an official announced an edict or delivered a speech. 3. The *contio* which preceded the *comitia* and in which, *e.g.* a proposal was defended; °Comitium.

conúbium. The right to marry legally, according to Roman law; °lex Canuleía; °marriage; °citizenship.

conveníre in mánum. °marriage.

Cópa. A poem dubiously ascribed to °Virgil, in which a landlady describes to a wayfarer the delights of her inn.

Córbulo, *Cn. Domítius Córbulo.* General under °Claudius and °Nero, famous for his victories over the Germans (47 AD), the Armenians and the Parthians. Jealous of his success, Nero had him condemned to death (66).

Corínna (Κόριννα). Greek lyric poetess (c. 500 BC).

Córinth (Κόρινθος). The city on the Isthmus between northern Greece and the Peloponnese. It was a flourishing city with three harbours. Destroyed by °Mummius (146 BC); °Isthmus; °Canal of Corinth, °ill. 58.

Corínthian order. The richest of the Greek orders of architecture and last in the period of development. It was more imposing than either °Doric or °Ionic; the columns were sometimes fluted and the °capitals variously ornamented and supported by elaborate °acanthus foliage; °ill. 59.

Corinthian War. The war of Athens, Corinth, Thebes and Argos against Sparta (395-387 BC). It ended with the peace of °Antalcidas, favourable to Sparta; °Agesilaus.

Coriolánus, *Cn. Március Coriolánus.* According to tradition a nobleman who wanted to deprive the °plebeians of the tribunate, and was banished because of it (491 BC). He went over to the Volsci and marched on Rome at the head of an army. Only his mother's

58. The Corinth canal.

59. A Corinthian capital.

supplications made him turn back (Liv. 2, 33-40).

Cornélia 1. Daughter of L. Cornélius °Cínna, married to °Caesar (c. 85) Their daughter °Julia married °Pompey. **2.** Daughter of °Scípio Africánus Maíor, married to T. Sempronius °Gracchus, who was many years her senior. After his death (c. 153 BC) she devoted herself entirely to the education of her twelve children, of whom only three survived: Ti. °Gracchus, C. Gracchus and °Sempronia. She was often quoted as the ideal Roman mother.

Cornélius. °Celsus; °Fronto; °Gallus; °Nepos; °Scipio; °Sulla; °Tacitus.

cornice. The upper member of the entablature; °frieze.

córnu cópiae. °Amalthea.

coróna. Middle part of the °cornice, between the °cymatium and the ᵕbed moulding.

Coronéa (Κορώνεια). City in Boeotia; °Agesilaus.

Corónis (Κορωνίς). Daughter of °Phlegyas, mother of °Asclepius by °Apollo.

Córpus iúris civílis. A collection of Roman legal texts compiled by order of the emperor °Justinian. It consisted of: 1. *Digésta* (523), 9123 fragments of the works of thirty-nine jurists from Q. Múcius Scaévola (died 83 BC) to °Constantine the Great; 2. *Institutiónes Iustiniáni* (533 AD), a manual to replace that of °Gaius; 3. *Códex* (534), containing 4652 °constitutiónes, for the greater part °rescrípta; the oldest is of °Hadrian; 4. The so-called *Novéllae*, a collection of '*constitutiones*' of °Justinian of 535-565, compiled during the reign of Tiberius II (578-582).

Corybántes (Κορύβαντες). Priests of °Cybele, who honoured her with wild music and ecstatic dances.

coryphaéus (κορυφαῖος). Leader of the chorus in the Greek theatre.

Cos (Κώς). Island opposite Caria, where thin, transparent garments were manufactured, the *véstes Cóae* or *Cóa*. There was a sanctuary of °Asclepius.

cothúrnus (κόθορνος). Soft leather boot, worn especially by actors. It was raised on a thick wooden sole; °ill. 60.

Cóttus (Κόττος). °Centimani.

Counting systems:
1. *Greek.* The Greeks had two systems. In the older of the two, *e.g.*:

60. Cothurnus.

I = 1,
Γ = 5,
Δ = 10,
H = 100,
X = 1,000
M = 10,000 (*e.g.* M is the initial letter of 'μυρίοι' = 10,000)
Later the alphabet was used thus:

1	α´	10	ι´	100	ρ´
2	β´	20	κ´	200	σ´
3	γ´	30	λ´	300	τ´
4	δ´	40	μ´	400	υ´
5	ε´	50	ν´	500	φ´
6	ς´	60	ξ´	600	χ´
7	ζ´	70	ο´	700	ψ´
8	η´	80	π´	800	ω´
9	θ´	90	ϙ	900	ϡ

(to indicate thousands, the accent was put underneath on the left, *e.g.* ͵β = 2,000.)

2. *Roman.* The Roman system is more familiar:

e.g.:
I = 1
V = 5
X = 10
L = 50
C = 100
D = 500
M = 1,000

Both IIII and IV could represent 4; similarly VIIII and IX equalled 9.

cranes. °Ibycus.
Crássus, *M. Licínius Crássus Dives* (*dives* = rich). Defeated °Spartacus (71 BC). Consul (70) with °Pompey, member of the first °triumvirate (60). His lust for gold made him raise an army and march against the Parthians, by whom he was defeated and murdered (°Carrhae, 53).
Crátes (Κράτης). **1.** °Cynic philosopher from Thebes, pupil of °Diogenes. **2.** *Crates of Mallos* (in Cilicia). Philologist who wrote about °Homer (2nd cent. BC).
Créon ((Κρέων). **1.** King of Thebes, brother of °Jocasta. He reigned after Laius' death and again after °Oedipus had gone into exile; °Sophocles; °Antigone. **2.** King of Corinth, father of °Creüsa.
crépida. °Solea.
crepídula. °Solea.
Crete (Κρήτη). Island south of Greece. 'Cretan art' dates from the 3rd and 2nd millennia, and flourished particularly from the Early to Late Minoan periods; °Knossos; °Minoan civilisation; °Phaestos.
créticus. A metrical foot: _ ⌣ _.
Creüsa (Κρέουσα). **1.** Daughter of °Priam, married to °Aeneas. She disappeared when Aeneas fled from Troy (Virg. *Aen.* 2, 671, ff.). **2.** Daughter of °Creon 2, also called Glauce. °Jason repudiated °Medea for her sake; °Euripides.
Críspus, *C. Sallústius Passiénus Críspus.* Favourite of the emperor °Gaius, married first to Domitia, °Nero's aunt. His second wife was °Agrippina (44 AD), who had him murdered so that she could marry °Claudius; °Domítii p. 68; °Julio-Claudian dynasty p. 101.
Crítias (Κριτίας). Uncle of °Plato (who called one of his dialogues after him), one of the °Thirty Tyrants of Athens (404 BC). He was killed fighting °Thrasybulus (403); °oligarchy.
Croésus (Κροῖσος). Son of °Alyattes, last king of °Lydia (560-546), defeated by °Cyrus (549), famous for his riches and his conversation with Solon on this subject (Hdt. I, 26-33).

Crónus. °Kronos.
Cróton (Κρότων). Flourishing Greek colony in Bruttium; °Pythagoras.
Ctesíbius (Κτησίβιος). Engineer of Alexandria (c. 250 BC), teacher of °Heron.
cúbitus. °Weights and measures 2a.
Cúlex. A poem sometimes ascribed to °Virgil. (A shepherd was startled from his sleep by a mosquito just in time to avoid the bite of a snake. He has already killed the mosquito, whose ghost visits him in his dream.)
Cunáxa (Κούναξα). A place in Babylonia on the river Euphrates, where °Cyrus was killed fighting against °Artaxerxes (401 BC); °Clearchus; °Xenophon.
Cunctátor. °Fábius Máximus.
Curétes (Κουρήτες). Priests of °Rhea in Crete.
Cupid. °Amor.
cúria. 1. °Curiae. **2.** Assembly hall of the Roman senate. The most ancient was the *Cúria Hostília* built by °Túllus Hostílius, restored by Faústus Súlla (50 BC), son of °Sulla, but pulled down by °Caesar (47 BC), who built the *Cúria Iúlia* nearer to the °forum.
cúriae. The Roman families (*gentes*) made up thirty *curiae*, ten of which made a °tribus: Rámnes, Títies, Lúceres. Each *curia* had a place of assembly (°curia) and was led by a *curio*. About 240 BC the °comitia curiata lost their importance.
Curiátii. °Horatii.
Cúrius Dentátus, *M. Cúrius Dentátus.* Roman general who defeated the °Samnites (290 BC) and Pyrrhus (275 at °Beneventum). He was famous for his simplicity and incorruptibleness.
Cúrtius. 1. *M. Cúrtius.* He threw himself, according to legend, fully armed and on horseback, into the chasm that had suddenly opened in the forum. An oracle had said that it would disappear when the chief strength of Rome had been sacrificed to it. The spot was afterwards called *Lácus Cúrtius;* °plan p. 80. **2.** *Q. Cúrtius Rúfus.* Historian of the time of

°Claudius, author of a history of °Alexander the Great, partly extant.

cúrule magistracies. °magistratus.

cýathus. °kyathos; °Weights and measures.

Cyáxares (Κυαξάρης). King of the Medes (634-584 BC), captured °Nineveh and destroyed the Assyrian empire (Hdt. I, 73 ff.).

Cýbele (Κυβέλη). An Asiatic goddess, worshipped especially in Phrygia, where her worshippers were called °Corybantes; °Rhea; °ill. 61.

61. A priest of °Cybele in full regalia. He is wearing a diadem with in front a statuette of Attis and at the sides two of Sozon. In his right hand are a pomegranate and three twigs (symbols of fertility); in his left hand a dish of fruit. At his side hangs a 'flagellum'. On the wall are musical instruments.

Cýclades (αἱ Κυκλάδες). Islands regarded as 'circling' the island of °Delos, whence the name; °Cycladic civilisation.

Cycládic civilisation. The prehistoric civilisation of the °Cyclades (from c. 3000 BC); °Minoan civilisation; °Helladic civilisation.

Cýclic Poets (Κυκλικοί). Imitators of °Homer.

Cýclopean masonry. The prehistoric use of very large, close-fitting, irregular stones. The walls of °Tiryns, °Mycenae, °Argos, and other prehistoric cities elsewhere, were built in that way; °Cyclopes.

Cýclopes (Κύκλωπες). The three one-eyed sons of °Uranus and °Gaea, who helped °Zeus in his battle against the °Titans. They were °Hephaestus' assistants in his smithy under mount Etna. According to legend they built °Cyclopean walls. In °Homer they were a lawless people.

Cydíppe (Κυδίππη). Wife of °Acontius.

Cýgnus (Κύκνος). 1. Son of °Poseidon and supposedly invincible. He fought on the side of the Trojans but was strangled by °Achilles. Poseidon changed him into a swan (Ovid *Met.* 12, 64-170). 2. Son of Sthenelus, legendary king of Liguria. He mourned °Phaëthon deeply and was turned into a swan by Apollo (Ovid. *Met.* 2, 367-380).

Cylléne (Κυλλήνη). Mountain on the border between °Achaea and °Arcadia, where °Hermes was born.

cymátium. The uppermost moulding of a °cornice.

Cynegética. °Grattius; °Nemesianus.

Cýnics. The followers of °Antisthenes.

Cynosárges (Κυνόσαργες). A wrestling place outside Athens, where °Antisthenes had his school.

Cynoscéphalae (Κυνὸς κεφαλαί). Two hills in south-east Thessaly, where T. Quinctius °Flamininus defeated °Philip V of Macedon in 197 BC.

Cýnthia. 1. Name of °Artemis, from Mount Cynthus in °Delos, where she was born. 2. Beloved of °Propertius. Her real name was Hostia.

Cyparíssus (Κυπάριττος), from Keos. He mourned his pet stag which he had accidentally killed, and was turned into a cypress (Ovid *Met.* 10, 106-142).

Cypriánus. *Tháscius Caecílius Cypriánus* (c. 200-258 AD). Teacher of rhetoric, who was converted to Christianity in 245 and appointed bishop of Carthage (249). Some of his letters and other writings are extant. He was martyred in the time of °Valerian.

Cýpselus (Κύψελος). Tyrant of °Corinth, father of °Periander.
'Cyrenáics'. °Aristippus.
Cyropaédía (Κύρου παιδεία). °Xenophon.
Cýrus (Κῦρος). **1.** Son of °Cambyses and °Mandane, grandson of °Astyages, who defeated the Medes and founded the Persian Empire (559 BC). He conquered Lydia (°Croesus) and Babylon and was killed fighting the Massagetae (529; °Tomyris). He was succeeded by his son °Cambyses. **2.** *Cyrus the Younger.* Son of °Dareios II Óchos, °satrap of Lydia, who tried to depose his brother °Artaxerxes, but was killed in the battle of °Cunaxa (401).
Cýzicus (Κύζικος). Town on the south coast of the Propontis, where °Alcibiades defeated the Spartans (401 BC). Its gold coins were famous everywhere ('κυζικηνοί').

D

Dácia. Country on the frontier of the Roman Empire on the north bank of the Lower Danube. °Trajan conquered it and made it a Roman province (102-106 AD), but the country was abandoned in 275.
dáctyl (δάκτυλος. A metrical foot: ‒ ◡ ◡.
Daédalus (Δαίδαλος). Legendary sculptor, architect and inventor. He fled from Athens because he had killed his nephew Perdix, who surpassed him in skill, and went to Crete where he built the labyrinth for °Minos to house the °Minotaur. Because he had assisted °Ariadne, he was imprisoned by Minos, but escaped, having made wings for himself and his son Icarus. Icarus flew too close to the sun, so the wax which held his feathers melted and he fell into the sea, which was called the 'Icarian' after him (Ovid *Met.* 8, 183-235). Daedalus reached Cumae safely. He was reputedly the first to make statues with their eyes open and their feet apart as if walking.
daémon (δαιμόνιον). °Socrates referred thus to his 'inner voice', by which he probably meant 'conscience'.
Dámocles (Δαμοκλῆς). A courtier of °Dionysius I of Syracuse, who praised the tyrant's happiness. Dionysius had a sword hung over his head by a single hair during a banquet, to show him what the real position of a °tyrant was like.
Dámon and Phíntias (Δάμων; Φιντίας). Famous for their friendship. When Phintias had been condemned to death by °Dionysius II but given leave to visit his family, Damon stood bail for him. When Phintias returned at the last moment Dionysius pardoned him and requested their friendship.
Dánaë (Δανάη). Daughter of °Acrisius, mother of °Perseus by Zeus, who visited her in a shower of gold.
Danáïds. The fifty daughters of °Danaüs, who with one exception (Hypermnestra) murdered their husbands, the fifty sons of °Aegyptus, on their wedding night. The only one who was saved, Lynceus, killed Danaüs and his daughters.
Dánaüs (Δαναός). Son of °Belus, fled from his brother Aegyptus to Argos. The fifty sons of Aegyptus followed and asked his daughters in marriage; °Danaids.
Dáphne (Δάφνη). Daughter of the river god Peneius in Thessaly, fled from Apollo and was turned into a laurel tree (Ovid *Met.* 1, 452-567).
Dáphnis (Δάφνις). **1.** Son of °Hermes, flute-player and inventor of °bucolic poetry. **2.** *Daphnis and Chloë,* °Longus.

59

Dardánidae

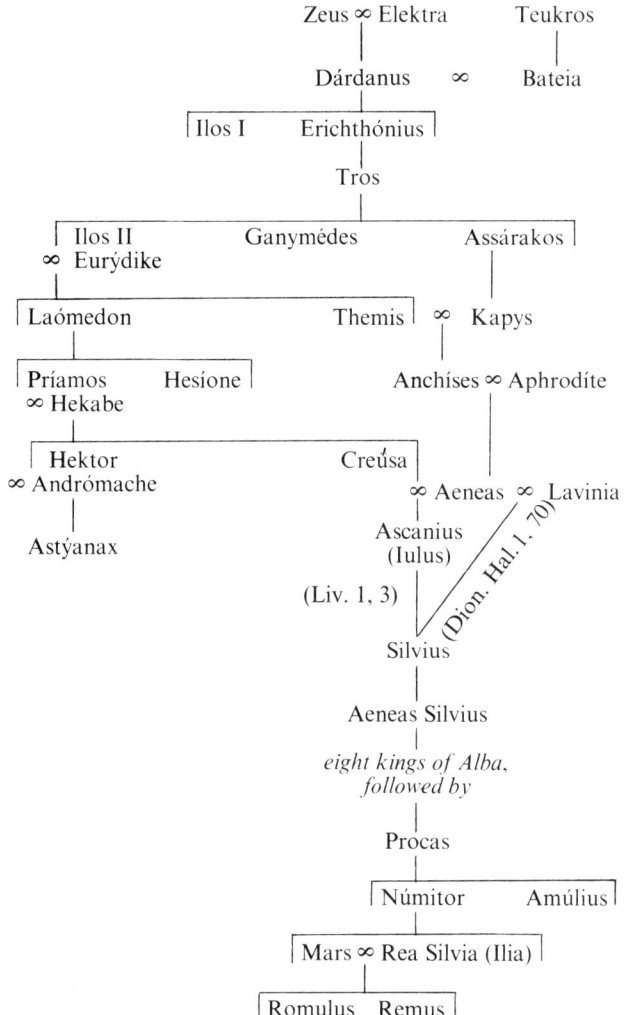

Zeus ∞ Elektra   Teukros

Dárdanus ∞ Bateia

Ilos I   Erichthónius

Tros

Ilos II   Ganymédes   Assárakos
∞ Eurýdike

Laómedon   Themis ∞ Kapys

Príamos   Hesíone   Anchíses ∞ Aphrodíte
∞ Hekabe

Hektor   Creúsa
∞ Andrómache   ∞ Aeneas ∞ Lavinia

Astýanax   Ascanius
    (Iulus)

(Liv. 1, 3)   (Dion. Hal. 1, 70)

Silvius

Aeneas Silvius

eight kings of Alba,
followed by

Procas

Númitor   Amúlius

Mars ∞ Rea Silvia (Ilia)

Romulus   Remus

60

Dárdanus (Δάρδανος). Legendary ancester of the Trojans; °Dardánidae p. 60.

dareíkos (= *dáric*). Persian gold coin (8.41 gr.). The oldest coin with the obverse showing a royal head; ill. p. 85.

Dáres Phrýgius. A history of the °Trojan War by an unknown author translated in the 5th cent. AD is said to have been written by this Phrygian eye-witness. This work was, together with that of °Dictys Cretensis, the source of knowledge of the Trojan War in the Middle Ages.

Darius (Δαρεῖος). 1. *Dareíos Hystáspes*. King of Persia (521-485 BC). He was one of the noblemen who killed the usurper °Smerdis. °Herodotus' story of his accession (3, 80-87) is confirmed by inscriptions in three languages (Babylonian, Old-Persian and Elamite) found near Behistun in western Persia. He enlarged and reorganised the empire, founded a postal service along his new network of roads and regulated the monetary system. He was unsuccessful on his foreign expeditions and was defeated by the Scythians (°Histiaeus) and by the Greeks at °Athos. 2. *Dareíos II Óchos*. King of Persia 424-405. 3. *Dareíos III*. King of Persia (336-330), who lost his empire to °Alexander the Great.

Deceléa (Δεκέλεια). Small town in Attica, occupied by the Spartans in 413 BC. The last part of the °Peloponnesian War was called the Decelean War (413-404).

decémviri (*X viri*). A board of ten officials: 1. *X viri légibus scribéndis*, who prepared the Twelve Tables, a collection of the principal rules of the oldest Roman laws (451-450 BC). 2. *X viri sácris faciéndis* (or *sacrórum* or *líbris Sibyllínis inspiciéndis*), originally *duumviri*, later *quindecimviri*. They kept and consulted the °Sibylline books and led the public services, which were held 'Graeco ritu' (according to Greek rites). 3. *X viri stlítibus iudicándis*, judged suits to decide whether a man was free or a slave.

Décius. 1. *P. Décius Mús*. Gave himself wholeheartedly to the battle with the Latins (340 BC). 2. *P. Décius Mús* (his son), acted similarly against the °Samnites at Sentinum (295).

decréta. °constitutiónes.

decumátes ágri. A territory between the Rhône and Danube, annexed by °Vespasian in 73-74 AD.

deféctive. Nouns and verbs are called defective when they lack one or more of the usual forms of declension or conjugation (*e.g.* vis, vim, vi) and verbs when not all tenses are formed from the same stem (*fero, ferre, tuli, latum*).

Deïaneíra (Δηιάνειρα). Wife of °Heracles, to whom the °centaur Nessus gave his poisoned robe; °Sophocles, *Trachiniae*.

Deïdameía (Δηιδάμεια). Daughter of °Lycomedes, mother of °Neoptolemus by °Achilles.

Deínarchus (Δείναρχος). Born c. 360 BC at Corinth. Orator and politician, supporter of °Cassander.

Deíphobus (Δηίφοβος). Son of °Priam, who married °Helen after the death of °Paris. He was killed by °Menelaus on the capture of Troy.

delátor. °sycophant.

Délia. 1. Epithet of °Artemis. 2. In °Tibullus' poems, the name of his beloved.

Delian Confederacy (Delian League). Founded in 477 BC by °Themistocles, organized by Athens and many islands to continue the naval war against Persia. All members cast one vote. Its treasury was first in °Delos, later at Athens, a move which caused resentment among the members.

Délos (Δῆλος). One of the °Cyclades. According to legend it was originally a floating island, but anchored by Zeus for the sake of °Leto, who gave birth to °Apollo and °Artemis there. It was a centre of the cult of °Apollo, and of international trade; °Delian Confederacy.

Délphi (Δελφοί). Town in Phocis on the southern slope of Mt Parnassus. The Greeks regarded it as the centre of the earth (ὀμφαλός). In the great temple of °Apollo the °Pythia pronounced the oracles of the god through the mouth of the priestess; °tripod.

Deméter (Δημήτηρ). The mother-goddess of the earth, and of fertility, daughter of °Kronos and °Rhea. Her daughter was °Persephone, her foster-son °Triptolemus. Her principal sanctuary was at °Eleusis. She was represented (in sculpture, etc.) seated with a diadem and ears of corn; °Ceres.

Demétrius (Δημήτριος). **1.** *Demétrius Poliorcétes*, son of °Antigonus I. He held all Asia until he was defeated at °Ipsus (301 BC). Demetrius was taken prisoner by °Seleucus and died in 283; °Diadochi. **2.** *Demétrius Phaléreus*, pupil of °Theophrastus, governed Athens 317-307 BC. None of his writings are extant.

Demócritus (Δημόκριτος). Philosopher from °Abdera, born c. 460 BC. He thought all matter to consist of indivisible atoms (ἄτομα), which differed in size, shape and weight. When these 'invisible reals' collided and coalesced all things came to be.

démos (δῆμος). Subdivision of °Cleisthenes' °phylae. He divided a hundred 'demoi' among ten 'phylae'. Later their number was increased.

Demósthenes (Δημοσθένης). The most famous of Attic orators (c. 385-322 BC). He was also a politician and opposed the growing influence of Macedon. Eight of his speeches against °Philip ('Philippicae') are extant. When Demosthenes had been awarded a golden crown (330), °Aeschines protested and Demosthenes defended himself with his famous oration 'De Corona'; °Olynthiacs.

demótic. °Hieroglyphics.

denárius. Roman silver coin; its value was ten times that of an °as (after c. 180 BC); ill. p. 164.

Deucálion (Δευκαλίων) and his wife Pyrrha were the only people left alive after the Great Flood. The oracle of Themis told them to throw 'the bones of their mother' over their shoulders. They took this to mean the stones of Mother Earth and obeyed. From the stones arose a new people (Ovid. *Met.* 1, 324-415); those thrown by Deucalion became men, those thrown by Pyrrha women.

déus ex machína. In Greek drama a deity could suddenly appear on the stage standing on a 'machina', to resolve the action of the play.

Diádes (Διάδης). An engineer who took part in Alexander's expedition and invented several siege engines.

Diádochi (Διάδοχοι). The generals who ruled over the different parts of the empire of Alexander the Great after his death; °Antigonus; °Seluecus; °Lysimachus, etc.

Diadúmenus. °Polycleitus.

diálogue (διάλογος). **1.** The spoken parts of a Greek drama. **2.** Conversation; °Plato.

Diána. Roman moon-goddess, identified with °Artemis.

Dicaeárchus (Δικαίαρχος). of Messana. Pupil of °Aristotle, author of a cultural history of Greece, which is lost.

Di Conséntes. The name which the Romans gave to the twelve superior gods, the *Di maiórum géntium*: 'Iuno, Vesta, Minerva, Ceres, Diana, Venus, Mars, Mercurius, Iovi, Neptunus, Vulcanus, Apollo' (°Ennius' lines).

dictator. Magistrate of Rome, nominated by a °consul on the senate's proposal to undertake a special task in a time of crisis. He resigned after six months. A dictator was usually appointed in times of war: *dictátor réi geréndae caúsa* or *seditiónis sedándae caúsa*. This happened for the last time in 216 BC with M. Iúnius Péra. Dictators were later nominated for lesser reasons: *comitiórum caúsa*, °*clavi figendi caúsa*, *senátus legéndi caúsa*. °Sulla in 82 and Caesar took the title of dictator to gain absolute power: *dictátor réi públicae constituéndae*; Quíntus °Fábius Máximus.

Díctys Creténsis. A history of the °Trojan War was translated from Greek into Latin by Lucius Septimus (4th cent. AD).

It is reputed to have been written by an eye-witness: Dictys: °Dares Phrygius.

Dído (Διδώ). Sister of the legendary king of Tyre, Pygmalion. He killed her husband and she fled to Africa to King Iarbas. There she was given so much land as might be covered by a bull's hide cut into thongs. According to Virgil she committed suicide out of despair at °Aeneas' departure (Virg. *Aen.* 2 and 4).

dídrachm (δίδραχμον). Coin of two drachmaes; °drachma; ill. p. 85.

dies Alliénsis. Unlucky day; °Allia.

Digésta. °Corpus iuris civilis.

dígitus. °Weights and measures 2a.

diïambus. A metrical foot: ⌣ ⏑ ⌣ ⏑.

Di Indígetes. Gods, originally Roman heroes.

Dinárchus. Born c. 360 BC at Corinth. Orator and politician, supporter of °Cassander.

dínos (δῖνος). Name sometimes used instead of °lebes; ill. 62.

62. Dinos on a stand.

Dío (Δίων). **1.** *Dio Cassius* (*Cassius Dio Cocceiánus*), grandson of °Dio Chrysostom (c. 155-235). Orator and politician, author of a history of Rome in eighty books, of which 36-60 are extant. **2.** *Dío Chrýsostom* (*Dío Cocceius Chrysostómus*), born at Prusa,

philosopher and orator of the reigns of °Nerva and °Trajan, one of the best stylists of his day. His orations are extant. **3.** *Dio of Prusa,* °Dio Chrysostom.

Dioclétian, *C. Valérius Aurélius Diocletiánus.* Son of a freedman, became governor of Moesia and was proclaimed emperor in 284 AD. He made the Roman Empire an absolute monarchy and appointed a co-emperor (286) °Maximianus and two °'caesars' (273) °Galerius and °Constantius Chlorus. At this time the term 'plurális maiestátis' came into use. Diocletian harshly persecuted the Christians, introduced an elaborate court ceremonial and built a large palace on the Dalmatian coast (Spalato, Split) to which he retired shortly before his death in 305; ill. p. 164.

Diodórus, of Sicily. Roman historian during the reign of °Augustus, author of a universal history of which books 1-5 and 11-20 are extant.

Diógenes (Διογένης). **1.** Of Sinope. °Cynic philosopher (404-323 BC), pupil of °Antisthenes. He lived according to the Cynic doctrine in great poverty and was the subject of many anecdotes. **2.** *Diógenes Laértius,* from Laërte in Cilicia, author of a work in ten books on the lives and doctrines of famous philosophers.

Diomédes (Διομήδης). **1.** Son of Tydeus, one of the bravest heroes at Troy. Together with °Odysseus he stole the Palladium; °Glaucus. **2.** King of the Bistones in Thrace. He fed his horses on the strangers who arrived in his country. °Heracles killed him and threw him to his own horses. **3.** Author of a Latin grammar in the 4th cent. AD.

Dío(n) (Δίων). Brother-in-law and son-in-law of °Dionysius I. With °Plato's help he tried to exert a favourable influence on the young °Dionysius II. He failed and was banished. He returned to liberate Syracuse, tried to rule according to Platonic ideas, but was murdered.

Dionýsia (Διονύσια). Festival of

°Dionysus: **1.** The Rustic or Lesser Dionysia, celebrated in Attica in December. **2.** The Greater Dionysia, instituted in °Peisistratus' time on the occasion of the performance on three consecutive days of new dramas; celebrated in early April. **3.** Lenaía (Λήναια), a wine festival in January. **4.** Anthestéria ('Αθεστήρια), February 11-13th, when the new wine was tasted.

Dionýsius (Διονύσιος). **1.** *Dionýsius I.* Tyrant of Syracuse (406-367 BC), cruel and suspicious; °Damocles. **2.** *Dionýsius II.* Tyrant of Syracuse (367-357 and 346-344). He was first expelled by his brother-in-law °Dion and when he had returned, was expelled again by °Timoleon; °Damon. **3.** *Dionýsius of Halicarnássus* (late 1st cent. AD). Greek historian, who wrote a history of the Roman Empire in twenty books of which eleven are left. Of greater importance are his rhetorical writings: 'On the arrangement of words' and his studies of Demosthenes, °Thucydides and others. **4.** *Dionýsius Periëgétes.* Author of a geographical work in the time of °Hadrian; °Avienus. **5.** *Dionýsius Thráx* (c. 170-90 BC). Author of a work on grammar which was a standard work for many centuries.

Dionýsus (Διόνυσος). Son of °Zeus and °Semele, god of trees and fruit, especially the vine, worshipped with °Demeter in the °Eleusinian mysteries. The festivals were celebrated with revelry and merrymaking, later drunkenness and debauchery prevailed. °Dionysia; °Bacchanalia. Dionysus' companions were °satyrs and °maenads; °Ariadne.

Diophántus (Διόφαντος), of °Alexandria, Mathematician (3rd cent. AD). He was the first to solve the quadratic equation.

Dioscúri (Διόσκουροι). The twin sons of °Zeus and °Leda; °Castor and Pollux.

díphros. °chairs.

Dípylon (Δίπυλον). One of the town gates of Athens. The important °Geometric style vases that were discovered in the proximity are called 'Dipylon vases'.

Dís. °Hades.

Discóbolus (Δισκοβόλος). The 'discus-thrower', a well-known statue by °Myron, a copy of which is in Rome in the Terme Museum.

Disk of Phaéstos. Disk of baked clay, 16cm in diameter, found in 1908 in °Phaestos (°Crete), now in the museum of Heraklion (Iraklion). On each face is an impressed inscription in a spiral, consisting of symbols which have not been found elsewhere, of a °hieroglyphic type; °ill. 63; °Minoan civilisation, °Phaestos.

63. The Phaestos disk.

dispondéus. A metrical foot: _ _ _ _.

dísticha Catónis. Collection of 142 maxims attributed to °Cato, popularly read until late into the Middle Ages.

dístichon. Couplet of two unequal lines of verse, especially °hexameter and pentameter; *i.e.* elegiac couplet.

dithyramb (διθύραμβος). Originally a °hymn to °Dionysus. °Arion converted it into a literary composition with a set subject. It formed a basis for later Greek tragedy.

ditrochaéus. A metrical foot: _ ᴗ _ ᴗ.

divérbia. The spoken part of a Roman comedy, as opposed to the °canticum.

Djóser (Zoser). Egyptian pharaoh of the 3rd dynasty. His tomb was the step-pyramid at °Saqqara.

dóchmius (δόχμιος). A metrical foot: ᴗ _ _ ᴗ _, in which every long element could be replaced by two short ones.

Dodóna (Δωδώνη). Town in Epirus, seat of an ancient oracle of °Zeus. The rustling of the leaves of an oak and the clashing of the metal cymbals in it foretold the future.

dokimásia (δοκιμασία). An examination of candidates for a public office in Athens.

Domítia 1. °Domítii p. 68. **2.** *Domítia Longína.* Daughter of Cn. Domítius °Córbulo, wife of the emperor °Domitian.

Domítian, *T. Flávius Domitiánus.* Emperor 81-96 AD, son of °Vespasian, brother and successor to °Titus. Although severe, early in his reign he was efficient. He diminished the power of the senate, persecuted the Christians, and his reign ended in terror. He was murdered by his wife and others; °Agricola; °Flavii p. 79.

Domítii. p. 68.

Domitílla. °Flavia Domitilla.

Domítius. 1. *Cn. Domítius Ahenobárbus.* Son of L. Domítius Ahenobárbus and °Antónia Maior, married to °Agrippina (28), died in 40 AD, father of the emperor °Nero; °Domitii p. 68; °Julio-Claudian dynasty p. 101. **2.** *L. Domítius Ahenobárbus;* °Nero. **3.** °Corbulo. **4.** °Ulpian.

dómus. 1. The *Greek* house of the older period is known only from literature, probably because it was made of mud bricks. Houses of °Hellenistic times in °Delos and °Priëne have been excavated: their fronts have no windows and one enters along a corridor, leading to a courtyard surrounded by rooms. **2.** The centre of the *Roman* house was the °atrium, from which the rooms opened. The principal room, the °atrium, was directly opposite the entrance. In later times the back-wall of the *tablinum* was left out and behind it lay the peristyle, a courtyard surrounded by columns, of Greek origin. Originally, houses had a ground floor only, but the use of bricks and mortar made higher buildings possible. After 80 BC social changes made big many-storied buildings necessary; °ill. 64.

Donátus. 1. *Aélius Donátus* (c. 350 AD). Author of a Latin grammar, used until the late Middle Ages, and a commentary on °Terence. **2.** *Claúdius Donátus* (c. 400 AD). Author of a commentary on the °Aeneid.

Dórians (Δωριεῖς). One of the Greek tribes, chiefly in the eastern Peloponnese, Crete and the south-west part of Asia Minor. They reputedly invaded Greece, c. 1000 BC, and ended the °Mycenaean civilisation in that area.

Dóric dialect. Spoken by the °Dorians. In many ways this dialect kept its original form. Characteristic are the first person plural —μες, infinitive —μεν.

Dóric order. One of the three Greek orders of architecture (Doric, °Ionic, °Corinthian) of which it was the oldest, strongest and simplest. It had sturdy, fluted columns, without a base, and the °frieze was divided regularly into °triglyphs and °metopes; beneath each triglyph is a row of *guttae*; ills. 65-67; °Paestum.

Dorýphorus. °Polycleítus.

dráchma (δραχμή). **1.** °Weights and measures 3d. **2.** Greek silver coin, originally of 4.36 g, later 3.41 g. The Romans used this for their foreign trade. The next coin struck (after 269 BC) was the °didrachm, weighing twice as much as the drachma.

Dráco (Δράκων). °Archon and first legislator of Athens (624 BC). Though his laws greatly diminished the privileges of the aristocracy, they did not succeed in meeting the grievances of the lower classes, as they were extremely severe; °Solon.

Dracóntius, *Blóssius Aemílius Dracóntius* (end of the 5th cent. AD). Author of a poem 'De laudibus Dei'.

dress. 1. Greek dress, °Chiton, °chlaina, °chlamys, °exomis, °himation, °peplos, °pharos. **2.** Roman dress, °Toga, °trabea, °tunica, °palla, °stola, °lacerna, °laena; °footwear.

Drusílla. 1. *Julia Drusilla.* Second

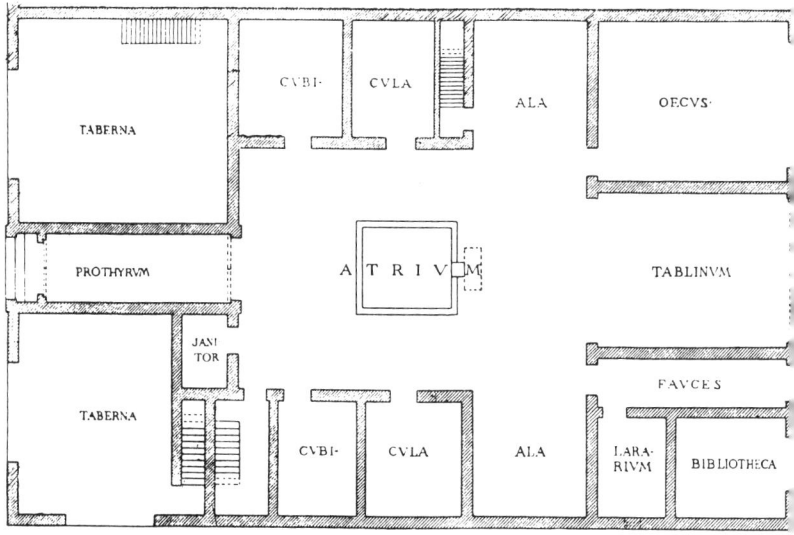

64. A large Roman

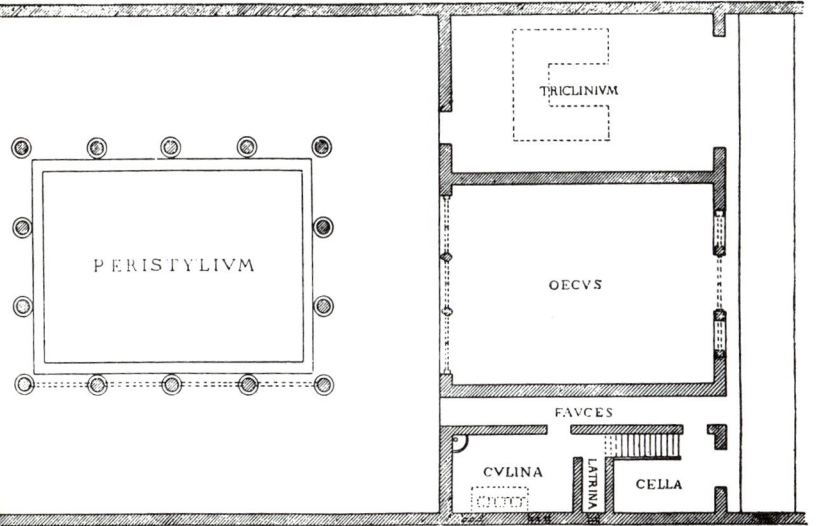

PERISTYLIVM

TRICLINIVM

OECVS

FAVCES

CVLINA

LATRINA

CELLA

·ivate house.

Domitii

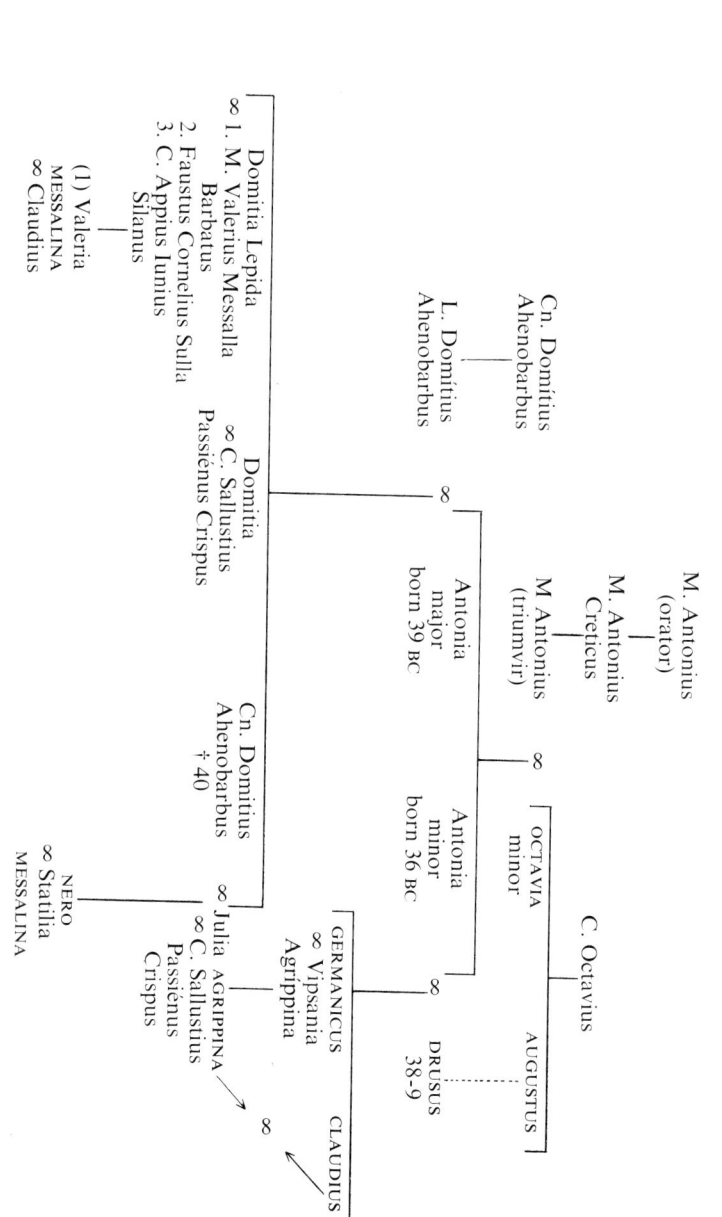

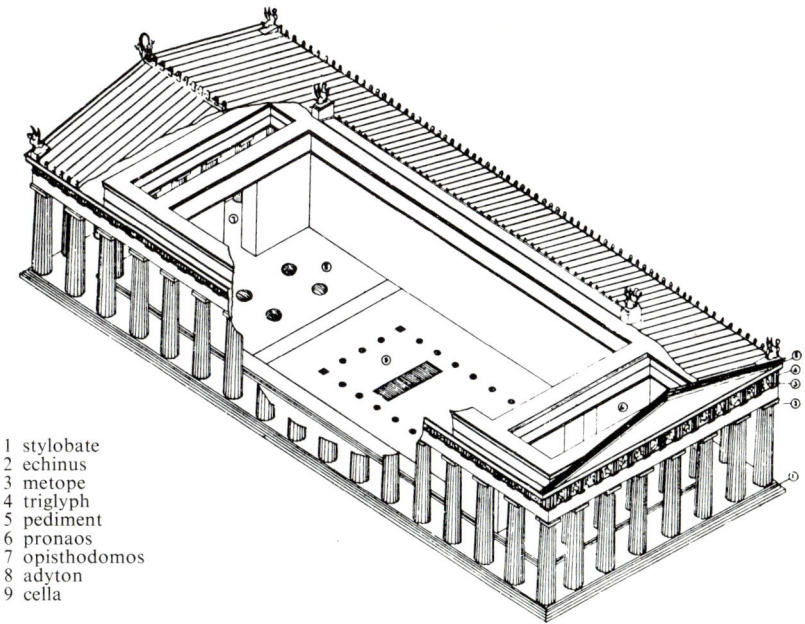

1 stylobate
2 echinus
3 metope
4 triglyph
5 pediment
6 pronaos
7 opisthodomos
8 adyton
9 cella

65. A Doric temple

66. A Doric capital.

daughter of °Germanicus and °Agrippina, born 16 AD, married to L. Cássius Longínus and secondly to M. Aemílius Lépidus. She died 38 AD; °Julio-Claudian dynasty p. 101. **2.** *Iulia Drusilla.* Daughter of the Emperor °Gaius and Milónia Caesónia, born 40 AD, died January 24th, 41, with her parents.

Drúsus. 1. *Claúdius Drúsus.* Son of the Emperor °Claudius and Plautia °Urgulanilla; engaged to be married to the daughter of °Sejanus. He died between 23 and 31; °Julio-Claudian dynasty p. 101. **2.** *Néro Claúdius Drúsus.* Stepson of °Augustus, brother of °Tiberius. He was the son of °Livia (Drusilla) and Ti. Claudius Néro, born 38 BC, married to °Antonia Minor; °Domitii p. 68; °Julio-Claudian dynasty p. 101. **3.** *Drúsus Iúlius Caésar.* Son of °Tiberius and Vipsánia °Agrippína, born c. 15 BC, married to Livilla. At Sejanus' instigation she poisoned him; °Julio-Claudian dynasty p. 101. **4.** *Drúsus Iúlius Caésar.* Second son of °Germanicus and °Agrippina, born 8 AD, married to Aemília Lépida. He died in prison 33 AD; °Julio-Claudian dynasty p. 101. **5.** *Nero Claudius Drusus Germanicus* = the Emperor °Nero.

Drýads (Δρυάδες). °Nymphs.

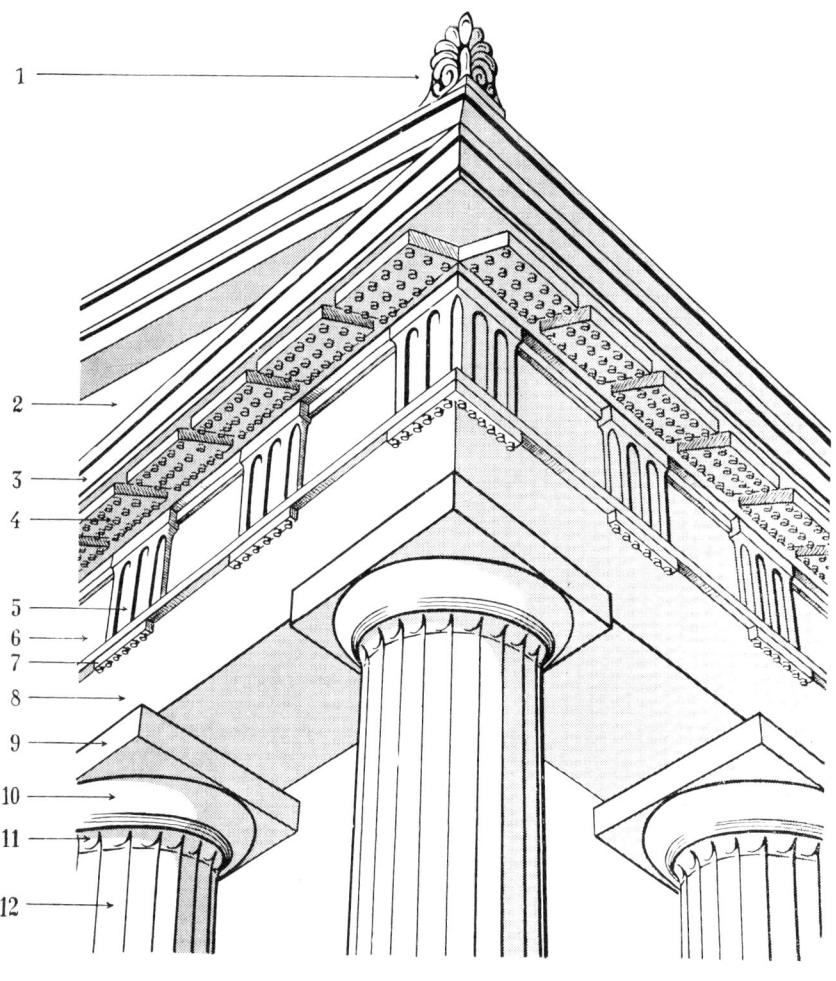

67. Doric order.

1 acroterion
2 pediment
3 cornice
4 mutule
5 triglyph
6 metope

7 guttae
8 architrave
9 abacus
10 echinus
11 hypotrachelium
12 fluted shaft

duélla. °abacus (= 1/36).
Duílius, *C. Duílius.* Consul in 260 BC. At °Mylae he gained the first victory over the Carthaginians. To commemorate this victory the °Columna Rostrata was erected.
dupóndius. Roman copper coin in use from imperial times (until 250 AD). Its value was twice that of the °as; °ill. p. 164.
Dúra-Európus. The ruins of a town on the Euphrates in Syria, discovered in 1921. It was founded (c. 300 BC) by °Seleucus I Nicator and destroyed by the Persians in 256 AD. The excavations, which are as important as those of Pompeii, revealed a 'gridiron' street plan, typical of the period, and later copied by the Romans; °Priene.
duúmviri víis extra úrbem purgándis. Magistrates whose task it was to keep the roads clean outside Rome.
Dýscolus (Δύσκολος). °Apollonius; °Menander.

E

ə. °alphabet.

ecclésia (ἐκκλησία). Assembly of the people at Athens, of which every citizen older than twenty was a member. It decided all matters not provided for by the laws. It assembled on the °Pnyx.
Echínades (Ἐχινάδες). Five islands at the mouth of the river °Acheloüs near Acarnania. According to legend they had been nymphs who failed to sacrifice to the river-god (Ovid *Met.* 8, 573-610).
echínus (ἐχῖνος). The convex moulding of a °Doric capital between °abacus and °hypotrachelium. In the °Ionic order it has °volutes, in the Corinthian order it has °acanthus leaves; °ill. 66.
Écho (Ἠχώ). A nymph whose love for °Narcissus was not returned. She pined away, was turned into stone, and retained only her voice.

Éclogues. Pastoral poems; °Virgil, °Bucolica.
edíctum. The higher Roman magistrates, before their accession to office, proclaimed by 'edicta' the legal provisions which they intended to observe. In the time of °Hadrian, a revised edition was composed: the 'edíctum perpétuum'; °constitutiónes.
Egéria. 1. A water nymph, who was said to have been the adviser of °Numa Pompilius (Ovid *Met.* 15, 479-496). **2.** °Peregrinátio.
ekklésia (εκκλησία). °ecclésia.
Elagábalus, *Várius Avítus Bassiánus.* Roman emperor (218-222 AD), cruel and intemperate. Murdered by his soldiers; °Sevéri p. 172.
Eleátic school. Philosophical school at Elea, founded by °Xenophanes; °Parmenides; °Zeno.

Eléctra (Ἠλέκτρα). Daughter of °Agamemnon and °Clytaemnestra who led °Orestes to safety after the murder of Agamemnon and incited him to vengeance; °Aeschylus; °Euripides; °Sophocles; °Tantalidae p. 182.

elegía (ἐλεγεῖα). Originally poems written in °disticha on various subjects, later dirges.

élegiac dístich. Two lines of verse, consisting of a dactylic °hexameter and a °pentameter; °distichon.

Eleusínian Mysteries (Ἐλευσίνια). The secret religious rites in honour of °Demeter and °Persephone at °Eleusis. The celebrations took six days and ended with a procession from Athens to °Eleusis along the 'Sacred Road' (ἱερά ὁδός).

Eleúsis. Town in Attica near the frontier with Megaris.

Elgin marbles. Marble sculptures of the °Parthenon, brought to London by Lord Elgin, the British ambassador in Constantinople (1802-1812). Originally he intended to have copies and drawings made, but seeing how the sculptures were being neglected and bartered to tourists, he got the government's permission to take them to England (*Journal of Hellenic Studies, XXXVI*, 1916). °Aegina.

Elícius. Name of °Jupiter as rain-god.

elísion (ἔκθλιψις). Omission of the last short vowel of a word when it is followed by a word beginning with a vowel.

ellípse. Omission of a word or part of a word.

Elýsium (Ἠλύσιον πεδίον). A region in the Underworld where the virtuous found complete happiness; °asphodel.

Empédocles (Ἐμπεδοκλῆς), of Agrigentum (494-434 BC). Politician, poet and philosopher. He taught that there were four elements from which everything originated: fire, air, earth, water. His verses were universally esteemed and recited at the °Olympian games, with those of °Homer and °Hesiod.

enállage (ἐναλλαγή). A substitution of one grammatical form for another, *e.g.*

past tense for present, singular for plural.

Endýmion (Ἐνδυμίων). A beautiful youth loved by Selene.

Énneades. °Plotinus.

Énnius, *Q. Ennius.* Born 239 BC at Rudiae in Calabria, one of the friends of °Scipio Africanus Maior. He became a Roman citizen in 184. Author of **1.** Tragedies, of which we have fragments. **2.** An epic poem 'Annales', written in hexameters, a history of Rome, a deliberate imitation of °Homer, of which some 600 lines are extant. **3.** Satires.

entáblature. The architectural superstructure carried by the °columns, including °architrave, °frieze and °cornice.

Éos (Ἠώς). Goddess of dawn.

Epaminóndas (Ἐπαμεινώνδας). Theban politician. He first distinguished himself by his victory at °Leuctra (371 BC), using his own invention the 'λοξή φάλαλξ' (°phalanx). He led several expeditions to the Peloponnese, liberated Messene and finally defeated Sparta at °Mantinea (362), where he died of his wounds.

Epaphrodítus (Ἐπαφρόδιτος). Freedman and secretary of °Nero, who helped the emperor to commit suicide.

Épaphus (Ἔπαφος). Son of °Zeus and °Io, king of Egypt and supposed founder of Memphis.

epeisódia. In Greek tragedy the dialogue between two songs of the chorus, spoken in °iambic trimeters; °stasimon.

Epeüs (Ἐπειός). Builder of the wooden horse of Troy; °Homer.

epexegésis (ἐπεξήγησις). The addition of a word or words by way of further elucidation; *e.g.*: 'hic in Epheso'; 'iudicium Paridis spretaeque iniuria formae'.

éphebe (ἔφηβος). Youth. In Athens the young citizens aged eighteen to twenty enlisted as frontier guards.

Éphesus (Ἔφεσος). One of the principal cities of Ionia, member of the °Delian Confederacy. It was famous for the temple of °Artemis, which was burnt down in 356 BC, on the night °Alexander

the Great was born; °Herostratus.
Ephiáltes (Ἐφιάλτης). **1.** A Thessalian who (480 BC) betrayed to the Persians the pass by which they could outflank the Greeks at °Thermopylae; °Leonidas. **2.** Athenian democrat who reduced the power of the °Areopagus (462); °Pericles.

éphors (ἔφοροι). College of five annual magistrates at Sparta, originally nominated by the kings. In later times their power gradually increased, so that finally they could call the kings to account; °Cleomenes.

Éphorus (Ἔφορος), of Cyme on the west coast of Asia Minor (408-330 BC). He wrote a history of Greece in thirty books; a few fragments are extant.

Epic Cycle. A collective name for a number of epic poems, reputedly by very ancient authors, of which only fragments survive: *e.g.* 'Ilioupersis', 'Aethiopis', 'Cypria', 'Thebaïs'.

Epichármus (Ἐπίχαρμος). Greek comic poet at the court of °Hiero I of Syracuse; he died 460 BC.

Epictétus (Ἐπίκτητος), from Phrygia. Slave of °Epaphroditus, but later a philosopher. He was set free and attended the lectures of °Musonius Rufus, the °Stoic. When °Domitian banished all philosophers from Rome (c. 90 AD) he went to Epirus. One of his pupils was °Arrian, who collected his lectures in the so-called 'Diatribai', of which four books are extant, and in the handbook 'Encheiridion'. His maxim was: 'ἀνέχου καὶ ἀπέχου' (='Endure and abstain').

Epicúrus (Ἐπίκουρος). Athenian philosopher (342-270 BC), founder of the Epicurean school, a fusion of the doctrines of °Democritus and °Aristippus. The highest good was life itself, according to him, and the end or aim of life pleasure, which was mainly negative, *i.e.* the absence of pain and trouble, imperturbability (ἀταραξία). The pleasures of the spirit ranked above those of the body and the wise man refrained from all pleasures which could later cause him pain; °Lucretius.

Epidaúrus (Ἐπίδαυρος). Greek city, noted today for its remarkably-preserved °theatre.

epideíctic oratory. The oratory of display, where more attention was given to the form than to the contents; °Isocrates.

Epígoni (Ἐπίγονοι). The sons of the heroes who were killed at Thebes. They undertook a second, successful expedition; °Adrastus. According to tradition, they were Alcmaeon, son of Amphiaraus; Aegialeus, son of Adrastus; Diomedes, son of Tydeus; Promachus, son of Parthenopaeus; Sthenelus, son of Capaneus; Thersander, son of Polyneices; Euryalus, son of Mecistheus.

épigram. Originally an inscription, later a poem, usually a °distichon, in which a saying, thought or mood was tersely expressed. °Simonides. Some 3,600 epigrams were collected in the °Anthology. The Romans mostly wrote vituperative epigrams (*e.g.* °Martial).

Epimétheus (Ἐπιμηθεύς). Brother of °Prometheus.

epíphora. Repetition of a word at the end of several parts of a sentence.

épistyle (epistýlium). °architrave.

Epitrepóntes (Ἐπιτρέποντες). °Menander.

épitrite (ἐπίτριτος). A metrical foot consisting of one short element and three long ones: first ᴗ _ _ _; second _ ᴗ _ _; third _ _ ᴗ _; fourth _ _ _ ᴗ.

épode (ἐπῳδός). **1.** Part of a lyric which followed the °strophe and antistrophe. **2.** A kind of lyric poem in which a long line is followed by a shorter one (not an °elegiac distich).

Epóna. Originally a Gallic goddess of horses, stables, etc.

épos (ἔπος = word). Name of the dactylic hexameter. Epic poetry; °Aeneid; °Homer; °Virgil.

epýllion (ἐπύλλιον). A short °epic poem.

éques. °knight.

Eráto (Ἐρατώ). °Muses.

Eratósthenes (Ἐρατοσθένης). **1.** One of the °Thirty Tyrants at Athens. **2.** *of Cyrene.* Second head of the library of °Alexandria (c. 234 BC), mathe-

68. The Erechtheum (°plan, p. 4). On the same spot where once stood the sacred olive-tree a young olive-tree has been planted (in modern times).

matician and geographer, but also poet, philosopher and historian; because he was going blind, he starved himself to death in 194. Almost all of his writings have been lost; °Strabo.

Eréchtheum (Ἐρέχθειον). Temple of °Erechtheus on the °Acropolis; °ill. 68.

Eréchtheus (Ἐρεχθεύς). Legendary king of Attica, who founded the cult of °Athena. He was worshipped with Athena and °Poseidon in the °Erechtheum; °Oreithyia.

Erichthónius (Ἐριχθόνιος). **1.** = °Erechtheus. **2.** Son of °Dardanus, father of Tros, famous for his three thousand mares; °Dardanidae, p. 60.

Erínyes (Ἐρινύες). The Furies, ministers of °Pluto's vengeance, tormenting criminals in their minds. There were

generally considered to be three: Tisiphone (who punished murderers), Alecto (eternal punishment) and Megaera (grudge). Euphemistically they were called 'Euménides' (= 'The kindly Godesses'); °Aeschylus.

Eríphyle (Ἐριφύλη). Daughter of °Adrastus, married to °Amphiaraüs.

Éris (Ἔρις). Goddess of Discord; °Peleus.

Éros (Ἔρως). °Amor.

Erymánthus (Ἐρύμανθος). Mountain of Arcadia, where a wild boar devastated the land; °Heracles.

Erysíchthon (Ἐρυσίχθων). Son of Triopas, king of Thessaly, cut down the trees in a grove sacred to °Demeter, who punished him with insatiable hunger. He had a daughter, °Mestra, who had the power to change shape. She was sold in the form of various animals, but always returned to be sold again, and he lived on the proceeds. Eventually he devoured his own limbs (Ovid *Met.* 8, 738-878).

Erytheía (Ἐρύθεια). Legendary island of °Geryon.

Ésquiline. One of the °Seven hills on which Rome was built.

Etéocles (Ἐτεοκλῆς). Son of °Oedipus and Jocasta. When Oedipus had left Thebes, he and his twin brother °Polyneices agreed to rule in alternate years. Eteocles would not give up the throne at the end of his year, so Polyneices called in the aid of °Adrastus and so started the expedition of the °Seven against Thebes. Both brothers were killed.

éthics. That part of philosophy which treats of virtues and vices, and the criteria of right and wrong.

Etrúscans. A people, possibly from Asia Minor, who settled in Central Italy and whose influence spread to Campania in the 6th cent. BC. The kings °Tarquinius Priscus and °Tarquinius Superbus were Etruscans. The power of the Etruscans diminished and finally °Sulla completely Romanized the country. The civilisation of the Etruscans greatly influenced the Romans (in pottery, bronze-casting, °augury, °theatre, politics, architecture, etc). Our knowledge of them is largely based on the excavations of many tombs (from which most complete Greek vases have come) and their language is still under discussion; °Agram.

Eúclid (Εὐκλείδης). **1.** Mathematician at °Alexandria (c. 300 BC). Modern mathematics are founded on his principal work 'Στοιχεῖα' (Elementa). **2.** Pupil of °Socrates, founder of the °Megarian School; he held that there was one supreme 'good'.

Eudóxus (Εὔδοξος), of Cnidus (c. 390-340 BC). Mathematician, astonomer and pupil of °Plato, creator of the general theory of proportion. He worked on the determination of geo-

graphical position.

Euhémerus (Εὐήερος). Expounder (c. 300 BC) of the theory that the Greek gods and heroes had been historical persons, worshipped by mankind out of gratitude for their great deeds.

Eumaéus (Εὔμαιος). The faithful swineherd of °Odysseus (Hom. *Od.* XV, 403-484).

Eúmenes II. King of Pergamum (197-159 BC), son of Attalus I. He continued his father's policy of co-operation with Rome.

Euménides (Εὐμενίδες). **1.** °Erinyes. **2.** Tragedy of °Aeschylus.

Eunuch. A play by °Terence.

Euphórbus (Εὔφορβος). A Trojan, killed by °Menelaus; °Pythagoras.

Euphórion (Εὐφορίων), of Chalcis (c. 275 BC). Librarian at Pergamum, and an epic and epigrammatic poet, much admired in °Cicero's day.

Euphrósyne (Εὐφροσύνη). One of the three °Graces.

Eurípides (Εὐριπίδης). One of the three great tragic poets in Athens (480-406 BC). He is notable for his insight into female psychology. Eighteen of his 120 dramas are extant:
1. *Alcéstis.* She offered to die in her husband's place (°Admetus), but was saved at the last moment by °Heracles who defeated °Hades.
2. °*Medéa.* In return for °Jason's infidelity, she killed his new wife, father-in-law, and (unwillingly) her children.
3. *Hippólytus.* Loved by his young stepmother °Phaedra, Hippolytus refused her love. She killed herself and accused him in a letter, so that he was banished by his father °Theseus and trampled to death by his horses.
4. *Hécuba.* The misery of Troy's captive queen and the death of her children °Polyxena and °Polydorus.
5. *Andrómache.* The fate of °Hector's widow when a slave and beloved of °Neoptolemus.
6. *Heraclídae.* °Alcmena, mother of °Herades, fled from Argos with her children after his death, pursued by °Eurystheus. They reached Marathon

as suppliants.

7. *Súppliants.* The mothers of the °Seven against Thebes asked leave of the Thebans to bury their sons; they refused. The Athenians defeated the Thebans and the bodies were burnt at Eleusis.

8. *Trojan Women.* The fate of the women of Troy after the sack of the city.

9. °*Héracles.* He saved his family from death, but afterwards in madness killed them. He was stopped by °Theseus from committing suicide.

10. *Iphigeneía in Tauris.* When she was priestess of °Artemis in Tauris, her brother °Orestes and his friend °Pylades were wrecked on the coast and about to be sacrificed to the goddess; by the intervention of Athena as °deus ex machina they were all saved.

11. *Íon.*

12. *Helena.* Helen supposedly stayed in Egypt, faithful to °Menelaus and was brought back by him.

13. *Eléctra.* She lived in poverty at the mercy of °Clytaemnestra and °Aegisthus, who murdered her father °Agamemnon, when her brother °Orestes returned and killed them with her help.

14. *Phoenician Women.* The battle of the °Seven against Thebes.

15. *Oréstes.* Having killed his mother, who had murdered his father °Agamemnon, Orestes and his sister °Electra were condemned to death. They were saved by °Apollo.

16. *Iphigeneía in Aulis.* She was supposedly sacrificed to °Artemis to get fair winds for the Greek fleet.

17. *Bácchae.* Triumph of °Dionysus over the opponents of his cult.

18. *Cýclops.* A °satyric drama.

Európa (Εὐρώπη). Sister of °Cadmus, raped by Zeus in the shape of a bull (Ovid *Met.* 2, 833-875). She was the mother of °Minos, °Rhadamanthus and °Sarpedon.

Eurýale (Εὐρυάλη). °Gorgons.

Eurýalus (Εὐρύαλος). Companion of °Aeneas, famous for his friendship with Nisus (Virg. *Aen.* 9, 176-449).

Eurycleía (Εὐρύκλεια). The old foster-mother of °Odysseus, who recognized him on his return from Troy by his scar (Hom. *Od.* XIX, 349-502).

Eurýdice (Εὐρυδίκη). **1.** Daughter of °Adrastus, married to the Trojan Ilus; °Dardanidae, p.60. **2.** Wife of °Orpheus.

Eurýmedon (Εὐρυμέδον). A river in Pamphylia; °Cimon.

Eurypóntids (Εὐρυπωντίδαι). A royal house of Sparta, to which °Archidamus belonged; °Agids.

Eurýstheus (Εὐρυσθεύς). Son of Sthenelus, king of Argos and Mycenae. He was born earlier than °Heracles, and °Zeus had decided the younger would serve the elder; he charged Heracles with the °twelve labours.

Eusébius (Εὐσέβιος). **1.** Bishop of Caesarea in Palestine (315-340 AD), the first Greek church historian. Author of 'Historia Ecclesiástica'; his other book 'Παντοδαπὴ ἱστορία' was translated into Latin by °Hieronymus (Jerome) and continued ('Chrónicon Eusébii'). **2.** Bishop of Emesa in Phoenicia.

Eutérpe (Εὐτέρπη). °Muses.

Eutrópius. By order of the emperor °Valens he composed a short history of Rome, which was widely read.

Evánder (Εὔανδρος). Son of °Hermes, who came from Arcadia to Italy before the °Trojan War and founded °Pallanteum. He fought with °Aeneas against °Turnus.

evocáti. Roman veterans who enlisted again voluntarily and enjoyed special privileges.

éxodos (ἔξοδος). Last song of the chorus in Greek drama; therefore the last part of the play.

exómis (ἐξωμίς). A man's narrow °chiton which left one or both shoulders bare; °ill. 49.

explorers. The expedition of the °Argonauts, probably based on some historical event, may be considered one of the first voyages of discovery. One true explorer was the pharaoh °Neccho (Hdt. 4, 42); also °Hanno; °Alexander the Great; Colasus to Platea (Hdt. 4, 152); Aristeas (Hdt. 4, 13; 4, 16). However, it must be remembered that, in the Mediterranean area from prehistoric times onwards, the constant movement of peoples or individuals was such that 'exploration' as we know it was not deemed necessary. The Mediterranean Sea is notoriously treacherous, even in summer, and all ancient navigators tried to 'hug the coast'.

F

F; Ⅎ. °alphabet.
Fábius Máximus, *Q. Fábius Máximus Verrucósus.* °Dictator after the Roman defeat at Lake Trasimene, nicknamed *Cunctátor* for his delaying tactics of avoiding battle, thus undermining °Hannibal's strength (217 BC).
Fábius Píctor, *Q. Fábius Píctor* (c. 225 BC). °Annalist, author of a history of Rome in Greek up to the 2nd Punic war.
Fabrícius, *C. Fabrícius Luscínus* (consul 278 BC). He warned °Pyrrhus that the king's physician had offered to murder him.
fásces. °lictor; °ill. 69.

69. Fasces.

fásti. 1. The Roman calendar of festivals; originally a list of the days on which legal and public business was allowed (*dies fásti*) or not (*dies néfasti*). **2.** *Fásti consuláres,* the list of eponymous magistrates, after °Augustus' time inscribed on marble along the walls of the °regia. **3.** °Ovid.
Fates. They decreed a man's fate at birth: Clótho, who spun the thread of life; Lachésis, who defined its length; Átropos, who cut it off. °Homer defined Fate as 'Moíra'.
Faúnus. Ancient Italian deity of woods and fields; son of Picus; identified with °Pan; °Lupercalia.
Faustína. 1. Wife of °Antoninus Pius; °Aurélii p. 31. **2.** Wife of °Marcus Aurelius, mother of °Commodus; °Aurelii p. 31.
Faústulus. A herdsman, who, according to legend, found °Romulus and Remus and, with his wife °Acca Larentia, reared them.
M. Favónius. Admirer of °Cato Uticensis; at first adversary, later supporter of °Pompey, and one of °Caesar's murderers. He was killed after the battle of °Philippi.
Ferália. Roman festival in honour of the dead, celebrated in February.
Féstus, *Sex. Pompeíus Féstus.* He wrote a summary of the work of °Verrius Flaccus. The first half of his work is lost.
fetiáles. Roman priests, whose task it was to declare war, make treaties and conclude peace. Their spokesman was called *páter patrátus.*

fíbula. A decorative brooch, the equivalent of a modern safety pin, to replace buttons; °ill. 70.

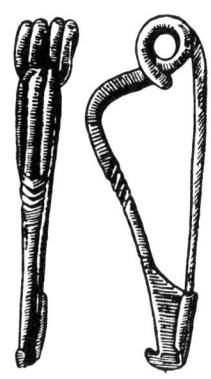

70. A fibula.

Fírmicus Matérnus. Author of an astrological treatise (c. 335 AD). When converted to Christianity (337), he wrote a passionate treatise on paganism: *De erróre profanárum religiónum*.

Fishbourne. A Roman site near Chichester, discovered in 1960, built c. 70 AD. It has revealed one of the most lavish villas of the period, with a courtyard, mosaic-floored rooms and complete sets of baths; °Britain.

Fláccus. °Horace, °Priscus.

flámen. The special priest of various deities, *e.g.*: *flámen Diális*, of °Jupiter; *flamen Martiális*, of °Mars; *flámen Quirinális*, of °Quirinus. The twelve other *flamines* looked after the cult of lesser gods. *The flamen Diális* wore a °toga praetexta, sat on a °sélla curúlis and was a member of the Senate; he was subjected to an elaborate system of restrictions. His wife (*flamínica*), was a priestess of °Juno.

lex Flamínia. An agrarian law, passed by C. °Flaminius Népos (232 BC), to distribute the *Ager Gallicus* and *A. Picenus* among the poor.

vía Flamínia. Road from Rome to Arimínum; °Flaminius.

flamínica. °flamen.

Flaminínus, *T. Quínctius Flaminínus*. The Roman general who, when °proconsul, defeated the Macedonian army at °Cynoscephalae (197 BC) and afterwards (196), during the °Isthmian Games, proclaimed the freedom of Greece.

Flamínius, *C. Flamínius*. Tribune of the people (232 BC), who despite senatorial opposition passed his agrarian law (°lex Flamínia). In 220, when °censor, he built the via °Flaminia and the °circus Flaminius. He was killed in the battle of Lake Trasimene (217).

Flávia Domitílla. °Flavii p. 79.

Flávii. p. 79.

Flavius. 1. *Flávius Clémens.* °Flávii p. 79. 2. °Domitian. 3. *Flávius Joséphus.* Born 37 AD of an aristocratic Jewish family, he incited the Jews to rebel against Rome. Taken prisoner by °Vespasian, he was afterwards set free, in the time of °Titus, and was an eye-witness to the siege of Jerusalem (70). The rest of his life was spent in Rome, where he wrote a history of the Jewish people to 66 AD, a history of the Jewish war and a treatise against the anti-Semite Apion of Alexandria. 4. *Flávius Philóstratus.* Sophist or rhetorician, in Rome (born c. 170 AD) at the court of °Julia Domna. At her request, he wrote a biography of °Apollonius of Tyana. He (or his nephew) was also the author of other biographies and of the 'Images' (Εἰκόνες), descriptions of famous paintings and sculptures. 5. °Sabinus. 6. °Titus. 7. °Valens. 8. °Valentian. 9. °Vespasian.

Flóra. Roman goddess of flowers and spring. After 238 BC the 'Florália' were celebrated in her honour; °Chloris.

Flórus, *P. Ánnius Flórus.* Author of a short history of Rome, based on °Livy. He lived in the time of °Hadrian.

fluting (stria). The vertical concave grooves on the shaft of a column. On °Doric columns the twenty flutes

Flavii

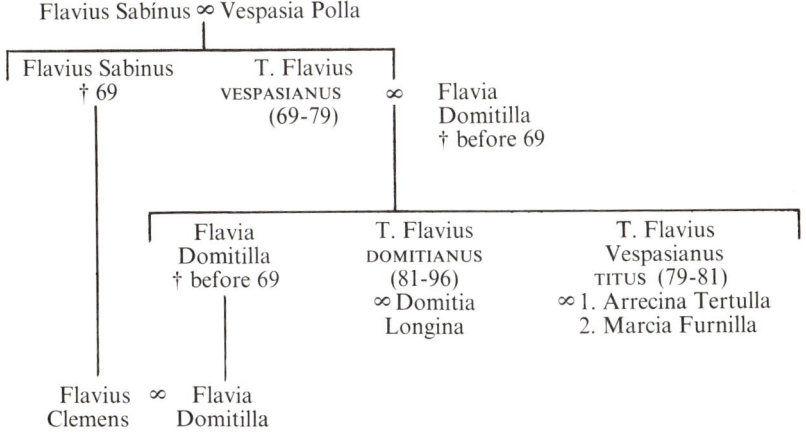

Flavius Sabínus ∞ Vespasia Polla

| Flavius Sabinus † 69 | T. Flavius VESPASIANUS (69-79) ∞ | Flavia Domitilla † before 69 |

| Flavia Domitilla † before 69 | T. Flavius DOMITIANUS (81-96) ∞ Domitia Longina | T. Flavius Vespasianus TITUS (79-81) ∞ 1. Arrecina Tertulla 2. Marcia Furnilla |

Flavius ∞ Flavia
Clemens   Domitilla

touched each other; °ill. 71(a) and on °Ionic columns the twenty-four flutes were separated by fillets; °ill. 71(b).

71A. Doric fluting.

71B. Ionic fluting.

fóllis. A silvered bronze coin (indicative of devaluation), first used by °Diocletian (284-304 AD); °ill. p. 164.

footwear. °baxea, °calceus, °caliga, °cothurnus, °soccus, °solea.

fork. °furca.

Fórum Boárium. A market place in °Rome; map p. 81.

Four Hundred (οἱ τετρακόσιοι). **1.** °Boule. **2.** The °oligarchic government at Athens consisting of 400 citizens (411 BC). After four months it was deposed.

Fránçois Vase. A volute °krater by Kleitias, one of the oldest °Black-figured vases (c. 570 BC), 66 cm high and decorated with more than 200 figures, arranged in six rows. It was found shattered at Vulci in 1845 in an °Etruscan tomb and is named after its excavator; now in Florence; °ill. 72.

frieze (ζφοφόρος). That member of the °entablature of an architectural order between the architrave and the cornice decorated with sculpture. In the °Doric order it consisted of °triglyphs and °metopes; in the °Ionic order it consisted of a continuous sculptured panel. Above the frieze was the projecting cornice inclined slightly downward and consisting of a moulding, surmounted by a plain vertical member; °mutule; °guttae.

72. The 'François vase'.

Frontínus, *Sex. Iúlius Frontínus* (c. 35-103 AD). °Proconsul in °Britain, afterwards *curátor aquárum* (supervisor of the aqueducts) in Rome. Author of a collection of strategems, *Strategémata,* and a book about the water-supply of Rome, *De áquis urbis Rómae.*

Frónto, *M. Cornélius Frónto.* Teacher of °Marcus Aurelius. Their correspondence was discovered in 1815 on a °palimpsest.

fúnus censórium. °censor.

furca. In antiquity, a fork was not used for dinner. It was introduced probably about the 12th century.

Furies. °Erinyes.

Fúrius. °Camillus.

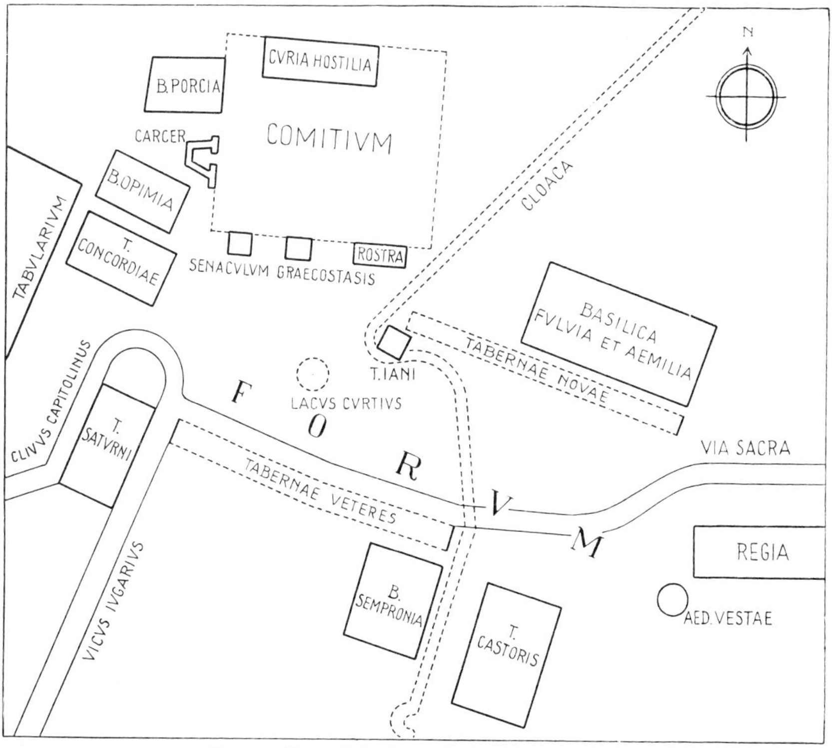

Surroundings of the forum in Republican times.

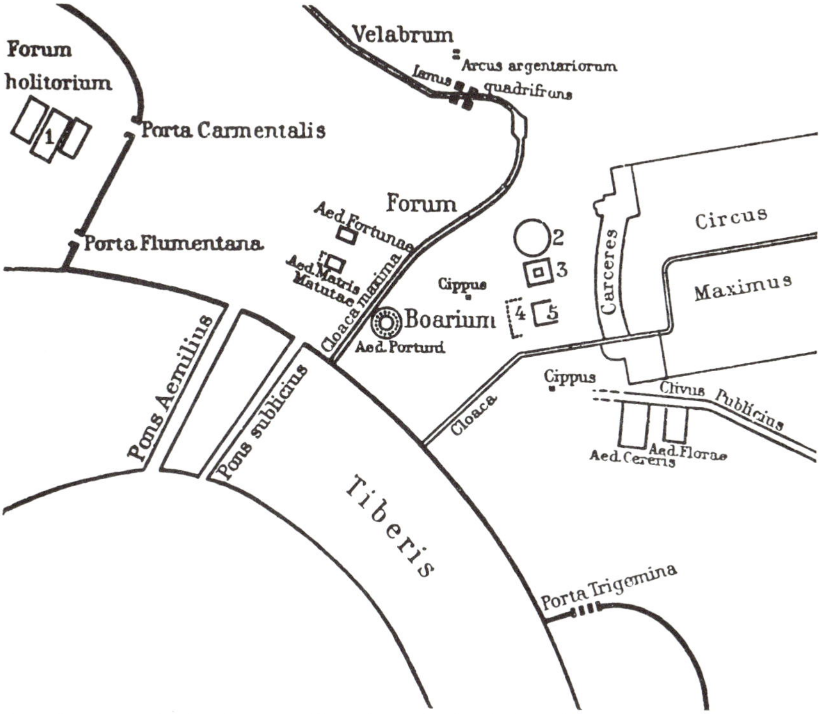

The 'forum Boarium' and surroundings. (1. 'aedes Spei'; 2. 'aedes Herculis invicti'; 3. 'Ara maxima'; 4. a portico; 5. 'aedes Herculis Pompeiani'.)

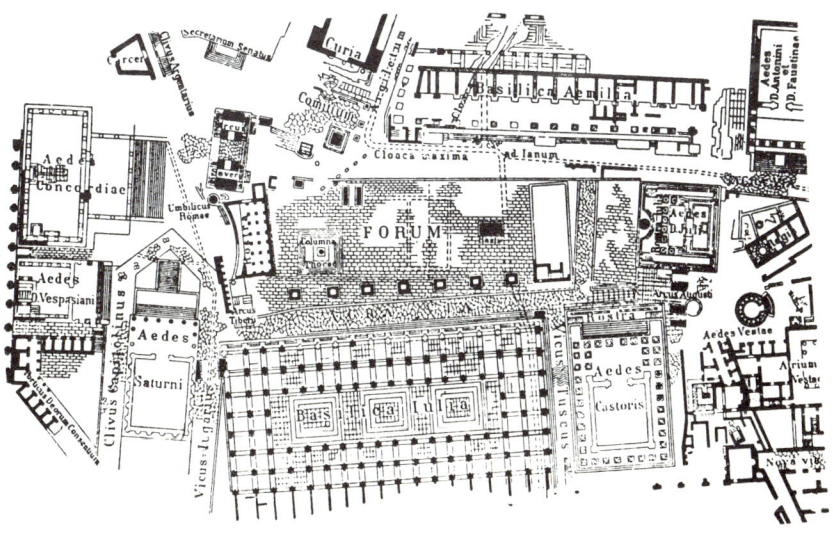

The buildings round the forum in Imperial times.

G

lex Gabínia, passed by the °tribune A. Gabínius (67 BC), establishing the command against the pirates for °Pompey, with the right to appoint his own legates.

Gabínus. *Cínctus Gabínus.* °toga.

Gaéa (Γαῖα: Γῆ). The earth goddess, mother of the °Centimani, the °Giants, the °Cyclopes and the °Titans; °Chaos.

gaésum. Gallic throwing-spear; the Romans used this name for a kind of spear unknown to us.

Gaíus. 1. *Iúlius Caésar Germánicus.* Usually called the emperor Gaius or Caligula (37-41 AD), son of °Germanicus and °Agrippina, born 12 AD; °Julio-Claudian dynasty, p. 101. **2.** *C. Caésar* (*C. Iúlius Caésar*). Son of °Agrippa and °Julia, born 20 BC, died 4 AD, married to °Livilla; °Julio-Claudian dynasty p. 101. **3.** *Gaíus.* Roman lawyer (c. 150 AD), whose manual on Roman law 'Institutiónes' is extant. The manuscript was discovered in Verona in 1816, and more fragments were found in Egypt in 1933.

Galatéa (Γαλάτεια). A nymph, one of the Nereids; °Acis.

Gálba. *Ser. Sulpícius Gálba.* Roman emperor (June 68, to 15th January 69 AD). He succeeded °Nero, was murdered by his soldiers and was succeeded by °Otho.

gálea. Originally a leather °helmet. Later there were metal helmets. °cassis.

Gálen, *Claúdius Galénus* (Γαληνός) (129-199 AD). Born at Pergamum, physician in Rome (from 164). About 100 of his writings are extant, a number of them in Latin and Arabic translations only.

Galérius. *C. Galérius Valérius Maximiánus.* Son-in-law of °Diocletian. He became emperor in 293 AD, and in 305 succeeded Diocletian as Augustus of the East. On the 30th April 311, he granted the Christians the right to rebuild their churches and died on the 5th May.

galliámbus. A line of verse:

⌣ ⌣ ⌐ _ ⌣ ⌣ ⌣ ⌐ _ ⌣ ⌣ ⌐ ⌣ _ _ ⌣.

Many variations were possible by the expansion of the long and the contraction of the short elements.

Galliénus. *Licínius Galliénus.* Roman emperor (253-268 AD) with his father °Valerian; °ill. p. 164.

Gállus, C. *Cornélius Gállus.* Elegiac poet, friend of °Ovid and °Virgil. No work extant.

Gánymede (Γανυμήδης). Son of Tros, carried off by °Zeus because of his beauty and made cupbearer of the gods on Mount °Olympus (Ovid *Met.* 10, 155-161); °Dardanidae p. 60.

Gaugaméla (Γαυγάμηλα). Place in Assyria, where °Alexander defeated Darius (331 BC).

Gaul (Gallia). The lands of the Gauls or Celts was divided into: 1. *Gállia Narbonénsis* (or *província Gállia*) after 121 BC 2. *G. Aquitánia.* 3. *G. Lugdunénsis.* 4. *G. Bélgica.* Together they were called *Gállia Transalpína,* while the northern part of Italy was *Gállia Císalpina,* divided into *Gállia Cispadána* and *Gállia Transpadána.*

geese, sacred to °Juno, saved the °Capitol when it was besieged by the Gauls (390 BC). Their cackling roused °Manlius, when the enemy attempted a surprise attack at night (Liv. 5, 47).

geíson (γεῖσον). The Greek word for the °cornice; °Doric order.

Géllius, *A. Géllius.* Born c. 130 AD. Author of *Noctes Atticae,* in twenty books, written during the long winter evenings of his stay in Athens. They contained excerpts from many authors, covering a wide range of subjects.

Gélo (Γέλων). °Tyrant of Syracuse (485 BC onwards), who conquered the whole of Sicily. He defeated the Carthaginians led by °Hamilcar, near the river Himera,

on the same day as the battle of
°Salamis (480).
geminátio (ἐπαναδίπλωσις, ἐπίζευξις).
The instant repetition of a word: *e.g.*:
'fuit, fuit ista virtus'.
Gemóniae, *Scálae Gemóniae*. Steps on
the east side of the °Capitol where the
bodies of criminals were exhibited
before they were thrown into the Tiber.
Geométric. The name given to the style
of Greek art between c. 1000 and
700 BC. This name is now often considered inappropriate as other kinds
of decoration were also used in this
period, and 'geometric' type decoration
has been found on earlier vases;
°Dipylon.
Geórgics. °Virgil.
Germánicus. **1.** *Germánicus Iúlius Caésar*.
Son of °Drusus and °Antonia Minor
(15 BC-19 AD), adopted by Tiberius
(4 AD), married to °Agrippina. He
became popular after his three expeditions into °Germany (14-16). In
17 AD he went to the East, where he died
in the belief that he had been poisoned
by °Piso, the governor of Syria;
°Domítii p. 68; °Julio-Claudian dynasty p. 101. Of his literary works some
Latin and Greek epigrams and a
didactic poem on astronomy (after
°Aratus) are extant. **2.** *Germánicus
Iúlius Caésar*. Son of °Drusus and
°Livilla (19-23).
Germany (Germánia). After 17 AD there
were two Roman provinces on the
western bank of the Rhine: *Germánia
Inférior*, with the capital *Colónia
Agrippína* (Cologne), and *Germánia
Supérior*, capital *Mogontiácum*
(Mayence). Both provinces were
governed by a *legátus consuláris* with
four legions. As to civil administration
they were part of °Gallia Belgica.
Geroúsia (γερουσία). The council of
Elders at Sparta, consisting of the two
kings and twenty-eight citizens of over
sixty years of age. They were elected by
acclamation of the citizens. The
Gerousia prepared business for the
popular assembly and had judicial
functions.

Géryon (Γηρυόνης). °Giant with three
bodies, who lived on the island of
Erytheia in the far west. One of the
Labours of °Heracles was to carry off
his cattle.
Géta, *P. Septímius Géta*. Emperor (211-
212 AD) together with his brother
°Caracalla, by whom he was murdered;
°Sevéri p. 173.
Giants. (Γίγαντες, Gigantes). Sons of
°Gaea, giants with serpent-shaped legs,
who waged war (°Gigantomáchia)
against °Zeus and the Olympian gods;
°ill. 73. They heaped Mount °Ossa and
°Pelion to reach Olympus. The gods
killed or defeated them, with the help
of °Heracles, and imprisoned them
beneath islands and volcanoes;
°Typhon; Enceladus.
Gilgamesh. The hero of a famous
°Sumerian epic poem.
Gíza (Gizeh). Site south-west of Cairo,
famous for the three great °pyramids.
Glaúce (Γλαύκη). °Creüsa.
Glaúcus (Γλαῦκος). **1.** Fisherman from
Boeotia, who ate a magic herb and
leapt into the sea, whereupon he
became a sea-deity. His love for °Scylla
was not returned. He asked °Circe to
help him, but she fell in love with him
herself and changed Scylla into a
monster (Ovid *Met.* 13, 898-14, 74).
2. Son of Hippolochus, ally of the
Trojans, who exchanged his golden
armour for the bronze of °Diomedes.
Glýcera. °Menander.
glycóneüs (γλυκώνειος). A metrical
verse: ⏓ ⏓ ⏑ ⏑ ⏑ ⏓ ⏓.
gnómic poetry. Poems written in
°disticha, embodying wise maxims;
°Phocylides; °Theognis.
Golden Fleece. The fleece of the ram on
which °Phrixus and Helle fled:
°Argonauts; °Jason.
Górdium (Γόρδιον). Town in Phrygia,
where °Alexander the Great assembled
his army (335 BC) and cut the Gordian
knot, because he could not unravel it.
Górgias (Γοργίας) of Leontini in Sicily
(c. 483-375 BC). He came to Athens as
an ambassador (427) and became
famous on account of his orations and

73. Giants. (Mosaic in the Piazza Armerina.)

rhetorical teaching. He was a pupil of
°Empedocles and wrote, 'Περὶ τοῦ μὴ
ὄντος ἢ περὶ φύσεως', in which he said
that nothing existed. If anything existed
it was impossible to perceive it; if it
were possible to perceive it, the experience could not be communicated;
°sophist; °Plato.

Górgons (Γοργόνες). Three sisters,
daughters of Phorcys and Ceto. They
were called Stheno, Euryale and
°Medusa and represented as winged
monsters with serpents in their hair.
Whoever looked at them was turned
into stone. In later times they were
represented as beautiful maidens.
°Homer mentioned only one, Gorgo,
on the °aegis; °Perseus.

Goths. An east German race, which
intermittently attacked the Roman
Empire in the 3rd cent. AD. In 332,
°Constantine abandoned the region
north of the Danube to the Visigoths.
In c. 350 they were converted to
Christianity by Ulfilas. The Ostrogoths
invaded Italy under °Theoderic the
Great (471-526) and founded an empire
there, destroyed in 552 by °Narses.

Grácchus. *C. Semprónius Grácchus.*
Younger son of **2.**, tribune in 123 and
122 BC. He won the favour of the people
by lowering the corn prices and
weakened the power of the Senate by
giving the law-courts to the *equites*
(°Knights). In 121 he was not re-
elected, but was murdered together with
many supporters. **2.** *Ti. Semprónius
Grácchus.* Consul (177 and 163 BC),
married to °Cornelia. His sons were
the famous Gracchi: Tiberius and
Caius; his daughter Sempronia married
°Scipio Africanus minor. **3.** *Ti. Sém-
pronius Grácchus.* Elder son of **2.**,
who, disturbed by the bad living-
conditions of the peasants and the
proletariat, took action against the
large land-owners, by re-enacting the
lex °Licinia when tribune, but was
killed (133) when seeking re-election.

Graces. Daughters of °Zeus, goddesses
personifying charm, grace and beauty:
Euphrósyne, Aglaéa and Thália;
°Charites.

Gránicus (Γρανικός). River in Mysia,
where °Alexander the Great defeated
the Persians in 334 BC.

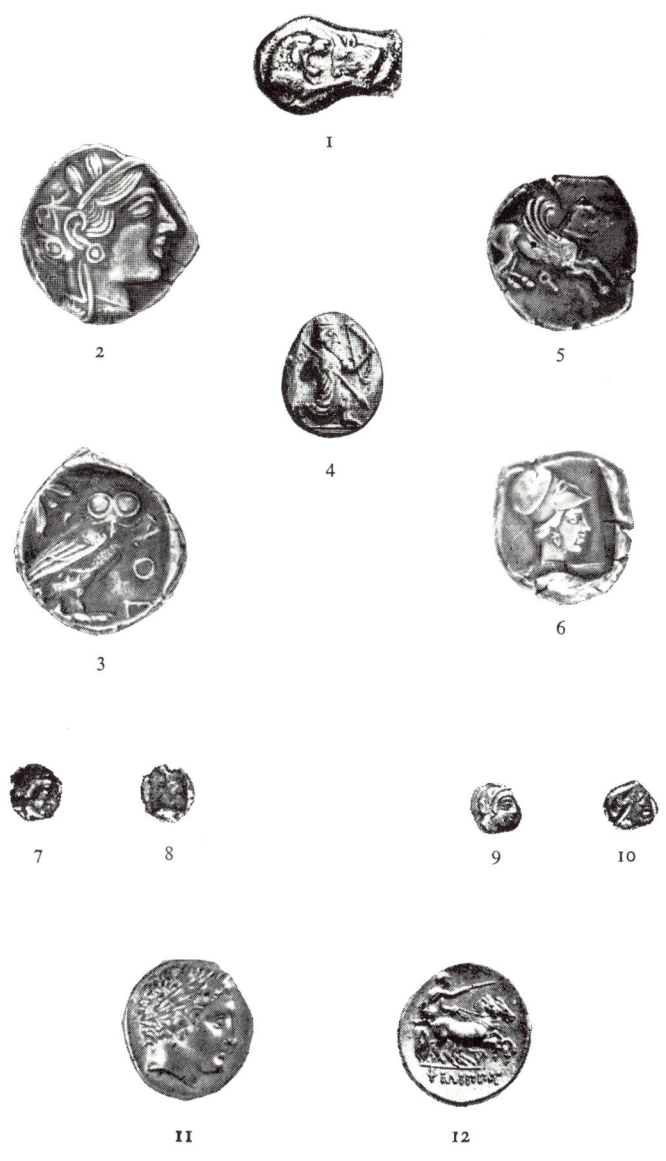

Greek coins 1-12 (all original size) – 1. gold stater of Croesus with lion's head and bull. – 2. and 3. Athenian tetradrachm; *obverse* Athena; *reverse* an owl. – 4. gold darlikos; *obv.* king with bow and arrow. – 5. and 6. didrachm of Corinth; *obv.* Pegasus; *rev.* Athena. – 7. and 8. Athenian obol; *obv.* Athena; *rev.* owl. – 9. and 10. Athenian hemiobolus; *obv.* Athena; *rev.* owl. – 11. and 12. gold stater of Philippus II; *obv.* head of the king; *rev.* two-horsed chariot; the charioteer holds a °stimulus.

85

Gráttius. Author of a didactic poem on hunting: 'Cynegética' (1st cent. AD).

Gregórius of Nýssa. Rhetorician, brother of °Basilius, who made him bishop of Nyssa in 371.

grýphon (γρύψ) **(griffin).** Mythical animal with the body of a lion and the head and the wings of an eagle.

gúttae. In the °Doric order the small peg-like projections beneath the °mutules and °triglyphs.

Gýas (Γύης). °Centimani.

H

Hádes ('Αίδης, ῎Αιδης, 'Αιδωνεύς). Son of °Kronos and °Rhea, god of the Underworld; as such he was the giver of wealth (metal and corn from the earth) and called Dis (*dives* = wealthy) or °Pluto (πλοῦτος = wealth); °Persephone.

Hádrian, *P. Aélius Hadriánus.* Roman emperor 117-138 AD, successor to °Trajan. His policy was one of peace. The expansion of the empire ended during his reign. He travelled widely, promoted the arts and sciences and he indulged his vanity by embellishing Athens, rebuilding Jerusalem (°Aélia Capitolína), and erecting the Athenaeum and the temple of °Venus and Roma in Rome. When he wanted to build a temple to *Iúppiter Capitolínus* on the site of Solomon's temple, the Jews revolted, led by °Bar Kochba (132-135); after that time he persecuted the Jews. He was buried in the °Mausoléum Hadriáni and succeeded by °Antoninus Pius; °Antinoüs, °Aurélii p. 31; °Sabina.

Hadrian's Wall. A fortified wall running for 121 km. from Bowness to Wallsend, to defend the northern frontier of Roman Britain, built by °Hadrian c. 122-126 AD; °Britain.

Haémon (Αἵμων). Son of °Creon, engaged to °Antigone.

Hámilcar. 1. *Hámilcar Bárcas* (= lightning). Carthaginian general in Sicily, who withstood the Romans 247-241 BC. After the Second °Punic War he quelled a mutiny of Carthaginian mercenaries in Africa, and in 238-229

conquered a large part of Spain. He was the father of °Hannibal. **2.** °Gelo.

Hammurábi. King of Babylon, c. 2000 BC, famous as a legislator. His laws were unearthed at °Susa in 1901, on a block of black diorite $2\frac{1}{2}$ m high (now in the Louvre).

Hánnibal ('Αννίβας). Son of °Hamilcar Barcas (247-183 BC), general of Carthage in the Second Punic War (218-201). After his initial victories on the °Ticinus and the °Trebia (218), at Lake °Trasimene (217) and at °Cannae (216), he was defeated at °Nola (215) by °Marcellus. Reinforcements were not sent from Carthage and he was recalled to defend his city against °Scipio (203). After the battle of °Zama (202) and the peace-treaty (201) he ruled in Carthage, but had to take refuge from the Romans (196), first with °Antiochus III of Syria, afterwards with °Prusias II of Bithynia. When the latter was about to deliver him to his enemies, he committed suicide (183).

Hánno (῏Αννων). **1.** Leader of the peace-party at Carthage, adversary of °Hamilcar and °Hannibal. **2.** A seafarer from Carthage, who sailed along the west coast of Africa as far as the equator (c. 500 BC).

Harmódius and Aristogeíton ('Αρμόδιος, 'Αριστογείτων). Two young Athenians, who planned to kill °Hippias and °Hipparchus, but failed (514 BC). Both were killed, but honoured as liberators in later times (°Antenor 2).

Harmónia. Daughter of °Ares and °Aphrodite, who married °Cadmus. At her wedding °Aphrodite gave her a necklace which was the cause of much trouble; °Amphiaraüs.

Hárpagus (Ἅρπαγος). A Persian nobleman, cruelly ordered by °Astyages to eat the flesh of his own son, since he had not killed the infant °Cyrus, who later started a revolt. He became a distinguished general under Cyrus.

Hárpalus (Ἅρπαλος). Treasurer of °Alexander the Great. After his treachery he was brought back into favour and made treasurer in Babylon.

Hárpies (Ἅρπυιαι). Storm-goddesses. Later associated with torment. °Phineus.

harúspices. °Etruscan priests who read the will of the gods from the intestines of sacrificial animals. They were consulted by the Senate when the Roman priests failed; after the conquest of Etruria they were summoned to Rome in such cases; °ill. 74.

74. Bronze model of a liver, used by the haruspices.

Hásdrubal (Ἀσδρούβας). **1.** Son-in-law and successor of °Hamilcar Bárcas. **2.** Brother of °Hannibal; he remained in Spain when the latter invaded Italy. In 207 he came to Hannibal's aid, but was defeated by the Romans under C. Claúdius Néro on the °Metaurus.

Heautontimoroúmenos. °Terence.

Hébe (Ἥβη). Goddess of youth and cup-bearer of the gods. Later she married °Heracles.

Hecabe. °Hecuba.

Hecataéus (Ἑκαταῖος) of Miletus (c. 500 BC). °Logographer; like °Herodotus he travelled to gain information. He did not support the °Ionian revolt. Only fragments of his work are extant.

Hécate (Ἑκάτη). Moon-goddess, who called up spirits from the Underworld and protected witches and witchcraft. She was worshipped especially on three-forked roads (whence her other name 'Trivia') and represented with three bodies and three heads.

Héctor (Ἕκτωρ). The bravest defender of Troy, son of °Priam and °Hecuba, married to °Andromache, father of °Astyanax. He was killed in single combat by °Achilles; °Dardanidae p. 60.

Hécuba (Ἑκάβη). Wife of °Priam, mother of °Deiphobus, °Hector, °Helenus, °Polydorus, °Paris, °Cassandra, °Polyxena. All her children were killed or taken prisoner and she herself became a slave of °Odysseus after the capture of Troy; °Euripides.

Hecýra. °Terence.

hegémony (ἡγεμονία). Leadership, by one state of a confederacy.

Hélen (Ἑλένη). Daughter of °Zeus (or Tyndareüs) and °Leda. Attracted by her beauty, nearly all the heroes of Greece sought her hand in marriage. On the advice of °Odysseus Tyndareüs made them all promise to honour her choice of a husband and to aid him in case of need. She chose °Menelaüs, but a few years later °Paris carried her off; °Trojan War. After the capture of Troy, Menelaüs took her back (°Homer). According to some, Paris and Helen were stranded in Egypt, where she stayed behind, while Paris unknowingly took her 'phantom' with him to Troy (°Eur. *Helena*); °Tantalidae p. 182.

Hélenus (Ἕλενος). Son of °Priam and °Hecuba, gifted with powers of prophecy. While a prisoner he told °Odysseus how Troy could be captured.

Héliades (Ἡλιάδες). Daughters of the Sun, sisters of °Phaëthon, whom they mourned until they were turned into poplar trees and their tears into amber (Ovid *Met.* 2, 340-366).

Heliaéa (ἡλιαία). A judicial tribunal at Athens; its members (ἡλιασταί) were citizens of at least thirty years of age.

Hélicon ('Ελικών). Mountain in Boeotia, abode of the °Muses; °Hippocrene; °Pegasus.

Heliópolis. °Baalbek.

Hélios (῞Ηλιος). The sun-god, who drove his chariot across the sky; identified with °Apollo; °Rhodes.

Helládic. The prehistoric civilisation of the continent of Greece is termed Helladic; c. 3000-1000 BC; °Cycladic civilisation; °Minoan civilisation, °Mycenae.

Hellanícus ('Ελλάνικος), of Lesbos. He made a collection of Greek legends at the time of the °Peloponnesian War.

Hélle (῞Ελλη). °Phrixus.

Hellénica. °Xenophon.

Hellenistic. The term used for the somewhat flamboyant art (and culture in general) of the Greek world after °Alexander's death. It was later absorbed by the Romans.

Héllespont ('Ελλήσποντος) (Dardanelles). **1.** The narrow strait between the Aegean and the Sea of Marmora,

called after Hélle, the sister of °Phrixus. **2.** The land bordering the Hellespont in Asia Minor.

helmet. The helmet made of boar's teeth described by °Homer (*Il.* X, 261-265) is identical with an ivory helmet found at °Mycenae. It has been reconstructed (°ill. 75). The Attic helmet covered the temples and cheeks and had a small neck-piece (°ill. 76). The Corinthian helmet covered the whole of the head with small openings for eyes and mouth (°ill. 127). The Romans after the time of °Camillus wore metal helmets (°cassis; °galea). After the time of °Marius a new type, with a larger neck-piece, came into use (*buccula*); °ill. 77.

76. An Attic helmet.

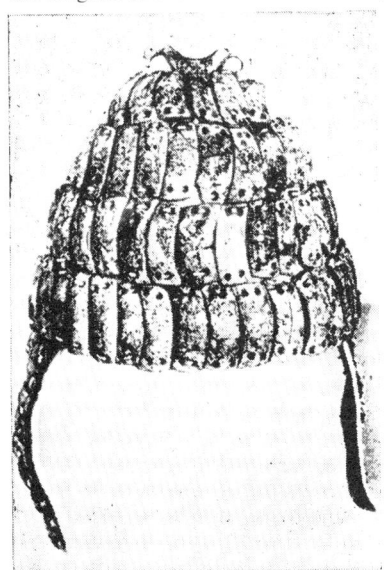

75. A Mycenaean helmet 20cm. high, as described by °Homer.

77. A Roman helmet.

Hélots (εἵλωτες). Serfs of the Spartan state.

hémina. °Weights and measures 2c.

Hémina. °Cassius.

hemióbol (ἡμιώβολον). Greek coin with the value of half a °drachma (°obol, °ill. p. 85).

hendecasýllable. A line of verse of eleven syllables:

‿ ‿ ⎵ ‿ ⎵ ‿ ⎵ ‿ ⎵ ‿ ⎵.

hendíadys (ἑν διὰ δυοῖν). A figure of speech in which a single idea was expressed by two words connected by a conjunction ('pateris libamus et auro').

Hephaéstus (Ἥφαιστος). Son of °Zeus and °Hera, god of fire and metal-working, represented as a lame, bearded man. His attributes were a hammer, tongs and bellows; °Charites.

Héra (Ἥρη). Wife and sister of °Zeus. Patroness of marriage; her principal sanctuaries were in °Olympia, Argos, °Paestum and Samos. She wore a diadem and a veil; the cow, peacock and pomegranate were sacred to her; °Juno.

Héracles (Ἡρακλῆς). Son of °Zeus and °Alcmena, hated by °Hera. In the service of °Eurystheus he had to perform twelve labours: 1. To kill the °Nemean lion; 2. To destroy the nine-headed hydra of °Lerna; 3. To catch the boar of °Erymanthus; 4. To capture, alive and unhurt, the swift hind of °Cerynea; 5. To scare away the man-eating birds of °Stymphalus; 6. To clean the stables of king °Augeas; 7. To catch the fire-breathing bull of Crete, sent by °Poseidon because °Minos had neglected to honour him; 8. To tame the man-eating horses of the Thracian king °Diomedes; 9. To fetch the girdle of °Hippolyta, the queen of the °Amazons; 10. To steal the cattle of the giant °Geryon; 11. To steal the golden apples of the °Hesperides; 12. To fetch °Cerberus from the Underworld. (°Antaeus, °Busiris, °Laomedon.) He sailed with the °Argonauts. He married °Deianeira, winning her by defeating the river-god °Acheloüs in a wrestling-match (Ovid

Met. 9, 1-97). On the way home he killed the °centaur °Nessus, who attempted to rape Deianeira, with an arrow dipped in the poisonous blood of the hydra of Lerna. Dying, the centaur advised Deianeira to keep some of his blood as a love-potion against Heracles' possible infidelity (Ovid *Met.* 9, 98-133). Some time afterwards Heracles won an archery contest in which king Eurytus of Oechalia had promised his daughter Iole as the prize. However, he refused her to Heracles, who then killed the king, devastated Oechalia and carried Iole off. To win him back Deianeira gave him a robe dipped in the blood of the centaur Nessus. However, the effect was that poison burned into his skin and, wracked with pain, he ascended a pyre at the foot of mount Oeta and died (Ovid. *Met.* 9, 134-272; Eur. *Trach.*; Sen. *Herc. Oet.*). After his death he became a demi-god and married °Hebe. In °Rome Heracles (= Hercules) had an altar, the °Ara Maxima (°Cacus) and a temple beside it, sacred to 'Hercules Invictus'; °map p. 81.

Heraclítus (Ἡράκλειτος), of Ephesus. Ionian philosopher. °Plato summed up his teaching as: πάντα ῥεῖ ('all things are in a state of flux'). Only fragments of his writings are extant.

Herculáneum. Small town at the foot of Mt Vesuvius, which was buried deep under volcanic ash in the eruption of 79 AD. The buildings collapsed more completely than at °Pompeii, but their furnishings were well preserved. Excavations were started in the 18th century.

Hércules, °Heracles.

Herénnius. Among °Cicero's writings a rhetorical manual, called 'De ratióne dicéndi ad C. Herénnium' and written c. 85 BC, is extant.

Hermaphrodítus (Ἑρμαφρόδιτος). A bi-sexual deity of Eastern origin (according to a Greek legend, son of °Hermes and °Aphrodite) who, out of love, became one with the nymph °Salmacis.

Hérmes (Ἑρμῆς). Son of °Zeus and

°Maea, born in a cave on Mt °Cyllene in Arcadia. He was the messenger of the gods, 'inventor' of the °lyre, guide of souls to the Underworld, protector of herds, boys in the °palaestra, orators, merchants, profit and deceit. He was represented as a young man with winged sandals, a herald's staff (°caduceus), sometimes with purse and lyre; °Praxiteles.

Hermíone ('Ερμιόνη). Daughter of °Menelaüs and °Helen, married to °Pyrrhus, the son of °Achilles, afterwards to °Orestes; °Tantalidae p. 182.

Hermocópidae ('Ερμοκοπίδης). The mutilators of the °herms at Athens, shortly before the Sicilian expedition; °Alcibiades.

herms. Pillars surmounted by a bust of °Hermes. They stood in large numbers in the streets and by the doors of Greek houses. They were worshipped and protected the houses. (°Alcibiades). In later times they could be surmounted by the busts of other gods or humans.

Héro ('Ηρώ). Priestess of °Aphrodite, who lived at Sestus on the Hellespont. Leander, at °Abydos on the other side of the strait, loved her. Every night he swam across until one night he was drowned in a storm; °Musaeus.

Hérod ('Ηρώδης). **1.** Nominated king of the Jews by °Antony in 37 BC; noted for his cruelty. **2.** *Heródes Agríppa*, °Július Agríppa. **3.** *Heródes Antípas*, Tetrarch of Galilee in Judaea (4 BC-39 AD). **4.** *Heródes Átticus* (*T. Claúdius Heródes Átticus*), 101-178 AD. Wealthy Athenian, orator and °sophist, friend of °Marcus Aurelius. He built the °odeum at Athens.

Heródas ('Ηρώδας), of Kos (c. 250 BC). Writer of °mimiambi. In 1891 some of them were discovered on a °papyrus.

Heródian ('Ηροδιανός). **1.** *Aélius Herodiánus*. Son of °Apollónius Dýscolus, grammarian. He dedicated his book on prosody to °Marcus Aurelius; extracts survive. **2.** Historian (3rd c. AD).

Heródotus ('Ηρόδοτος), of Halicarnassus (c. 484-425 BC). Historian of the °Persian Wars. He travelled throughout the then-known world and described the conflict between Europe and Asia, striving for historical truth and objectivity. The Alexandrians divided his work into nine books. He died at Thurii in Lucania; °ill. 78.

Heróïdes. °Ovid.

Héron (Ηρων), of Alexandria. Greek mathematician and physicist (c. 120 BC) who made several contrivances operated by means of water or steam, among them a 'penny-in-the-slot' machine for dispensing holy water (°ill. 79) and a °taxameter ('οδόμετρον).

Heróndas. °Herodas.

Heróphilus ('Ηρόφιλος), of Chalcedon. Physician in Alexandria (c. 300 BC). He wrote on anatomy and noted the rhythm of the pulse.

Heróstratus ('Ηρόστρατος). An incendiary who set fire to the famous temple of °Artemis at Ephesus in order to gain immortal fame.

Hésiod ('Ησίοδος). Poet from Ascra in Boeotia (8th cent. BC?). Extant are his: *Theogony* (on the origins of the gods and the origin of the world), *Works and Days* ("Εργα καὶ ἡμέραι) (a didactic poem on agriculture and sea-faring, addressed to his wayward brother) and other fragments.

Hesíone ('Ησιόνη). Daughter of °Laomedon (°Dardanidae), wife of °Telamon; °Aeacidae p. 3.

Hespérides ('Εσπερίδες). Daughters of °Atlas, who guarded a tree which bore golden apples, far away in the West; °Heracles.

Héstia ('Εστία). Daughter of °Kronos and °Rhea, goddess of the hearth, consequently of the family and the state (°Vesta).

hexámeter. The dactylic hexameter was a line of verse of six feet, of which the first five were °dactyls or °spondees and the last a spondee or a °trochee:

‾‿‿ ‾‿‿ ‾‿‿ ‾‿‿ ‾‿‿ ‾‿.

The fifth foot was nearly always a dactyl; °Homer.

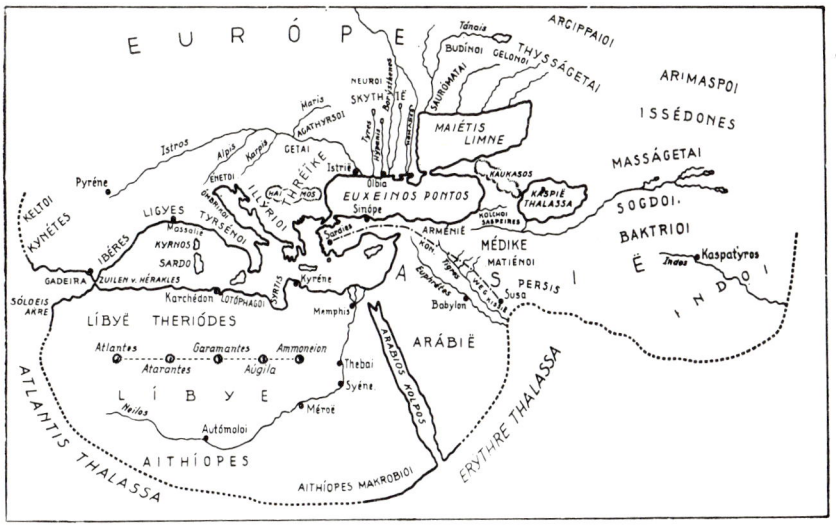

78. The world according to Herodotus.

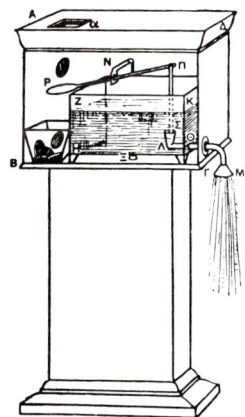

79. Automatic machine for dispensing water designed by Heron. When the coin touches the end of the lever (P), the outlet (Σ) is opened at (Λ) and the water flows from the reservoir (Z). Meanwhile the coin falls into the tray (B), the lever goes up again and the flow of water is stopped.

héxapla. An edition of the Old Testament by °Origenes, in six languages: 1. Hebrew; 2. Transcription in Greek; 3. Translation of °Aquila; 4. Translation of °Symmachus; 5. °Septuagint; 6. Translation of °Theodotion.

Híempsal. °Adherbal.

hierátic. °Hieroglyphics.

Hiéro ('Ιέρων). **1.** *Hiero I.* °Tyrant of Syracuse (478-467 BC). Successor to °Gelo. A patron of artists. **2.** *Hiero II.* Tyrant of Syracuse (269-215 BC); after 263 he was a loyal ally of the Romans.

hieroglýphics. The pictorial script of the Egyptians. There were characters which represented a word (ideograms), others representing phonetic signs for groups of consonants and the third class of hieroglyphics, the determinatives, were ideographic signs annexed to words phonetically represented, to give some hint of their meaning. This was necessary because, as only consonants were used in hieroglyphics, there were many homonyms. For the purpose of ordinary writing this system was simplified to a cursive style, called hieratic script, and from that, in about 1000 BC, a still simpler style, the demotic, developed. Decipherment of the hieroglyphics began in 1822 by J. F. Champollion, who started his studies using the °Rosetta Stone.

Hierónymus (Ἱερώνυμος) (Jerome), *Sophroníscus Eusébius Hierónymus* (c. 348-420 AD). Church-father, translator of the Bible into Latin (°Vulgate), and of °Eusebius, author of a number of theological writings.

Hilárius, of Poitiers (c. 315-367 AD). He was opposed to the doctrines of °Arian; his most famous work was 'De fíde contra Ariános', about the Trinity.

himátion (ἱμάτιον). A Greek cloak; °ill. 80.

Hímera (Ἱμέρα). River in northern

80. Relief from Sparta (37cm. high). A girl wearing a °chiton and °hination, of which she lifts a corner, pours wine.

Sicily; °Gelo.

Hippárchus (Ἵππαρχος). Son of °Peisistratus, killed by °Harmodius and Aristogeiton (514 BC).

Híppias (Ἱππίας). **1.** Son of °Peisistratus, °tyrant of Athens (527-510 BC), at first with his brother °Hipparchus. He was expelled by the influence of the °Alcmaeonids (510); °Cleomenes. **2.** of Elis. °Sophist of °Socrates' day. He considered it necessary for a sophist to know and to be able to do everything. He rigorously trained his memory and could repeat any fifty words in the right order.

Hippócrates (Ἱπποκράτης). **1.** *Hippócrates of Cos* (459-c. 350). The greatest physician of antiquity. Many of his writings are extant. **2.** *Hippócrates of Chios* (c. 450 BC). Wrote mathematical treatise.

Híppocrene (Ἵππου κρήνη). Fountain on Mount °Helicon, sacred to the °Muses; °Pegasus.

Hippodameía (Ἱπποδάμεια). **1.** Wife of °Pelops, mother of °Atreus and °Thyestes; °Tantalidae. She was the daughter of Oenomaüs, king of Elis, who had promised her to the man who would defeat him in a chariot race. Pelops succeeded, by bribing his adversary's charioteer °Myrtilus; °ill. 81. **2.** °Pirithoüs.

Hippólyta (Ἱππολύτη). Queen of the °Amazons, whose girdle °Heracles had to fetch for °Eurystheus' daughter Admete. She married °Theseus.

Hippólytus (Ἱππόλυτος). Son of °Theseus and °Hippolyta (or °Antiope). His stepmother °Phaedra loved him but, angry at his indifference, she accused him to Theseus, who put a curse on him. °Poseidon heard the curse and sent a sea-monster to frighten Hippolytus' horses as he drove along the shore, and they trampled him to death. °Euripides.

Hippómenes (Ἱππομένης). °Atalanta.

Hippónax (Ἱππῶναξ), of Ephesus. He fled from the Persians to Clazomenae (542 BC). Writer of lampoons, inventor of the °choliambi.

81. Pelops abducting °Hippodameia (from an °amphora *c.* 415 BC).

Hírtius, *A. Hirtius.* Consul 43 BC, killed at °Mutina fighting °Antony. He was the author of the eighth book of 'De Bello Gallico' (Julius °Caesar), and of 'Bellum Alexandrínum'.

Híssarlik. Modern name of the place where °Schliemann (in 1870) started excavations to find Troy; °Trojan War.

Histiaéus (Ἱστιαῖος). Tyrant of Miletus, who saved the army of °Darius by preventing °Miltiades from destroying the bridge across the Danube (514 BC). Later he instigated the rising of the °Ionians against Persia and eventually was killed by the Persians.

História Augústa. An indifferent collection of imperial biographies (from Hadrian to °Carinus) by various writers.

Históriae. °Tacitus.

Híttites. A group of tribes in Asia-Minor, flourishing 1650-1530 BC and 1480-1200 BC. Their civilisation is known to us from excavations at Boghazköy (near Ankara) which brought to light thousands of clay-tablets.

Hómer (Ὅμηρος). The oldest known Greek poet. Very little is known about his life and many towns boasted of being his birthplace. He probably lived in western Asia Minor c. 800 BC. His extant works are: 1. *Iliad.* An episode in the Siege of Troy, ending with °Hector's burial. 2. *Odyssey.* The return of °Odysseus to °Ithaca. Traditionally, some other poems were said to have been composed by him: the °epic cycle and the °Homeric hymns, but as early as the 4th century BC only the *Iliad* and the *Odyssey* were ascribed to him, while some scholars (°Chorizontes) assume even these to have been written by different authors.

The conflict about the unity of *Iliad* and *Odyssey* in modern times was inaugurated by F. A. Wolf with his 'Prolegómena ad Homérum', 1795. He explained the discrepancies in the poems by assuming that separate poems were collected at Athens in Peisistratus' time. Many theories were brought forward later. K. Lachman (1847) attempted to single out separate poems from the whole. The 'Unitarians' assume the unity of the poems, but suppose some passages to have been interpolated. G. Hermann (1831) championed the theory that the original poem has been enlarged gradually. Kirchhoff (1859) thought that the Odyssey originally consisted of three poems; the problem may never be solved.

Homeric hymns. A collection of °hymns, traditionally attributed to °Homer, *e.g.* one to Delian °Apollo, to Pythian Apollo, to °Hermes, to °Aphrodite, to °Demeter, and °Dionysus.

Homeric Question. °Chorizontes; °Homer.

Homeromástix (Ὁμηρομάστιξ). 'Scourge of Homer', nickname of the orator Zoílus (284-247 BC), for his sharp criticism of °Homer.

hómo mensúra. °Protagoras.

Honórius, *Flávius Honórius.* Son of °Theodosius the Great, who was allotted the western half of the Roman Empire, when it was divided. He reigned 395-423 AD. His counsellor and general was °Stilicho.

Horace, *Q. Horátius Fláccus.* Famous Roman lyric poet (65 BC-8 AD). His extant works are: 1. *Odes* (Cármina); 2. *Épodes*; 3. °*Satires*; 4. °*Cármen saeculáre*; 5. *Epistles*; 6. *Ars Poëtica.* Horace was the first Roman poet to be inspired by Greek poets of Classical times (°Alcaeus; °Sappho). His subjects were largely conventional (love, death, worldly wisdom), but the first six odes of the third book sing the praises of Augustus for his moral rejuvenation of the Roman people. Horace had patrons of power and distinction. °Maecanas and °Augustus, but managed to keep his independence.

Hórae (Ὧραι). Daughters of °Zeus and °Themis: Eunómia, Díke and Eiréne. They opened and closed the gates of the Heavens for the Sun chariot. In later times they were the goddesses of Justice and Order.

Horátii. Three Roman brothers who, in the reign of °Tullus Hostilius, fought the three °Curiatii from Alba (Liv. 1, 24-25).

Horátius Cócles. A Roman who, alone, held the bridge across the Tiber against the °Etruscans (Liv. 2, 10).

Hóremheb. King of Egypt and general (1345-1314 BC), who reacted against the revolutionary ideas of °Amenhotep IV.

lex Horténsia. A law passed in 287 BC, by the °dictator Q. Hortensius (°secessio plebis).

Horténsius, *Q. Horténsius Hortálus.* Consul 69 BC, who was the most famous orator in Rome, apart from °Cicero. He defended °Verres.

Hórus. The Egyptian god of light, son of °Osiris and °Isis, identified with °Apollo by the Greeks.

Hostília. °curia.

house. °domus.

hýacinth (ὑάκινθος). The same plant was called by this name in antiquity as the one we know today; °ill. 82.

Hyacínthus ('Υάκινθος). Beloved of °Apollo, who accidentally killed him with a discus and changed him into the °hyacinth (Ovid. *Met.* 10, 162-219). His festival 'Hyacínthia' was chiefly celebrated at Amyclae in the Peloponnese.

Hýades ('Υάδες). Daughters of °Atlas, who mourned their brother Hyas until they died. They were placed in the constellation Taurus.

Hýdra. (ὕδρα). A water snake; °Lerna; °Heracles.

hýdria (ὑδρία). A Greek jar in which water was carried from the well. It had three handles, one vertical for holding and pouring, and two horizontal for lifting; °ill. 83.

Hygieía ('Υγίεια). Goddess of Health, usually said to be a daughter of °Asclepius.

Hýksos. Name of the tribes from Asia which dominated Egypt from c. 1700-1600 BC.

Hýmen ('Υμέναιος). God of marriage.

hymn. A song or poem in honour of a deity or hero. The oldest are called the °Homeric hymns; °Callimachus.

hypállage (ὑπαλλαγή). Connection of an adjective with the 'wrong' noun: *e.g.* 'omnium génera avium'; 'a nice cup of tea'; °enallage.

Hyperboréans. ('Υπερβόρειοι, -εοι). A legendary people of the distant north.

82. The Greek sculptured head dates from the 7th cent. BC, and shows possible influence from the formation of the flowers (of the °hyacinth). Hair has been likened to this flower in °Homer.

83. An Attic °black-figured hydria *c.* 500 BC. Harnessing the horses. On the shoulder is a battle scene.

Hypérides (‘Υπερείδης). °Attic orator (390-322 BC), a contemporary supporter of °Demosthenes. He was executed by °Antipater. Seven of his speeches survive.

Hypermnéstra (‘Υπερμνήστρα). °Danaids.

Hýphasis (‘Υφασις). River in India which marked the limit of °Alexander the Great's march.

hýpocaust (ὑπόκαυστον). A Roman 'central-heating' system, by which warm air from a central fire circulated below a raised floor ('suspensúra'), supported on low tiled pillars ('pílae'). The smoke escaped *via* specially constructed hollow tiles at intervals inside the walls, thus warming these as well; °ill. 84. A good example in °Britain is at Bath ('Aquae Sulis').

hypotrachélium (ὑποτραχήλιον). In the °Doric order, the groove(s) between the necking of the °capital and the shaft.

'hýsteron próteron' (= ὑστερον πρότερον). Inversion of the natural sequence of events: 'moriamur et in media arma ruamus'.

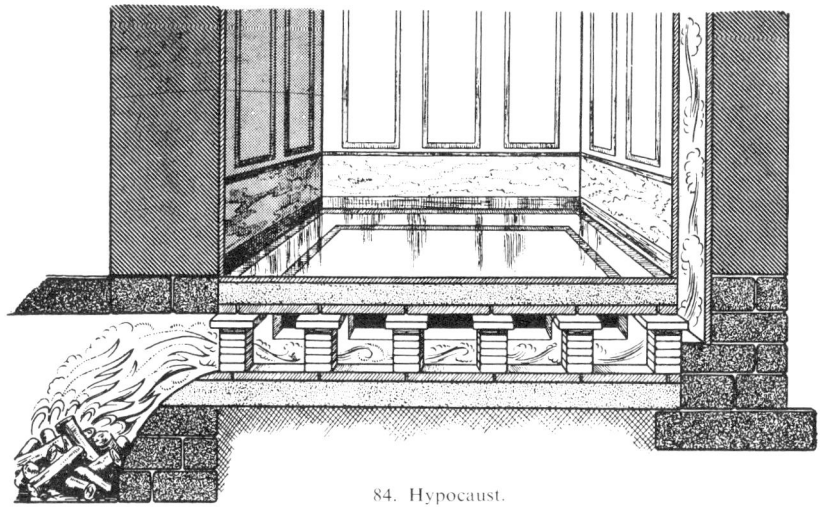

84. Hypocaust.

I

Iacchos (Ἴακχος). Son of °Zeus and °Demeter, the deity worshipped at the °Eleusinian Mysteries, identified later with °Bacchus.

iamb (ἴαμβος). A metrical foot: ◡ ‒.

Iamblichus (Ἰάμβλιχος). °Neo-Platonist and mystic (4th cent. AD). His writings on °Pythagoras and the Egyptian °mysteries are extant.

Iapetus (Ἰαπετός). One of the °Titans, father of °Atlas, Menoetius, °Prometheus and °Epimetheus; °Zeus threw him into °Tartarus.

Ibycus (Ἴβυκος). Greek lyric poet from Rhegium in Bruttium (c. 540 BC). According to a later story he was killed by robbers, who were brought to justice by a flock of cranes who had seen the murder.

Icarus (Ἴκαρος). Son of °Daedalus.

Ictinus (Ἰκτῖνος). Architect of the °Parthenon; °Callicrates.

ideogram. A sign or symbol representing a word (not a letter); °hieroglyphics.

Idomeneus (Ἰδομενεύς). King of Crete, grandson of °Minos, commander of the Cretans at Troy; °Meriones.

Idus (Ides). Name for the 15th day of March, May, July and October, and of the 13th day of the other months; °Kalendae; °calendar; Nonae. °Caesar was murdered on the Ides of March (44 BC).

Ignatius. Bishop of Antioch, who died a martyr in the reign of °Trajan. Seven of his letters survive.

Iliad (Ἰλιάς). °Homer.

Ilissus (Ἰλισσός). A small river near Athens.

Ilus (Ἴλος). °Dardanidae p. 60.

ímbrex. °tiles.

Imhótep. The architect of the step-pyramid of °Saqqara in Egypt. He was physician and adviser to the pharaoh °Djoser. After his death he was worshipped as a god of medicine and identified with °Asclepius by the Greeks. Recent excavations (1972) appear to have located his tomb.

impérium. The supreme power of some Roman magistrates involving command in war and the interpretation and execution of law. Power limited to special activities was called *potestas*.

implúvium. °atrium; °domus.

Ínachus (Ἴναχος). Father of °Io.

inchóative. Inceptive, expressing the beginning of an action, *e.g.* 'cogno-sc-o'.

induméntum. °tunica.

infix. A modifying element inserted in the body of a word, *e.g.* 'ing-, iungo; λαθ-, λανθάνω'.

Íno ('Ινώ). Daughter of °Cadmus and °Harmonia, second wife of °Athamas, step-mother of °Phrixus and Helle. °Juno sent °Tisiphone to make Athamas mad; Ino threw herself into the sea and became the goddess Leucothea (Ovid *Met.* 4, 481-542).

Institutiónes Justitiáni. °Corpus iuris civilis.

intercéssio. °tribunus plebis.

interréx. When both consuls in Rome had died or been unable to hold new elections, all magistrates resigned and the patrician senators appointed an 'interrex', to exercise the function of the consuls for five days, at the end of which he nominated a successor ('interregem pródere'). This continued until elections had been held.

intérula. °tunica.

Ío ('Ιώ). Daughter of Inachus, king of Argos (Ovid *Met.* 1, 583-750).

Ióbates ('Ιοβάτης). King of Lycia, father of Stheneboea; °Bellerophon.

I.O.M. Abbreviation of 'Iuppiter Optimus Maximus'; °Jupiter.

Íon (Ἴων). A poet from Ephesus; one of °Plato's dialogues is called after him.

Ionian Revolt. Uprising of the °Ionian cities of Asia Minor against their Persian overlords, instigated by °Aristagoras (499 BC). After initial victories, the Greek fleet was defeated near °Lade (494).

Iónians (Ἴωνες). A Greek tribe living chiefly in Attica, Euboea, the °Cyclades and Ionia; °Dorians.

Ionic dialect. The form of Greek spoken by the °Ionians; °Attic dialect.

Ionic order. One of the three orders of Greek architecture, characterized by the two volutes of the °capital, with a fluted °shaft; it rests on a composite base; °ills. 85, 86.

85. An Ionic capital.

86. Ionic entablature.

iónicus. A metrical foot: *ionicus a maiore*
_ _ ⌣ ⌣, *ionicus a minore* ⌣ ⌣ _ _.

Iphigeneía ('Ιφιγένεια). Daughter of
°Agamemnon and °Clytaemnestra. Her
father was compelled to sacrifice her
to °Artemis, who held back the Greek
fleet at Aulis with contrary winds and
could only be appeased by this. (°Eur.
Iph. in Aul.) The goddess supposedly
saved her and made her a priestess in
the Tauric Chersonese, where °Orestes
and °Pylades found her (°Eur. *Iph.
in Taur.*); °Tantalidae p. 182.

Íphis (⸗Ιφις). A youth who killed himself when his love for Anaxarete was
not returned. The gods turned her into
stone (Ovid *Met.* 14, 698-771).

Ípsus (῎Ιψος). Town in Phrygia, where
°Antigonus I and his son °Demetrius
Poliorcetes were defeated by the other
°Diadochi.

Irenaéus (Εἰρηναῖος). Bishop of Lyons
(178-202 AD). Apologist and champion
of the Church, who died a martyr.

Iron Age. The period in which iron
replaced bronze as the chief material
for tools and weapons began in Europe
c. 1000 BC.

Isaéus ('Ισαῖος). Attic orator, teacher of
°Demosthenes, °logographer. Ten of
his speeches (all dealing with cases of
inheritance) survive.

Isidórus. Bishop of Seville (600-636 AD).
He wrote an encyclopaedia, 'Ety-
mológiae' (or 'Origines'), and another
work, 'De fide catholica contra
Iudaeos'.

Ísis. Egyptian goddess of life and fertility.
She was the wife of °Osiris and mother
of °Horus. In °Hellenistic and Roman
times her cult became widespread;
°Mysteries; °sistrum; °Apuleius 2.

Isméne ('Ισμήνη). Sister of °Antigone.

Isócrates ('Ισοκράτης). °Attic orator
(436-338 BC), pupil of °Gorgias. He was
principally a teacher of rhetoric. Politically he was in favour of a Greek nation
comprising all the small city-states,
under the leadership of °Philip of
Macedon. Of his speeches twenty-one
survive, the larger part °epideictic,
written in the °Attic dialect, excellent
for its simplicity and beauty.

Íssus ('Ισσός). Coastal town of Cilicia,
where °Alexander the Great defeated
°Darius (333 BC).

Ísthmian Games. Athletic competitions
held at °Corinth every second year in
honour of °Poseidon. They became an
international festival in 581 BC. It was
at the Isthmian Games of 196 BC that
°Flaminius proclaimed the freedom of
Greece; °Pindar; °Nemean, °Olympian,
°Pythian games.

Isthmus (῎Ισθμος). A narrow neck of
land, especially that of °Corinth; °Canal
of Corinth.

Íthaca ('Ιθάκη). The island home of
°Odysseus, probably the modern
'Levkas' (Hom. *Od.* IX, 21-26; XXI,
347).

iúgerum. °Weights and measures 2 b.

Iúlus. °Ascanius.

ius Aeliánum. °Paetus.

ius honórum. Roman °citizenship.

ius Látii. The rights enjoyed by the
coloniae Latinae (°colonia). They
shared °*conubium* and °*commercium*
with Rome; in special conditions they
could acquire Roman °citizenship.

Íxion ('Ιξίων). King of the °Lapiths,
favourite of °Zeus, tried to make love
to °Hera. In the Underworld he was
bound to a wheel which turned for ever.

J

Jánus. Roman god of doors, thus of beginnings. His two-faced head appears on the °'as'; °ill. 87 and p. 164.

Jáson ('Ιάσων). Son of °Aeson, who had been expelled from Iolcus by his brother °Pelias. Pelias promised to return the kingship to Jason if the latter would fetch the °Golden Fleece from Colchis on the Euxine. Jason, accompanied by fifty heroes, the °Argonauts, sailed for Colchis in the ship Argo.

On arrival he had to overcome the fire-breathing bull, which he achieved with the aid of °Medea, King Aeëtes' daughter, who also helped him to capture the °Golden Fleece (Ovid *Met.* 7, 1-158). Fleeing the country with Jason and pursued by Aeëtes, she killed her brother °Absyrtus and scattered his limbs to delay her father. Thus Aeëtes could not overtake them.

Back in Iolcus Medea renewed the youth of Aeson (Ovid *Met.* 7, 159-293) and persuaded the daughters of Pelias to try the same with their father; they failed and killed him (Ovid *Met.* 7, 297-346). Medea had to flee with Jason to Corinth, where he fell in love with °Creüsa, King °Creon's daughter; threatened with rejection, Medea killed Creon, Creusa and her own children and fled (Eur. *Medea*; Ovid *Met.* 7, 350-403).

Jéricho. Town in Palestine, north of the

87. The Arch of Janus, built 315 AD as an entrance gate to the °Velabrum to honour °Constantine the Great after his victory over Maxentius.

Dead Sea. Excavations have shown it to be the oldest city in the world, dating from at least c. 7000 BC.

Jocásta (Ἰοκάστη). Mother and wife of °Oedipus; °Sophocles.

John Chrýsostom. Saint, (c. 344-407 AD), patriarch of Constantinople; a great number of his homilies survive.

Joséphus. °Flavius Josephus.

Jugúrtha. King of Numidia, who murdered his two nephews °Adherbal and Hiempsal to acquire the kingdom, which he defended against the Romans, chiefly by intrigue and bribery (112-105 BC). He was defeated by °Marius and taken prisoner by Marius' °quaestor °Sulla. He was led through Rome in the triumphal procession of Marius in 106 and strangled in the °carcer. The story of the war with Jugurtha was told by °Sallust.

Júlia I. Name of the female members of the Júlian family. The best-known are **1.** *Júlia.* Daughter of °Caesar, born c. 83 BC, married in 59 to °Pompey. **2.** *Júlia.* Daughter of °Augustus and °Scribonia, born 39 BC, married in 25 BC to M. Claúdius Marcéllus, in c. 21 BC to M. °Vipsánius Agríppa and in

11 BC to °Tibérius. She was banished to Pandateria by °Augustus in 8 AD; °Julio-Claudian dynasty p. 101. **3.** *Vipsánia Júlia.* Daughter of M. Vipsánius Agríppa and °Julia **2** (c. 19 BC-28 AD), married in 4 BC to L. Aemílius Paúllus (a daughter, Aemília Lépida, born 3 BC); °Julio-Claudian dynasty p. 101. **4.** *Julia.* Daughter of °Drúsus and °Livílla, born c. 4 AD, married 20 AD to Néro Germánicus and in 33 to C. Rubéllius Blándus. Her son was Rubéllius Plaútus. She died in 43 AD; °Julio-Claudian dynasty p. 101. **5.** *Júlia Livílla.* Daughter of °Germánicus and °Agrippína, born 17 AD, married in 33 AD to M. Vinícius. She was murdered in 42 AD; °Julio-Claudian dynasty p.101.

2. Name of several imperial princesses: **1.** *Júlia Dómna.* Second wife of °Septimius Severus; °Sevéri p. 173. **2.** *Júlia Maesa;* °Sevéri p. 173. **3.** *Júlia Mamaéa.* Mother of °Alexánder Sevérus; °Sevéri p. 173. **4.** *Júlia Soaémias;* °Sevéri p. 173.

basílica Júlia. °basilica.

lex Júlia. *De civitáte sociórum;* °Social War.

Jugurtha

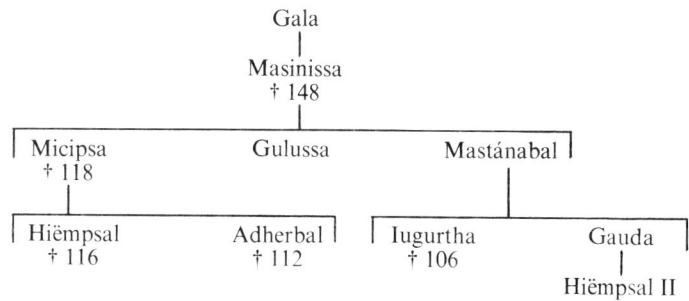

```
                        Gala
                         |
                     Masinissa
                       † 148
    ┌────────────────────┼──────────────────────┐
  Micipsa            Gulussa              Mastánabal
  † 118                                        |
    ┌──────────────┐          ┌────────────────┴────────┐
 Hiëmpsal       Adherbal    Iugurtha                  Gauda
  † 116          † 112       † 106                      |
                                                  Hiëmpsal II
```

Júlian calendar, the reformed °calendar of °Caesar; °Sosigenes.

Juliánus. 1. (=Júlian the Apóstate), *Flávius Claúdius Juliánus.* Roman emperor (361-363), son of Constantius, °Constantine the Great's brother. He was well grounded in philosophy, an adherent of °Neo-Platonism and greatly opposed to the Christian faith. He was an able soldier and died fighting the Persians. **2.** *Juliánus,* °Salvius Juliánus (c. 130 AD). Jurist. His principal work was 'Digesta'.

Julio-Claudian dynasty. pp. 102, 103.

Július. 1. °Agrícola. **2.** *Július Agríppa I* (10 BC-44 AD). Jewish king, educated in Rome. °Gaius sent him to Judaea in 37 as king of two °tetrarchies and °Claudius made him king of all Judaea. In the Acts of the Apostles he is called 'Heródes Agríppa'. **3.** *M. Július Agríppa II* (28-c. 93). Son of **2,** became king of Chalcis (50) and later of other territories; he remained loyal to Rome. **4.** *Agríppa Július Caesar* (=*Agríppa Póstumus*). Son of M. Vipsánius Agríppa and °Julia. He was born posthumously, hence his name (12 BC) and adopted by °Augustus. °Livia caused him to be banished to Planasia, where after Augustus' death he was murdered by the command of °Tiberius (Tac. *Ann.* 1, 6); °Julio-Claudian dynasty p. 101. **5.** *C. Július Caesar.* Roman politician, general and author. He was a member of the first °triumvirate with °Pompey and °Crassus (60 BC), conquered Gaul (58-50) and explored °Britain. In 49 he marched against Pompey (°Rubicon) and started the 2nd °Civil War (49-48), which ended with Pompey's defeat at °Pharsalus. In 45 Caesar became °dictator. On the 15th March (the Ides of March) 44 BC he was killed in the Senate by °Cassius and °Brutus. His extant works are: 1. *De bello Gállico,* covering the years 58-52 in seven books (the eighth was written by °Hirtius); 2. *De bello cívili,* starting with the crossing of the Rubicon and ending with Pompey's death in Egypt. **6.** *C. Július Caésar,*

adoptive name of °Augustus. **7.** *Július Civílis,* leader of the Batavian rebellion against Rome (69-70 AD). Through a mistaken interpretation of Tac. *Hist.* 4, 13 he has been called 'Claudius Civilis' for many centuries. **8.** °Frontínus. **9.** °Paulus. **10.** °Solinus.

Júnia Claudílla. Daughter of M. Június Silvánus, married in 33 AD to C. Caesar, afterwards the emperor °Gaius. She died in 38 AD; °Julio-Claudian dynasty p. 101.

Június. 1. °Brutus. **2.** °Columella. **3.** °Juvenal. **4.** *M. Junius Pera;* °dictator.

Júno. Roman goddess, daughter of °Saturn and °Rhea, wife of °Jupiter. She was worshipped in a temple on the °Capitol, the so-called temple of *Juno Moneta* (from Latin *monére*=to warn?), in later times the Mint of °Rome (°plan p. 165). She was identified with the Greek °Hera.

Júpiter. The supreme god of the Romans, son of °Saturn, consort of °Juno. He was the omnipotent and benevolent king and father of the gods, the creator of thunder and lightning, rain and sunshine. His principal temple stood on the °Capitol (hence his name ('J. Capitolínus'); identified with the Greek °Zeus; °I.O.M.

Justínian. Roman Emperor of the East (527-565 AD). His greatest achievement was the codification of Roman law (°corpus iuris civilis). His generals °Belisarius and °Narses subdued large parts of Italy and Africa (533-540), but in the last years of his reign he suffered much at the hands of the Persians.

Justínus. 1. Philosopher, father of the church and martyr (c. 100-c. 165 AD). **2.** *M. Juniánus Justínus* (3rd cent. AD). Made an abstract of the works of °Pompeíus Trogus, which is extant.

Júvenal, *D. Junius Juvénalis* (c. 62-142 AD?), satirist. In sixteen brilliant° satires he attacked the moral decline of his day.

Juvéncus, *C. Véttus Aquilínus Juvéncus.* A Spanish priest (c. 330 AD), who turned the Gospels into an epic of four books of °hexameter verse.

Julio-Claudian dynasty

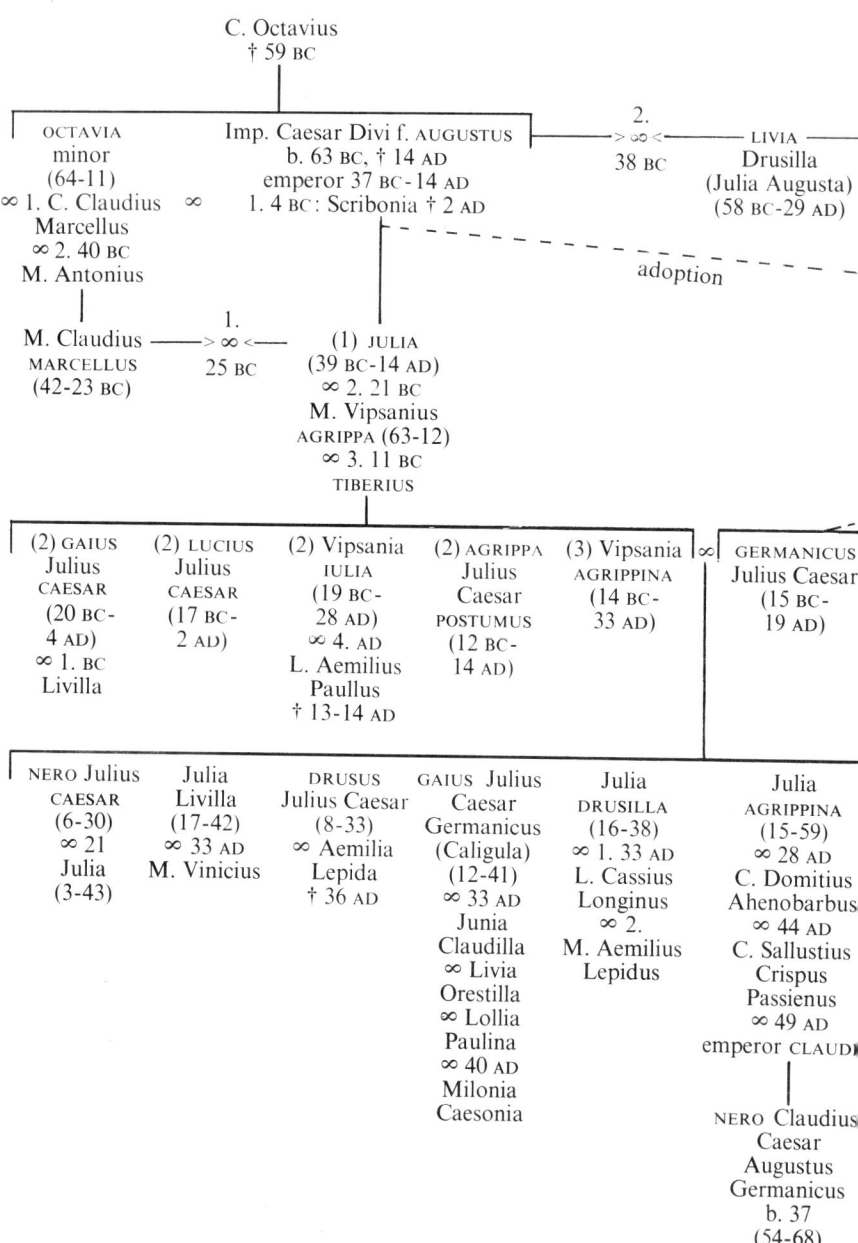

C. Octavius
† 59 BC

OCTAVIA minor (64-11)
∞ 1. C. Claudius Marcellus
∞ 2. 40 BC M. Antonius

Imp. Caesar Divi f. AUGUSTUS
b. 63 BC, † 14 AD
emperor 37 BC - 14 AD
1. 4 BC: Scribonia † 2 AD

2. > ∞ < ——— LIVIA ——— Drusilla (Julia Augusta) (58 BC-29 AD)
38 BC

adoption

M. Claudius MARCELLUS (42-23 BC) ——— 1. > ∞ < ——— (1) JULIA (39 BC-14 AD)
25 BC
∞ 2. 21 BC M. Vipsanius AGRIPPA (63-12)
∞ 3. 11 BC TIBERIUS

(2) GAIUS Julius CAESAR (20 BC-4 AD) ∞ 1. BC Livilla

(2) LUCIUS Julius CAESAR (17 BC-2 AD)

(2) Vipsania IULIA (19 BC-28 AD) ∞ 4. AD L. Aemilius Paullus † 13-14 AD

(2) AGRIPPA Julius Caesar POSTUMUS (12 BC-14 AD)

(3) Vipsania AGRIPPINA (14 BC-33 AD) ∞ GERMANICUS Julius Caesar (15 BC-19 AD)

NERO Julius CAESAR (6-30) ∞ 21 Julia (3-43)

Julia Livilla (17-42) ∞ 33 AD M. Vinicius

DRUSUS Julius Caesar (8-33) ∞ Aemilia Lepida † 36 AD

GAIUS Julius Caesar Germanicus (Caligula) (12-41) ∞ 33 AD Junia Claudilla ∞ Livia Orestilla ∞ Lollia Paulina ∞ 40 AD Milonia Caesonia

Julia DRUSILLA (16-38) ∞ 1. 33 AD L. Cassius Longinus ∞ 2. M. Aemilius Lepidus

Julia AGRIPPINA (15-59) ∞ 28 AD C. Domitius Ahenobarbus ∞ 44 AD C. Sallustius Crispus Passienus ∞ 49 AD emperor CLAUDIUS

NERO Claudius Caesar Augustus Germanicus b. 37 (54-68)

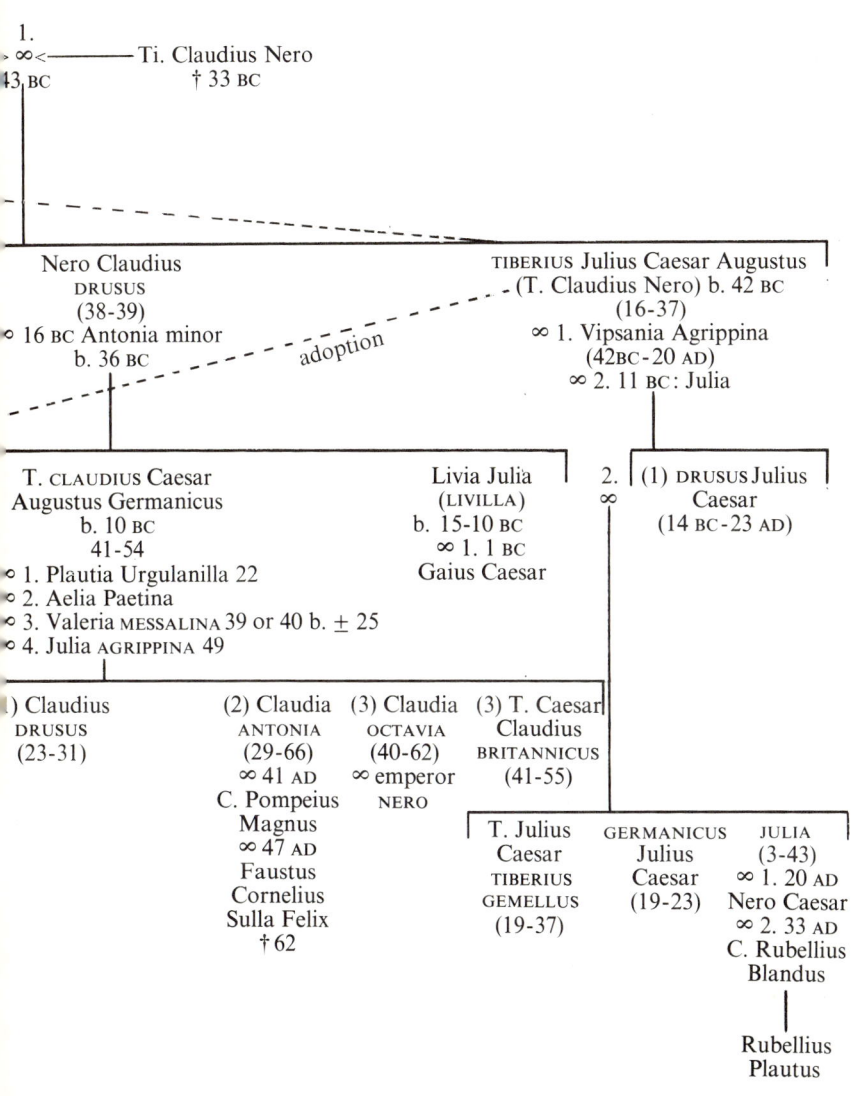

1.
∞<————— Ti. Claudius Nero
43 BC   † 33 BC

Nero Claudius
DRUSUS
(38-39)
∞ 16 BC Antonia minor
b. 36 BC

adoption

TIBERIUS Julius Caesar Augustus
(T. Claudius Nero) b. 42 BC
(16-37)
∞ 1. Vipsania Agrippina
(42BC-20 AD)
∞ 2. 11 BC: Julia

T. CLAUDIUS Caesar
Augustus Germanicus
b. 10 BC
41-54
∞ 1. Plautia Urgulanilla 22
∞ 2. Aelia Paetina
∞ 3. Valeria MESSALINA 39 or 40 b. ± 25
∞ 4. Julia AGRIPPINA 49

Livia Julia
(LIVILLA)
b. 15-10 BC
∞ 1. 1 BC
Gaius Caesar

2.
∞

(1) DRUSUS Julius
Caesar
(14 BC-23 AD)

(1) Claudius
DRUSUS
(23-31)

(2) Claudia
ANTONIA
(29-66)
∞ 41 AD
C. Pompeius
Magnus
∞ 47 AD
Faustus
Cornelius
Sulla Felix
† 62

(3) Claudia
OCTAVIA
(40-62)
∞ emperor
NERO

(3) T. Caesar
Claudius
BRITANNICUS
(41-55)

T. Julius
Caesar
TIBERIUS
GEMELLUS
(19-37)

GERMANICUS
Julius
Caesar
(19-23)

JULIA
(3-43)
∞ 1. 20 AD
Nero Caesar
∞ 2. 33 AD
C. Rubellius
Blandus

Rubellius
Plautus

K

Kaléndae (Kálends). The first day of the month; °Idus (Ides); °calendar; °Nonae (Nones).

kálpis (κάλπις). A Greek vase; °ill. 88.

88. Kalpis.

89. Kalyx krater from Spina, c. 430 BC. The battle between the gods and the °giants.

kályx kráter. °Krater with body in the form of a 'calyx'. The body consists of two parts, the upper part is concave, the lower part convex; °ill. 89.

kántharos (κάνθαρος). Greek cup with two high vertical handles; °ill. 90.

kélebe (κελέβη). Column °krater.

Kháfre. Pharaoh of the 4th dynasty who built the second largest °pyramid at °Giza. He was the son of Khúfu.

Khúfu (Cheops). Pharaoh of the 4th dynasty who built the largest of the three °pyramids at °Giza.

klísmos (κλισμός). °chairs.

knight. One of the class of *equites* who originally formed the cavalry of the Roman army, and later were a wealthy and important class.

Knóssos (Cnossus, Κνωσός). Cretan pre-

90. Kantharos.

historic city with the famous palace excavated by Sir Arthur Evans; °Minoan civilisation; °labyrinth; °Crete.

kotýle (κοτύλη). A small Greek cup; a Greek liquid measure; °Weights and measures p. 199.

kráter (κρατήρ). Greek mixing-bowl with broad body and wide mouth in which wine was mixed with water.

There were four varieties: °column krater, °volute krater, °kalyx krater and °bell krater; °ill. 91.

Krónos (Κρόνος). °Saturn. Youngest of the °Titans, son of °Uranus and °Gaea, father of °Hades, °Poseidon, °Zeus, °Hestia, °Hera and °Demeter. He de-

posed his father and was killed by Zeus.

kýathos (κύαθος). Greek cup or ladle with one high handle used for drawing wine out of a °krater; °ill. 92.

kýlix (κύλιξ). Greek cup with a high stem and two horizontal handles just under the rim; °ill. 93.

91. The °krater from °Vix.

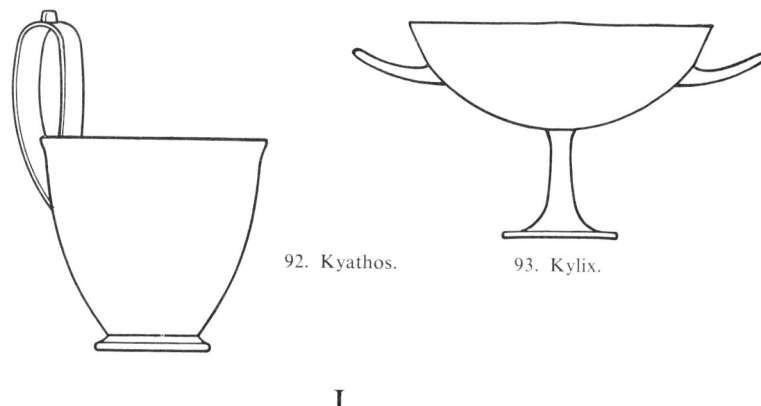

92. Kyathos.   93. Kylix.

L

Labdácidae. Descendants of °Labdacus, *i.e.* °Laius, °Oedipus, °Eteocles, °Polyneices.

Lábdacus (Λάβδακος). Father of °Laius, grand-father of °Oedipus.

Lábeo, *M. Antístius Lábeo.* Famous jurist in the time of °Augustus, opponent of °Ateius Cápito. The followers of Labeo were called Proculiani; °Proculus.

Labérius, *D. Labérius.* Roman °knight and °mimic poet. At the age of sixty he was compelled by °Caesar to act in his own play. Only fragments of his work survive.

Labiénus, *T. Labiénus.* °Legate of °Caesar, who deserted to °Pompey.

lábyrinth (λαβύρινθος). A maze. According to legend, one was built by °Daedalus in Crete to house the °Minotaur, which was killed by °Theseus.

In Egypt there was a building described by Herodotus (2, 148) also called a labyrinth; it was the funeral temple of °Amenemhet III, consisting of numerous rooms.

lacérna. A woollen cloak, fastened by a clasp and worn especially by soldiers and in bad weather.

Láches. °Plato.

Lachésis (Λάχεσις). °Fates.

Lactántius, *L. Caélius Firmiánus Lactántius,* born c. 250 AD. Rhetorician at Nicomedia, converted to Christianity in 300. His chief works were: *Divinárum institutiónum líbri VII* (a refutation of paganism and exposition of Christian teachings and morals) and *De opifício Déi* (proving the existence of Providence). *De mórtibus persecutórum* (about the fate of the emperors who persecuted the Christians) is often ascribed to him. He is called the 'Christian Cicero', writing oratorical prose, and seeking to persuade and to reconcile faith with reason.

lácus Cúrtius. °Curtius.

Láde (Λάδη). A small island off Miletus, where the rebellious °Ionians were defeated by the Persians (494 BC); °Ionian revolt.

Laélius, *C. Laélius,* given the name 'Sapiens'. Consul in 140 BC. None of his writings survive, but according to Cicero his language excelled in simplicity and purity; °Lucilius.

laéna. Thick woollen cloak, fastened with a clasp, originally the dress of the °flamen.

Laértes (Λαέρτης). Father of °Odysseus.

Laestrýgones (Λαιστρυγόνες). A mythical race of giants, in whose country the nights were so short that the morning immediately followed the evening (Hom. *Od.* X, 80-86).

Lagash. °Sumerian city in southern Mesopotamia; it flourished from c. 2500-c. 2350 BC. It is the centre of the excavations by which the civilisation of °Sumer was discovered.

Láïus (Λάϊος). Son of Labdacus, king of Thebes, father of °Oedipus.

Lake Trasimene. °Trasumennus Lacus.

Lanúvium. Town in Látium on the Via °Appia (not to be confused with °Lavinium). There was a well-known temple of °Juno.

Laócoön (Λαοκόων). Trojan priest, who warned the Trojans against the Wooden Horse, but shortly afterwards he and his sons were killed by two serpents (Virg. *Aen.* 2, 40-56; 199-227). The famous Laocoön sculpture dates from Hellenistic times, was discovered in 1506 and is now in the Vatican; ill. 94; °Hellenistic.

Laómedon (Λαομέδων). King of Troy, father of °Priam. When °Poseidon and °Apollo had built the walls of the city, he refused to pay them. Poseidon sent a sea-monster to which Laomedon had to sacrifice his daughter Hesione. °Heracles saved her, but when he too was refused a reward, he killed Laomedon and destroyed the city; °Dardanidae p. 60.

Lápis Níger. In the forum of Rome a slab of black marble was discovered in 1899. Beneath it was a square pillar on which is the oldest Latin inscription; °ill. 95.

95. The inscription under the °Lapis Niger. The text is written in °boustrophedon style. On the right-hand side:
ODIOVESTOD,
and the line over that
VELODNEQV,
but from right to left.

Lápiths (Λαπίθαι). Legendary people of Thessaly, famous for their battle with the °Centaurs at the wedding of their king, °Pirithoüs. In literature (Ovid *Met.* 12, 210-458) and in art (°François vase), temple of °Zeus at °Olympia,

94. °Laocoon and his sons according to the reconstruction of Caffarelli, who used the arm which was found in 1905.

Láres

metopes of the Parthenon) their battle is the theme.

Láres. Roman tutelary deities of the family and the house, usually worshipped together with °Vesta and the °Penates; °Manes.

Latin league. A league of cities, led by Alba Longa and afterwards by Rome. After the expulsion of °Tarquinius Superbus, Rome lost her leadership. The new league was dissolved in 338 BC and Rome made separate treaties with its members. Afterwards there was a legal difference between Roman citizens ('cives Romani'), Latin citizens ('nominis Latini') and allies ('socii').

Latínum nómen. °Latin league.

Latínus. King of Latium, who received °Aeneas hospitably and gave him his daughter Lavinia in marriage (Virg. *Aeneid*).

Latóna. °Leto.

latrína. Public lavatory; °ill. 96.

96. *Latrina* in °Ostia.

Laúrium (Λαύριον). Southern promontory of Attica with silver-mines, exploited by Athens from the 5th century BC. Its proceeds were divided among the citizens until °Themistocles succeeded in having the money reserved for building a fleet.

Lavínia. Daughter of °Latinus.

Lavínium. The town °Aeneas built in Latium and called after his wife Lavinia (°Latinus). In 1957 the remains were discovered 30 km from Rome at Prática di Máre. (Not to be confused with °Lanuvium).

Leánder (Λέανδρος). °Hero.

lébes (λέβης). Round-bottomed wine vessel without handles, placed on a stand (°ill. 97); °tripod.

Léda (Λήδα). Wife of °Tyndáreus, king of Sparta. She had three children by Zeus, who visited her in the shape of a swan: °Helen, °Castor, °Pollux.

legátus pro praetóre. 1. Second-in-command to the °proconsul in a senatorial province; the office originated from the *legati* of °Pompey (*lex* °Gabinia). They had five °lictors. **2.** *Legatus (Augusti) pro praetore.* Governor of an imperial °province, appointed for an indefinite time.

lékythos (λήκυθος). One-handled narrow-necked Greek oil jug with a cylindrical body; °ill. 98.

Lémnia. A statue of °Athena by °Pheidias, on the °Acropolis, offered by Athenians of Lemnos. The statue is lost, but a Roman copy survives.

Lenaéa. °Dionysia 3.

Leocháres (Λεωχάρης). Sculptor, who assisted at the building of the °mausoleum of Halicarnassus.

Leónidas (Λεωνίδας). King of Sparta, who defended the pass of °Thermopylae with 300 Spartans and 700 Thespians against the army of °Xerxes; °Ephialtes.

Lépidus. 1. *M. Aemílius Lépidus.* Consul 187 and 175 BC, °censor 179, built the via Aemilia, which extended from the via °Flaminia (°Flaminius), from Ariminum to Mediolánum, and the °basilica Aemilia. **2.** *M. Aemílius Lépidus.* Consul 6 AD, restored the °basilica Aemilia. He was the father-in-law of °Drusus and °Drusilla; °Julio-Claudian dynasty, p. 101. **3.** *M. Aemílius Lépidus.* Married to °Drusilla, sister of °Gaius. He was killed for conspiring against the emperor.

108

97. Attic °black-figured lebes (c. 575 BC).

Lérna. Settlement on the coast of Argolis. Recent excavations brought to light important remains from c. 2800 BC: °Heracles.

Lésbia. °Claudia.

Lésbos (Λέσβος). The largest island off the coast of Asia Minor, where °Alcaeus, °Sappho, °Arion and °Terpander lived.

Léthe (Λήϑη). River in the Underworld, the water of which was drunk by the dead in order to forget (λανϑάνομαι) their earthly life.

Léto (Λητώ). Beloved of Zeus, mother of °Apollo and °Artemis who were born on °Delos. She was worshipped in association with her children.

Leucíppus (Λεύκιππος). Philosopher of Abdera, teacher of °Democritus.

Leucóthea (Λευκοϑέα). °Ino.

Leúctra (τὰ Λεῦκτρα). Town in Boeotia, where °Epaminondas defeated the Spartans (371 BC).

Lévkas. °Ithaca.

lex = law; entered in this volume according to the lawgiver's name.

Libánius (Λιβάνιος), of Antioch (314-393 AD). Orator and teacher of °John Chrýsostom and the emperor °Julian. His many writings are almost wholly extant.

Líber. Ancient Italian god of viticulture, afterwards identified with °Bacchus.

Líbera. Ancient Italian goddess, female companion of °Liber, later identified with °Persephone.

líbra. Weights and measures 2 d.

libraries (βιβλιοϑήκη = library). The most famous of ancient libraries was that of the °Museum at Alexandria. Most of its collection of 700,000 scrolls was burnt during the fighting of Caesar's troops in the city (47 BC). There were also famous libraries at °Pergamum, Rome and many other towns. In the Athenian market place

98. Attic lekythos (5th cent. BC), showing Hermes with a ˚caduceus, sitting on a rock.

99. Inscription from the library in Athens.

βυβλίον οὐκ ἐξε
νεχθήσεται ἐπει
ὠμόσαμεν ἀνυγή
σεται ἀπὸ ὡρας πρώ
της μέχρι εκτης

the remains of a library have been excavated, including a stone tablet with an inscription. This library was given to the city by T. Flávius Pantaénus, a wealthy citizen (c. 100 AD). The inscription runs: "No book may be taken away for we have sworn an oath. Open from the first hour until the sixth"; ˚ill. 99.

lex Licínia Séxtia. The tribunes of the people C. Licínius Stólo and L. Séxtius Lateránus passed three laws (367 BC): 1. "that no one should possess more than fifty *iugera* (˚Weights and measures 2b) of the ˚ager publicus";

2. "that one of the two consuls should be chosen from the people"; 3. Intended to diminish debts.
Licínius. 1. *C. Licínius Calvus* (82-47 BC). Friend of ˚Catullus, who wrote wedding-songs, elegies and epigrams, of which fragments survive. **2.** ˚Crassus. **3.** *C. Licínius Mácer.* ˚Annalist. **4.** *C. Licínius Muciánus,* ˚Muciánus. **5.** *C. Licínius Stólo.* Tribune of the people 376-367 BC; ˚lex Licínia.
líctor. Attendant of a Roman magistrate. He preceded the magistrate, bearing the ˚fasces, a bundle of rods (when outside Rome, including an axe), as a symbol of authority. A ˚dictator had twenty-four lictors, a ˚consul twelve, a ˚praetor six, a ˚legatus pro praetore five; ˚ill. 100.
limes. Originally the frontier road between two territories. ˚Hadrian defined this as a fortified wall with ditch and stockade and fortresses at regular

100. Lictor.

intervals, as in °Britain. The German *limes* ran from the Rhine near Bonn to the Danube near Regensburg.

Linear B. Clay tablets were first discovered in 1900 at °Knossos by Sir Arthur Evans, and later at °Pylos in 1939 and °Mycenae in 1952. The earlier Cretan tablets were inscribed in Linear A, those from Greece in Linear B. The later kind, Linear B, was deciphered by the English architect Michael Ventris (died 1956) in 1952. Linear B had a syllabary of c. sixty symbols each representing a syllable of a vowel or a consonant followed by a vowel; also ideograms; the language was an early form of Greek of c. 1400-1200 BC. A year after the decipherment, in 1953, Ventris' theory was proved correct by a new tablet found at Pylos. This tablet, numbered Ta 641, is 18 cm long and contains three lines of inscription; °ills. 101, 102. *Cf. The Decipherment of Linear B* (J. Chadwick).

101. Tablet Ta 641.

The inscription runs as follows:

ti-ri-po-de	ai-ke-u	ke-re-si-jo we-ke	ti-ri-po	e-me	po-de	o-wo-we
τριποδε	?	χρησιοεργη	τριπος	ενι	ποδι	οιωης

111

ti-ri-po	ke-re-si-jo we-ke
τριπος	χρησιοεργης

a-pu ke-ka-u-me-no	ke-re-a ...
ἀποκεκαυμενος	σκελεα

qe-to

πιθοι(?)

di-pa	me-wi-jo	a-no-we
δεπας	μειον	ἀνωες

The translation runs:-

Line 1.
two tripod-cauldrons of Cretan workmanship, of ai-ke-u type;
one tripod-cauldron with a single handle on one foot;
one tripod-cauldron of Cretan workmanship;
burnt away at the legs . . . ;

Line 2.
three wine-jars (?);
one larger-sized jar with four handles;
two larger-sized jars with three handles;
one smaller-sized jar with four handles;

Line 3.
one smaller-sized jar with three handles;
one smaller-sized jar without a handle.

di-pa	me-zo-e	qe-to-ro-we	
δεπας	μεζον	τετρωες	

di-pa-e	me-zo-e	ti-ri-o-we-e	
δεπαε	μεζοε	τριωεε	

di-pa	me-wi-jo	qe-to-ro-we	
δεπας	μειον	τετρωες	

di-pa	me-wi-jo	ti-ri-jo-we	
δεπας	μειον	τριωες	

102. Clay tablet found at Mycenae, with the text in Linear B. (16½ cm. high).

Lion Gate. At °Mycenae, the main gate in the °Cyclopean Wall is surmounted by a lintel over which two sculptured lionesses face each other.

litótes. Understatement by means of a negative or quasi-negative: *e.g.*: 'non me fallit'; 'non mediocriter'.

líturgy (λειτουργία). In Athens a public function was compulsorily imposed upon a rich citizen or °metic. These included °*chorégia*, °*trierárchia*, *hippotróphia* (maintenance as a knight of a horse), and *architheória* (leadership of a public delegation to a foreign festival).

lítuus. 1. Crooked staff, with which the °augur marked out the quarters of the heavens in which he would look for signs, *e.g.* from the flight of birds. **2.** A wind instrument similar in shape to **1.**

Lívia. 1. Daughter of °Drusus and °Antonia Mínor; °Livilla. **2.** *Livia (Drusilla)*, daughter of M. Lívius Drúsus Claudiánus; (58 BC-29 AD), married (43 BC) Ti. Claúdius Nero and (38 BC) °Augustus. She possessed great beauty and was an active empress of intelligence and dignity. After Augustus' death she was adopted into the *gens* °Júlia and her official name became Júlia Augústa. She tried to maintain her position of empress beside her son; °Julio-Claudian dynasty p. 101; °ill. 103. **3.** *Lívia Orestílla*. Married to C. Calpúrnius Píso, from whom the emperor °Gaius took her away; °Julio-Claudian dynasty p. 101.

Livílla, *(Claudia) Livílla Julia.* Daughter of Néro Claúdius °Drúsus and °Antónia Mínor, born c. 12 BC, married to °Gaius Caésar in 1 BC, afterwards to °Drusus, °Tiberius' son; °Julio-Claudian dynasty p. 101.

Lívy. 1. *L. Lívius Andrónicus.* A slave from Tarentum, and later freedman at Rome (3rd cent. BC), author of a Latin translation of the °Odyssey in °Saturnian verse. First Roman lyric poet. **2.** *T. Lívius* (59 BC-17 AD). Born at Patávium, and author of a history of Rome in 142 books (°'Ab urbe

103. Livia as a priestess.
(Pompeii Villa dei Misteri)

cóndita') up to 9 BC. Books 1-10, 21-45 and short abstracts of other books survive. Livy's sources were °Polybius and the °annalists, but his interests were as literary as they were historical. During his lifetime many abstracts of his work were composed.

locátio, *locatiónes censóriae.* °censor.

Locústa. A notorious female poisoner, who poisoned °Claudius and °Britannicus; °Nero.

logógrapher. 1. A writer of traditional history in prose; °Acusilaus, °Hecataeus. **2.** A professional speech-writer; °Isaeus, °Lysias.

Lóllia Paulína. Married in 38 AD to the emperor °Gaius and shortly afterwards repudiated; °Julio-Claudian dynasty p. 101.

Longínus, *Dionýsius Cassius Longínus.* °Neoplatonist and orator at Athens and °Palmyra (3rd cent. AD). 'Περὶ ὕψους' (='de sublimitate') was wrongly ascribed to him; °Pseudo-Longinus.

Lóngus (3rd cent. AD?). Author of a pastoral novel, *Daphnis and Chloë*.

Lotóphagi (Δωτοφάγοι). A legendary people mentioned by °Homer (*Od.* IX, 82-104), who lived on the lotus, the effect of which was to make the eater forget his own country.

loutróphoros (λουτροφόρος). A tall vase with a high neck and flaring mouth, sometimes used for bringing water from the fountain Callirhoë for the nuptial bath and placed on tombs of unmarried people; °ill. 104.

104. Loutrophoros.

Lúcan, *M. Annaéus Lucánus* (39-65 AD). Born at Cordoba, epic poet at the court of °Nero. He soon fell into disgrace, took part in the conspiracy of °Piso and was forced to commit suicide. His chief work 'Pharsalia' deals with the civil war between °Caesar and °Pompey and is written in a brilliant rhetorical style, full of lively descriptions; °Annius p. 16.

Lucián (Λουκιανός). Greek satiric writer from Samosata on the Euphrates (c. 120-c. 180 AD). He travelled as a sophist and wrote, in Attic, a number of humorous works, ridiculing superstition and other human frailties.

Lucílius, *C. Lucílius* (c. 180(?)-102 BC). The first Roman satirist, belonging to the circle of °Scipio minor and °Laelius. A large number of fragments of his work are extant.

Lúcius Caesar, *L. Július Caésar.* Second son of °Agrippa and Júlia, adopted by °Augustus in 17 BC. He fell ill on a journey to Spain and died in 2 AD; °Julio-Claudian dynasty p. 101.

Lucrétia. Wife of L. Tarquínius Collatínus, who was raped by Sextus Tarquinius, the son of °Tarquinius Superbus. Having told her husband, she killed herself. This was the immediate cause of the expulsion of the kings of Rome (Liv. 1, 57-60).

Lucrétius, *T. Lucrétius Cárus* (c. 98-55 BC). Epic poet and Epicurean. His poem 'De rérum natúra' expounded the teachings of °Epicurus, with the intention of freeing people from fear of the gods and death. His language was simple, and in his many arresting images and in his glorification of Epicurus he shows himself to be a great poet.

Lucúllus, *L. Licínius Lucúllus* (c. 117-56 BC). Roman politician, quaestor of °Sulla, consul 74 BC, defeated °Mithridates and took great interest in the financial mismanagement of Asia by the *equites.* He lowered the rate of interest from 48 to 12 per cent and back interest of more than 100 per cent was remitted. He was hated by the *equites* (=°knights) for his reforms and recalled in 67. He was rich, had a large library and collected objects of art. He is still quoted as a gourmet and is supposed to have introduced the cherry into Europe.

Lupercália. The festival of °Faunus on 15th of February (Ovid *Fasti* 2, 267-452) to purify the city and ensure fertility.

Lusitánia (=Portugal). An area subject to Rome after 136 BC and a Roman province in 15 BC, bounded by the rivers Durius and Anas.

lústrum. The purification sacrifice of the °censors at the end of their term of office, every fifth year. It consisted of *suovetaurília,* the sacrifice of a pig, a sheep and a bull; °ill. 161.

Lycáön (Λυκάων). Legendary king of Arcadia, notorious for his cruelty. He was turned into a wolf by °Zeus (Ovid *Met.* 1, 163-252).

Lycéum (Λύκειον). The sacred domain of 'Apollo Lykeíos', in the north-east part of Athens, where °Aristotle founded his °Peripatetic school.

Lycomédes (Λυκομήδης). Legendary king of Scyros (island to the east of Euboea). When the °Trojan War broke out °Thetis sent her son °Achilles to hide himself in female dress among the companions of Lycomedes' daughter, where °Odysseus found him (°Deidameia; °Statius).

Lycophron (Λυκόφρων). of Chalcis (3rd c. BC). Writer of tragedies, one of which was 'Cassandra', in which °Cassandra uttered dark prophecies.

Lycúrgus (Λυκοῦργος). **1.** Legendary king of Thrace, who attacked °Bacchus, who drove him mad. **2.** Revered lawgiver of Sparta (c. 9th cent. BC). **3.** Athenian politician and orator (c. 390-325 BC), supporter of °Demosthenes. Some of his speeches survive.

Lýgdamus. 1. Obscure poet whose work survives with that of °Tibullus (4, 7-12 = 3, 13-18). Some suppose him to have been an elder brother of °Ovid. **2.** Lýgdamus I, a Naxian, ally of °Peisistratus.

Lýnceus (Λυγκεύς). °Danaids.

lyre (λύρα). A stringed instrument with a sound-box made from a tortoise-shell and played with a plectrum; °ill. 105. °Muses.

lyric poetry. Poetry recited to accompaniment on a °lyre. One may distinguish between choral songs and °monodic poetry, which expressed human emotions in various metres (°Lesbos). °Catullus was Rome's greatest lyric poet.

Lysánder (Λύσανδρος). Famous Spartan admiral. He defeated the Athenians near °Aegospotami (405 BC), and in 404 ordered the Long Walls of Athens to be taken down and appointed the °Thirty to rule; °oligarchy.

Lýsias (Λυσίας). One of the ten °Attic orators from Syracuse (c. 458-c. 380 BC), who lost his possessions under the

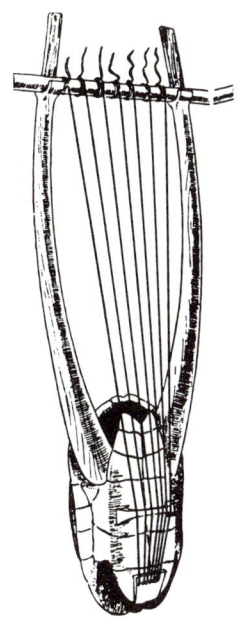

105. A lyre.

°Thirty. Not being an Athenian citizen he could not act as a barrister and wrote speeches for others (°logographer). He is thought to have written very pure Attic. His style was simple and entirely suited to his subject.

Lysímachus (Λυσίμαχος). One of the °Diadochi (c. 360-281 BC). After the death of °Alexander the Great he got Thrace and north-west Asia Minor. He fought with °Cassander and °Ptolemy against °Antigonus, who was killed (301) at °Ipsus, expelled (287) °Demetrius Poliorcetes, but at the height of his power fell a victim to the intrigues of his wife Arsinoë. Deserted by his allies, he was killed fighting °Seleucus.

Lysippus (Λύσιππος), of Sicyon. Sculptor at the time of °Alexander the Great, who only allowed himself to be portrayed by him and by °Apelles. His statues were more slender than those of °Polycleitus (°ill. 106). Of his many works only copies survive, the most famous of which is the 'Apoxyomenos', the athlete who is scraping himself clean (Vatican Museum).

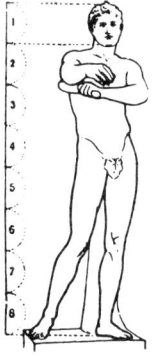 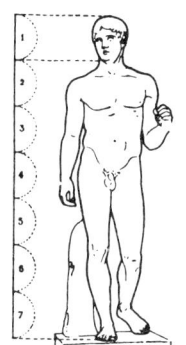

106.
The 'Apoxyomenos'   The 'Doryphorus'
   of °Lysippus.   of °Polycleitus.

M

Máccabees (Μακκαβαῖοι, Maccabaei). Jewish dynasty of priests who were kings of Palestine (164-37 BC). Juda began a revolt against the °Seleucids in 167.

Macedonian Wars. The first and second Macedonian Wars were waged against °Philip V by the Romans. Greece was then declared free in 196 BC. (°Flamininus). The third war was against °Perseus (171-168) and the fourth (148-146) resulted in the annexation of Macedon, which became a province of the Roman Empire.

Macháon (Μαχάων). Son of °Asclepius, a physician in the Greek camp outside Troy (Hom. *Il.* XI, 514).

Macróbius Theodósius. Proconsul in Africa (410 AD) who wrote a commentary on the °'Somnium Scipionis'

and seven books, 'Saturnalia', in which he discussed all kinds of interesting subjects.

Maéa (Μαῖα). Daughter of °Atlas, mother of °Hermes; °Pleiades.

Maeánder (Μαῖανδρος). River of Lydia, well-known because of its 'meandering' course, hence the name of the architectural ornament; °ill. 107.

107. Meander ornament, found in architecture and on vases.

Maecénas, *C. Cílnius Maecénas.* Roman °knight of ancient °Etruscan nobility, friend and counsellor of °Augustus. In antiquity his name was already proverbial as a patron of the arts. °Horace, °Virgil and °Propertius frequented his house; °ill. 108.

108. Maecenas (relief from the °Ara pacis).

109. A Maenad (from an amphora, early 4th cent. BC).

Maénads (μαινάς). Female companions of °Dionysus. They were represented wearing long clothes with a °thyrsos in their hands; °ill. 109.

Maénius, *C. Maénius.* °rostra.

mágister équitum. Second-in-command to the °dictator; appointed by and resigning with him.

magistrátus. Roman officials who had °imperium or °potestas and were therefore authorized to act in the name of the State. There were: *a.* 'Magistratus maiores', *b.* 'Magistratus minores', or *a.* 'Magistratus curules', *b.* 'Magistratus non curules': 1. *Magistratus maiores*, high officials elected or appointed with the °*auspicia maxima, i.e.* in the °*comitia curiata* and *centuriata*: °censor, °consul, °praetor, °dictator. 2. *Magistratus minores.* The other officials elected with the °*auspicia minora* in the °*comitia tribúta.* Among them were the °aedilis, °quaestor, °tribunus plebis, °vigintisexviri. 3. *magistratus curúles,* having the right to use the °sélla curúlis: (°ill. 148) °consul, °praetor, °censor, °dictator, °magister equitum, °aedilis curúlis.

Magna Mater = °Cybele, °Rhea.

Magnésia. A town in Lydia near the Sipylus, where in 190 BC Antiochus was defeated by the Romans.

Mamertíni. Mercenaries from Campania who fought for °Agathocles in Sicily. Later they treacherously killed the inhabitants of Messana and settled there.

Mamertínus. °carcer.

Mandáne (Μανδάνη). Daughter of °Astyages, mother of °Cyrus.

117

mandáta. °constitutiones.

Mánes (Di Manes). The spirits of the dead worshipped with great solemnity particularly by the Romans; °Penates.

lex Manília, *de império Cn. Pompeii.* A law proposed by the tribune C. Manílius (66 BC), by which the command in the war against °Mithridates was given to °Pompey. °Cicero defended the law in a speech.

Manílius. 1. *C. Manilius.* °Tribunus plebis in 66 BC; °lex Manília. **2.** *C. Manilius.* Poet at the time of °Augustus. He wrote a poem 'Astronómica'.

manípulus (= maniple). An army unit in the 4th cent. BC. Each legion consisted of thirty *manipuli*, each divided into two °centuriae; °signum.

Mánlius. 1. *M. Mánlius Capitolínus.* Saved the °Capitol in 390 BC during an attack by the °Gauls (Livy 5, 47); °geese. In 385 he tried to help the °plebeians against their patrician creditors. He was condemned and thrown from the °Tarpeian rock (Livy 6, 14-16). **2.** *T. Mánlius Imperiósus Torquátus.* With P. °Decius Mus defeated the Latins in 340 BC. When his son, against his father's orders, fought a duel with an enemy, he had him executed.

Mantinéa (Μαντίνεια). Town in Arcadia, well-known from two battles: in 418 BC the Spartan king °Agis defeated the troops of Argos, Athens and Elis, and in 362 BC the Spartans and Athenians were defeated here by °Epaminondas.

Mánto (Μαντώ). Prophetess, daughter of °Teirésias.

Márathon (Μαραθών). Village on the East coast of Attica, where °Miltiades defeated the Persians in 490 BC. The messenger (Pheidippides) who brought the good tidings of the victory to Athens ran 40 km without resting and died on arrival.

Marcéllus. 1. *M. Claúdius Marcéllus.* °Consul on several occasions. He defeated °Hannibal near Nola in 215 BC and took Syracuse in 212, whence he had all art treasures brought over to Rome. **2.** *M. Claúdius Marcéllus.* Son

of C. Claúdius Marcéllus and °Octávia, married °Julia, the daughter of Augustus, in 25 BC. He died in 23 BC, at about twenty years old, bitterly grieved by °Augustus, who had selected him as his successor; °Julio-Claudian dynasty p. 101.

Márcia Furnílla. Second wife of °Titus. She had a daughter Julia but was rejected by Titus; °Flavii p. 79.

Márcus Aurélius, *M. Aurélius Antonínus.* Roman emperor (161-180 AD), adopted by °Antoninus Pius. His love of the arts and sciences and his virtuous character were highly beneficial to the State. Unfortunately, he was compelled to wage war continuously. He was a °Stoic and his 'Meditations' have been preserved; °Aurélii p. 31.

Mardónius (Μαρδόνιος). Son-in-law and general of °Darius. When the latter withdrew after his defeat near °Salamis in 480 BC he left Mardonius behind in Thessaly. In 479 he was °defeated near °Plataea and killed.

Márius, *C. Márius.* Seven times consul. In 107 BC he, himself a man of the people, was acclaimed by the people, who were disillusioned by the misgovernment of the °Optimates, regarding the war against °Jugurtha. His success was the reason for his appointment as commander in the expedition against the °Cimbri and the °Teutones, whom he defeated near °Aquae Sextiae in 102, and near Vercellae in 101. In politics he was less successful. He became the self-constituted leader of the democrats against °Sulla and had to leave the city. When Sulla marched against °Mithridates, Marius returned to Rome with the help of °Cinna and took bloody revenge, hence the beginning of the 1st Civil War 88-82. He died in 86.

Mármor Párium. A marble column from the island of °Paros. It bears a long inscription with dates relevant to Greek history until 264 BC and is one of our more important sources of history.

marriage. In Athens a marriage was arranged by a contract between the bridegroom or his father and the father or guardian of the bride, except in the case of an heiress, when by law the closest unmarried relative was obliged to marry her. In Rome there were two kinds of marriage: the one by which the bride passed from the authority (*manus*) of her father into that of her husband and the other by which she remained under her father's authority. In the first case, there were three 'forms': *a.* the most solemn form, *confareátio*, between patricians in the presence of the °pontifex maximus and the °flamen Dialis, could not originally be dissolved. *Diffareátio* (divorce) only became possible under the Empire; *b. coemptio*, when by a mock-sale the bride passed into the *manus* of the husband; *c. usus*, from the late republic onwards, by which the bride passed into the *manus* of the husband after a year of marriage. Usually the bride did not pass into her husband's authority. The marriage was the result of a mutual agreement and by a marriage settlement the wife could remain mistress of her own property (*stipulátio réi uxóriae*).

Mars. Roman god of war, with °Jupiter and °Quirinus the patron deity of Rome. The wolf and the woodpecker were sacred to him; °Ares.

Marsian War. °Social War.

Mársyas (Μαρσύας). Legend has it that he (a °satyr) found the flute which °Athena had invented and thrown away. He challenged °Apollo to a musical contest, with the °Muses as judges, lost, and was flayed alive (Ovid *Met.* 6, 382-400).

Mártial, *M. Valérius Martíalis* (c. 40-102 AD). Satirist who was born at Bilbilis in Spain and lived in Rome after 64. By means of flattery he remained in the favour of °Nero and °Domitian. Many of his epigrams have been preserved.

Martiánus Capélla. Lawyer in Carthage, at the end of the 4th cent. AD. He wrote a learned work about the °Seven liberal arts under the title 'De núptius Mercúrii et Philológiae'.

Massiníssa. King of Numídia (238-148 BC). First fighting on the side of Carthage, he deserted to the Romans to whom he remained faithful. His fight against Carthage resulted in the Third °Punic War; °Jugurtha p.100.

mástaba. Mudbrick mound over the tombs of middle-class people in early Egypt.

Mausoléum Hadriáni (Móles Hadriáni, Castel Sant' Angelo). Sepulchral monument for °Hadrian, built 138-139 AD. His successors were also buried there.

Mausoléum of Halicarnássus. Monument erected over the grave of the °satrap Mausolus, by his widow °Artemisia in about 350 BC. It was one of the °Seven Wonders of the World. In the 14th century it was destroyed by an earthquake, and excavated in 1857.

Maxéntius. Opponent of °Constantine the Great, defeated near the Mulvian Bridge in 312 AD. °Mulvius.

Maximiniánus Hercúlius. Ruler with °Diocletian in 285 AD; abdicated with him in 305.

Medéa (Μήδεια). Daughter of °Aeëtes, king of Colchis; °Jason; °Euripides.

Medúsa (Μέδουσα). One of the °Gorgons beheaded by °Perseus (Ovid *Met.* 4, 772-803); °ills. 110, 111.

110. An early head of Medusa with fangs, and her tongue protruding.

119

111. Medusa portrayed with a less fierce aspect, in later sculpture.

Megaíra (Μέγαιρα). One of the °Erinyes.
Megárian School. Founded by the philosopher °Euclid, disciple of °Socrates. Like the °Eleatic philosophers, he denied the existence of movement and declared all sensory perception to be false; °Stilpo.
Méla. °Pomponius.
Meleáger (Μελέαγρος). **1.** Son of °Oineus and Althea, who took part in the expedition of the °Argonauts and the °Calydonian Hunt. He gave the skin of the boar to °Atalanta (Ovid *Met.* 8, 267-444). At his birth the Fates had given a fire-brand to his mother. As long as it remained intact, Meleager would stay alive. When, after the Calydonian Hunt, his uncles took the skin away from Atalanta, Meleager killed them. In a moment of resentment, to avenge the death of her brothers, Althea threw the stick into the fire and Meleager died (Ovid *Met.* 8, 445-525). **2.** *Meleager of Gadara,* c. 100 BC. Collected °epigrams, which are contained in the Greek °Anthology.
Meleágrides (Μελεαγρίδες). Sisters of °Meleager. They wept so bitterly at his death that, out of pity, °Artemis changed them into guinea-fowl (Ovid

Met. 8, 526-546).
Melétus (Μέλητος). Athenian poet, one of the principal accusers of °Socrates.
Melpómene (Μελπομένη). °Muses.
Mémnon (Μέμνων). **1.** Legendary son of °Eos, king of Ethiopia. He fought on the side of the Trojans and was killed by °Achilles. **2.** The *Colossi of Memnon.* Two statues 20 m high, erected by °Amenhotep III near Thebes on the western bank of the Nile. The two immense figures seated on thrones are carved out of sandstone conglomerate. The northern colossus emitted a musical note at sunrise, but after the restoration of the statue in the times of °Septimus Severus, the phenomenon ceased. The attribution to 'Memnon' is erroneous; ill. 112.
Menaéchmi. °Plautus.
Menánder (Μένανδρος). The greatest poet of the New °Comedy in Athens (c. 342-291 BC). All through antiquity his plays remained famous and he was imitated by °Plautus and °Terence. In 1907, large fragments of his work were found together with two thirds of a play, 'The Arbitration', and in 1958 a papyrus was published containing an almost complete play. 'Dyskolos' (= the Misanthropist).
Meneláüs (Μενέλαος). Son of Atreus, brother of °Agamemnon, husband of Helen and king of Sparta. Tantalidae, p. 182.
Menénius, *Agríppa Menénius Lanátus.* Consul c. 500 BC. He appeased the °plebeians who had left Rome c. 494 during the first °secéssio plebis and brought them back to Rome by telling them the parable of the 'Belly and the Limbs' (Livy 2, 32).
Meníppus, of Sinope. °Cynic philosopher (3rd-2nd cent. BC), who satirized in prose and poetry the relativity of all earthly things; °Varro; °satires.
Méntor (Μέντωρ). Friend of °Odysseus. °Athena took his shape to help °Telemachus.
Mércury. The god of trading and profit, messenger of the gods; Roman equivalent of °Hermes.

112. The Colossi of Memnon.

Meriónes (Μηριόνης). Friend of °Idomeneus, archer and javelin-thrower.

Mérope (Μερόπη). °Pleiades.

Mesolithic Age. The Middle Stone Age, period of transition between the °Palaeolithic and °Neolithic Ages which ended in Crete c. 3500 BC.

Messalína. 1. *Statília Messalína.* Wife of °Nero, who puts her fourth husband Átticus Vestínus to death in 65 BC. She was wealthy, beautiful and intelligent and so played an important part even after Nero's death; °Domitii, p. 68. **2.** *Valéria Messalína.* Third wife of °Claudius, mother of °Octavia and °Britannicus. She was cruel, greedy and immoral; °Domitii, p. 68.

Messálla, M. *Valérius Messálla Corvínus* (64 BC-13 AD). Consul 31 BC with °Octavian. He was the patron of °Tibullus. °'Panegýricus ad Messállam'.

Messénian War. In the first Messenian War (c. 740-720? BC) the Spartans con-

quered the fertile plain of Messéne in the south-west part of the Peloponnese. The Messenians revolted and were again subjugated in the 2nd war (c. 680-610?). In 369, after the 3rd war they regained their independence through °Epaminondas.

Méstra (Μήστρα). °Erysichthon.

Metamorphóses. Title of a poem by °Ovid; °Apuleius.

métaphor (μεταφορά). The figure of speech by which a name or descriptive term is applied to some object to which it is not properly applicable, *e.g.* 'ventus populáris'.

Metaphýsics. °Aristotle.

Metáurus. River in mid-Italy, flowing into the Adriatic Sea. °Hasdrubal was defeated here in 207 BC by C. Claudius Nero.

Metéllus. *Q. Caecílius Metéllus Numídicus* (consul 109 BC). Fought against °Jugurtha and was succeeded by °Marius. He was granted a °triumph.

121

metempsychósis. The supposed passage of the soul of a human being or animal after death into a new body of the same or a different species; °Pythagoras.

métics (μέτοικοι). Resident aliens in Greek towns distinguished by grants of special privileges, but having few civic rights. They could not contract legal marriages with citizens or own lands.

metónymy (μετωνυμία). The figure of speech in which one word is substituted for another related to it e.g. Ceres = corn, custodia = keeper.

métope (μετόπη). The rectangular panels between the °triglyphs of the °frieze of the °Doric order. Usually they were decorated with figures in relief.

Micípsa. °Adherbal.

Mídas (Μίδας). Legendary king of Phrygia. He asked °Dionysus to change everything he touched into gold (Ovid Met. 11, 85-145). His second act of stupidity was, when judging a musical contest between °Apollo and °Pan, to vote against Apollo, who then bestowed ass's ears on him (Ovid Met. 11, 146-193).

Mildenhall. Town in Suffolk, where (1942) a hoard of Roman silver, now in the British Museum, was found; °Britain.

Mílo, T. Annius Mílo. °Tribunus plebis in 57 BC. His gladiators killed °Clodius in 52. Milo was prosecuted in court and °Cicero published a speech in his defence, 'Pro Milone'.

Miltíades (Μιλτιάδης). Father of °Cimon, who administered the Attic possessions on the Thracian Chersonese. During the °Ionian revolt he had to flee from the Persians and in 490 BC he was the commander of the Greeks at °Marathon.

Mílvius. °Mulvius.

mime (μῖμος). Simple farcical drama with scenes from daily life. It flourished particularly after the decline of classical drama; °Herondas; °Laberius; °Publilius Syrus.

mimiámbi. Mimes in °choriambi, treating subjects from daily life in the form of a °dialogue; °Herondas; °mime.

Mimnérmus (Μίμνερμος). Elegiac and love poet c. 600 BC.

Minérva. Roman goddess of wisdom and skill. Her principal temple was on the °Capitol with that of °Juno and °Jupiter; identified with the Greek °Athena.

Minoan civilisation. This flourished c. 3000-1200 BC in °Crete and was contemporaneous with the °Helladic and °Cycladic civilisations.

Mínos (Μίνως). Legendary king and legislator of Crete, son of °Zeus °Europa, after his death one of the judges in °Hades; °Aeacus. His wife Pasiphaë fell in love with a bull and bore a creature half man, half bull (the °Minotaur). °Daedalus constructed a maze, the °labyrinth, for it to hide in. After °Androgeüs had been killed in Athens, the Athenians had to give a yearly tribute of seven youths and seven maidens whom Minos imprisoned with the Minotaur; °Ariadne; °Theseus; °Minoan civilisation.

Mínotaur. °Minos; °labyrinth.

Minúcius Félix, M. Minúcius Félix (2nd cent. AD). Author of a dialogue, 'Octávius', in defence of Christianity.

Minyádes (Μινυάδες). Daughters of Minyas: Leucippe (or Iris), Arsippe (or Leuconoë; Clymene) and Alcithoë. They refused to worship °Bacchus and were changed into a bat, an owl, and a crow (Ovid Met. 4, 1-30; 4, 389-415).

Mínyans (Μινύαι). Legendary tribe of Orchomenus in Boeotia, called after their king Minyas. The °Argonauts and their descendants were also called Minyans.

Míthras. A Persian god of light. He was widely worshipped in Rome and the provinces, e.g. on °Hadrian's Wall, °Britain. The Mithraic temple, 'Mithraeum', had a statue of Mithras killing a bull. Later the cult was superseded by that of Christ which at this time was better organised and more tolerant; °ill. 113.

Mithridátes. Name of several kings of Pontus. **1.** Mithridátes II. Ruled over Pontus after the death of °Alexander the Great. **2.** Mithridátes VI Eupátor

113. Mithras killing a bull in a vaulted grotto. Left and right are two cross-legged torch-bearers, Cautopates and Cautes. The vault is decorated with the signs of the Zodiac. In the frieze above are trees and four scenes with Mithras. Under the bull are a serpent and a lion.

('The Great') (132-63 BC). He raided all neighbouring countries and was a deadly enemy of Rome. In 88 he expelled the Romans from Asia and sent an army to Greece. In 84, he was defeated by °Sulla (1st Mithridatic War). In 83, the Romans under Murena invaded Pontus and were defeated, but in 81 Murena was recalled by Sulla (2nd Mithridatic War). In 74, Mithridates occupied Bithynia which had been given to the Romans by King Nicomedes. When Mithridates had won at Zela in 67 the war was entrusted to °Pompey (*lex* °*Manilia*) who finally defeated Mithridates (63) (3rd Mithridatic War).

Mnemósyne. Goddess of memory; °Muses.

Mnésicles (Μνησικλῆς). The architect of the °Propylaea.

Modestínus, *Herénnius Modestínus.* The last known classical lawyer (3rd cent. AD). Of his works only a few fragments survive, of which 345 are in the °*Digesta.*

módius. °Weights and measures 2c.

Moésia. Country between the Danube and the Black Sea, and a Roman province after °Tiberius' time.

Mogontiácum. Mayence; °Germany.

Moirai (Μοῖραι). °Fates.

molóssus. A metrical foot: _ _ _.

Monéta. °Juno.

Mons Sácer. A hill north of Rome just beyond the Anio; °secessio plebis.

Monuméntum Ancyránum. Inscription discovered in 1555 on the wall of a temple at Ankara (ancient Ancyra). It is a copy of the 'Rés géstae dívi Augústi' (achievements of °Augustus), composed by Augustus himself. The text is in Latin and Greek.

Monuméntum Antiochénum. Text of the 'Rés géstae dívi Augústi', found at Antioch in Pisidia in small fragments which help to complete the text of the °'Monumentum Ancyranum'.

Morália. °Plutarch.

Morétum. A poem in 122 lines attributed to °Virgil. It described how a farmer prepared his breakfast with his servant on a dark winter morning.

Mórpheus (Μορφεύς). God of dreams, son of Hypnos, god of sleep (Ovid *Met.* 11, 183-206).

Móschus. °Bucolic poet of Syracuse (2nd cent. BC), whose principal work is an °epyllion, 'Europa', in which the rape of °Europa by °Zeus was the subject.

Mosélla (=Moselle). Title of a poem by °Ausonius. River.

Muciánus, *C. Licínius Mucíanus.* Legate of Syria in 69 AD. On the news of the revolt of the troops on the Rhine and in Spain, he offered °Vespasian the crown and remained his principal adviser.

Múcius. **1.** *C. Múcius Scaévola.* He penetrated the camp of °Porsenna, who was besieging Rome. When he was caught, he allowed his right hand to be burned in order to show his contempt for death. Afterwards he was called 'Scaevola' (Livy 2, 12). **2.** *P. Múcius Scaévola.* °Pontifex Maximus (130-116 BC) and a famous lawyer. We have only fragments of his work. **3.** *Q. Múcius Scaévola* (c. 170-87). An °augur, and son-in-law of °Laelius, lawyer and teacher of °Cicero. **4.** *Q. Múcius Scaévola* (140-82). °Pontifex, son of **2.** He was the greatest lawyer of the family and wrote an important work on civil law. He was also a teacher of °Cicero. (*N.B.* **3.** and **4.** may have been the same person).

Múlvius, *Pons Múlvius* (or *Mílvius*). A bridge across the Tiber, north of Rome on the Via °Flaminia (now called Pónte Mólle). Here °Constantine the Great defeated °Maxentius on 28th October, 312 AD and from that time favoured Christianity.

Múmmius, *L. Múmmius.* Consul 146 BC, who conquered and destroyed Corinth. He shipped its art treasures to Rome.

Munda. Town in Spain, near Cordoba. Here °Caesar's victory in 46 BC ended the second °Civil War.

municípium. Town in Italy with Roman civil rights 'sine suffragio', but autonomous except as regards foreign policy; °citizenship.

Musaéus (Μουσαῖος). Epic poet of the later Roman Empire, who wrote 'Hero and Leander' in Greek.

Muses (Μοῦσαι). The nine deities of poetry, literature, music, dance, astronomy, philosophy, etc. They were the daughters of °Mnemósyne and °Zeus. Their home was °Helicon or,

Name	Function	Attribute(s)
Clío (Κλείω)	history	book and trumpet
Eutérpe (Εὐτέρπη)	flute-playing	flute
Thália (Θάλεια)	comedy	comic mask
Melpómene (Μελπομένη)	tragedy	tragic mask and lyre
Terpsíchore (Τερψιχόρη)	dance	cithara
Eráto ('Ερατώ)	love poetry	lyre
Polyhýmnia (Πολύμνια)	rhetoric, lyric poetry	sceptre
Uránia (Οὐρανία)	astronomy	celestial globe and rod
Calliópe (Καλλιόπη)	heroic poetry, eloquence	books and trumpet

The Muses

according to Roman poets, °Parnassus. They were presided over by °Apollo.

Museum. Particular name for the literary and educational institute at °Alexandria founded by Ptolemy I. About one hundred research scholars worked there; °libraries.

musical instruments. In antiquity the bow was unknown. Strings were sounded by plucking them either with the hand (°phorminx) or by a plectrum (°cithara, °lyre); °sambuca. As regards wind instruments: °aulos (tibia), °bucina, °lituus, °salpinx (tuba). The °sistrum was shaken.

Mutína. Town in Cisalpine °Gaul (Modena), where °Antony was defeated by °Hirtius and Pansa in 43 BC.

mútule. A projecting block of the Doric °cornice; °Doric order.

Mycále. Promontory opposite Samos, where in 479 BC the Persian fleet was defeated by the Greeks.

Mycénae (Μυκῆναι). Most important citadel in Argolis where °Atreus and °Agamemnon are said to have lived. It was first excavated by Schliemann in 1874. He found the enclosure of the First Grave Circle, the °Cyclopean Walls with the °Lion Gate and the °Treasury of Atreus. Excavations there still continue; °Mycenaean civilisation; °Helladic civilisation.

Mycenaéan Civilisation. A period in Greek pre-history, named after °Mycenae, marked by the expansion of the Greek culture as far east as the Levant. Concurrent with the Egyptian Empire between the eighteenth and twenty-fifth dynasties (1600-1200 BC). This civilisation was destroyed by the so-called °Dorian invasion; °Helladic civilisation.

'Mycerinus'. Pharaoh of the 4th dynasty who erected the third (the smallest) °pyramid at °Giza (c. 2510 BC).

Mýlae (Μυλαί). Town on a peninsula on the north-east coast of Sicily, well-known for the victories of °Duillius and °Agrippa (°Vipsanius).

Mýrmidons (Μυρμιδόνες). Legendary warlike Thessalian tribe who were commanded by °Achilles; °Aegina.

Mýron (Μύρων). Sculptor at Athens (c. 450 BC). He worked mostly in bronze and is known from later copies: °Athena, °Marsyas, °Perseus with the head of °Medusa and a discus-thrower (°Discobolos).

Mýrtilus (Μυρτίλος). Charioteer of Oenomaüs (°Hippodameia), thrown into the sea by Pelops.

Mysteries. Ceremonies mainly intended for purification. The initiated were sworn to the strictest secrecy. The cults offered a prospect of a happy life after death; °Bacchanalia; °Eleusis; °Isis; °Mithras, °Orphism.

N

Nabopolássar. First king of the New-Babylonian empire (625-605 BC). Together with °Cyáxares he destroyed the °Assyrian empire. His successor was °Nebuchadnezzar.

Naévius, *Cn. Naévius.* Born in Campania, one of the first known Roman poets. He wrote comedies, *fabulae °praetextatae* and an epic 'Béllum Púnicum', of which fragments have come down to us. In 204 BC he was exiled for political reasons, and retired to Carthage.

Naíads. °Nymphs.

Namatiánus. °Rutilius.

names. The Greeks gave their sons a name on the tenth day after their birth, usually a composite name (*e.g.* Xanthíppus, Péricles; Ξάνθιππος, Περικλῆς). It was often the name of the grandfather. For the sake of clarity the name of the father could be added in the genitive (in °Homer, sometimes an adjective), °patronymic. The Romans originally had two names; the first name (*praenomen*) and a family name (*nomen*). Sometimes another name (*cognomen* or *agnomen*) was added, possibly a nick-name, to denote a personal quality (*e.g.* P. Ovídius *Náso*), which could become hereditary later on. For most Romans, however (*e.g.* P. Cornélius *Scípio*), the *cognomen* represented the branch of the *nomen*.

Narbonénsis. °Gaul.

Narcíssus (Νάρκισσος). **1.** A youth who rejected the love of the nymph °Echo. To punish him °Nemesis made him fall in love with his own image reflected in a fountain (Ovid *Met.* 3, 339-510). **2.** Freedman of °Claudius. He was his secretary (*ab epistulis*) and had great influence. It was he who persuaded the emperor to put °Messalina to death.

Nármer. A king of the first dynasty in Egypt.

Nárses. A general of °Justinian (c. 478-574 AD). When °Belisarius had fallen into disgrace, Narses was entrusted with the command of the army and subjugated the whole of Italy in 552. In 567 he was dismissed; °Goths.

Naúplius. In legend, the father of °Palamédes and king of Euboea. When his son was stoned to death, for revenge he caused many Greek ships returning from Troy to run upon the rocks by false signals.

Nausicáä (Ναυσικάα). Daughter of °Alcinoüs. She was the first to meet °Odysseus when he landed in °Scheria (Hom. *Od.* VI).

Náxos (Νάξος). One of the °Cyclades; °Ariadne.

Neárchus (Νέαρχος). Admiral of °Alexander the Great.

Nebuchadnézzar. Second king of °Babylon (605-562 BC). He rebuilt Babylon in baked-brick instead of mud-brick; °Nabopolassar.

Nécho (Νεχώς). King of Egypt, c. 610-595 BC. He began to construct a canal between the Mediterranean and the Red Sea and organized an expedition round the African coast; °explorers.

necrópolis (νεκρόπολις). A cemetery or burial ground in or outside a city; °Etruscans; °Abydos 2.

Némea. Town in Argolis, where in honour of °Zeus the °Nemean games were held. °Heracles; °Pindar.

Némean Games. °Nemea; °Isthmian, °Olympian, °Pythian Games.

Némean Lion. Continually threatened the people of °Nemea in Argolis. It was crushed to death by °Heracles.

Nemesiánus, *M. Aurélius Olýmpius Nemesiánus* of Carthage (3rd-4th cent. AD). He imitated °Virgil's 'Eclogues' and wrote a didactic poem on hunting ('Cynegética').

Némesis (Νέμεσις). Greek goddess of vengeance and retribution.

Neolithic Age. The New Stone Age, when

man began to cultivate and store his food and domesticate animals (in Crete and in Greece c.(?) 5000-3000 BC); however stone or obsidian (volcanic glass-like substance) were still used for tools. Was succeeded by the °Aegean civilization.

Neo-Plátonism. The latest form of Greek philosophy, an admixture of Platonic ideas with Oriental mysticism, founded by Ammónius Sáccas (c. 175-242 AD) and represented in the writings of °Plotinus (205-270), °Porphyrius (232-304) and °Iamblichus (died 330).

Neoptólemus (Νεοππόλεμος) or Pyrrhus. Son of °Achilles and °Deidameia, killed °Priam when Troy was destroyed and sacrificed °Polyxena. When the captives were divided among the conquerors, he had for his prize °Andromache. He married °Hermione (°Euripides, 'Andromache'), and was murdered by °Orestes.

Néphele (Νεφέλη). °Phrixus.

Népos, *Cornélius Népos* (c. 99-c. 77 BC). Roman historian. Twenty-five of his biographies of famous men survive, written in a simple style, but full of inconsistencies.

Néptune (Neptúnus). Roman god of sea and water; °Poseidon.

Néreïds (Νηρεΐδες). Sea-nymphs, fifty daughters of the sea-god Nereus and Doris; °Amphitrite; °Thétis; °Galatéa.

Néro. 1. *Néro Claúdius Caésar Augustus Germánicus.* Emperor (54-68 AD), born at Antium as L. Domitius, son of Cn. °Domítius Ahenobárbus and °Agrippina the Younger. He married °Octavia, the daughter of °Claudius. After Claudius' death the praetorians put him on the throne. The first years of his reign were favourably influenced by °Seneca and °Burrhus. His true nature became apparent when he had °Britannicus poisoned, and then contrived Agrippina's death in 59 and that of Burrhus in 62. Octavia was repudiated and killed and Nero became dissipated and more cruel. His megalomania, arousing in others both fear and contempt, led to his death. After many

ill-fated conspiracies (*e.g.* that of °Piso) he was compelled to commit suicide (65 AD). **2.** *Néro Caésar* (*Néro Iúlius Caésar*). Eldest son of °Germanicus. He married °Julia, daughter of Drusus, in 21 AD. °Tiberius, believing the accusations of °Sejanus, caused his death at Pontia in 30 AD. °Julio-Claudian dynasty, p. 101.

Nérva, *M. Cocceíus Nérva,* born c. 35 AD. Emperor 96-98 AD, successor to °Domitian, whose ruthless reign he replaced by an enlightened and progressive administration. He adopted °Trajan.

Néssus (Νέσσος). A °centaur; °Heracles.

Néstor (Νέστωρ). King of °Pylos, who took part in the °Trojan War, where he was the oldest and wisest of all the kings. His sons were °Antilochus and °Peisistratus.

Nícias (Νικίας). Athenian politician, leader of the conservative party. After the failure of °Cleon's policy in the °Peloponnesian War, he was largely responsible for the peace with Sparta (421 BC). Together with °Alcibiades, he led the ill-fated expedition to Sicily, though he disapproved of it. He died in 413.

Nicoláus (Νικόλαος). of Damáscus. Court-historian of °Herod the Great and tutor to the children of °Antony and °Cleopatra. He wrote a 'Universal History' in 144 books of which fragments are extant, and a partial biography of °Augustus.

Níke (Νίκη). Winged goddess of victory. There were many statues of Nike which are lost, except for the badly damaged one by °Paeonius in the museum at °Olympia and the Nike of °Samothrace in the Louvre. She had an °Ionic temple on the °Acropolis, near the °Propylaea.

Níneveh. Town in Assyria on the Tigris, which flourished in the early 7th century BC, when it was made the capital by °Sennacherib, who had destroyed Babylon. It was destroyed by the Medes and Chaldeans c. 610.

Níobe (Νιόβη). Legendary daughter of °Tantalus, married to °Amphion, king of Thebes. Having seven sons and seven daughters, she thought herself superior to °Leto, who had only two children: °Apollo and °Artemis. The gods punished her by killing her children and she herself was turned into a weeping stone (Ovid *Met.* 6, 146-312); °Tantalidae, p. 182.

Níobids. The children of °Niobe; °ill. 114.

114. One of the daughters of Niobe.

Nísus (Νῖσος). **1.** Legendary king of Megara who was besieged by °Minos. His daughter Scylla, seeing Minos from the walls of the town, fell in love with him and when her father slept, stole the purple lock of his hair on which depended the fate of the city. Megara fell, but Minos despised Scylla's love and she drowned herself (Ovid *Met.* 8, 6-151); °Ciris. **2.** °Eurýalus.

Nóctes Átticae. °Gellius.

Nóla. Town in Campania where, in 215 BC, °Hannibal was defeated by °Marcellus. °Augustus died at Nola.

nómen Latínum. °Latin League.

Nónae (Nones). The 7th day of March, May, July and October; the 5th day of the other months; °Idus; °Kalendae; °calendar.

Nónius Marcéllus. Grammarian and philosopher (4th cent. AD), whose work 'De Compendiósa Doctrína' dealt with points of grammar and contained many quotations from earlier writers; he also wrote 'Doctrína de proprietáte Sermónum'.

Nónnos (Νόννος). Epic poet from Panópolis in Egypt (5th cent. AD). He was a Christian and wrote a paraphrase of St John's Gospel in verse and an epic in forty-eight books, 'Dionýsiaca', in accurate but pedantically precise hexameters.

nóta censória. °censor.

nótae Tironiánae. °stenography.

via Nóva. The oldest street in Rome but one, the Via °Sacra. It ran across the north slope of the °Palatine to the °Velabrum.

Núma Pompílius. Second king of Rome, possibly historical (c. 715-672 BC), who, according to tradition, reformed religion on the advice of the 'nymph' °Egeria; °ancile.

Númitor. King of °Alba Longa, father of °Rhea Silvia. His brother °Amulius deposed him. His grandsons °Romulus and °Remus were exposed but were suckled by a she-wolf, and Rhea Silvia became a °Vestal Virgin; °Dardanidae, p. 60.

nurághi. Prehistoric stone-built towers

peculiar to Sardinia. There were commonly two or three storeys, roofed by corbelling.

Nux elégia. An elegy in ninety-one °disticha, possibly by °Ovid. In it a nut-tree lamented that passers-by threw stones at her. It was allegorical, the victim representing the poet.

nymphaéum. Building (sometimes subterranean) with many niches from which water spouted into a basin. The greatest was in Rome, built by °Septimius Severus c. 200 AD.

Nymphs (νύμφη). Daughters of °Zeus, inhabitants (*e.g.*) of rivers (Naiads), hills (Oreads) and trees (Dryads).

O

óbelisk (ὀβελίσκος). A tapering monolithic shaft of stone with pyramidical apex, a characteristic monument of ancient Egypt. Some obelisks are now in Rome and Paris; one of a pair erected by Thothmes III at Heliopolis is now 'Cleopatra's Needle' in London, the other is in New York.

óbol (ὀβολός). **1.** °Weights and measures 1e; 2d. **2.** Smallest Greek monetary unit = 1/6 °drachma; °Attic stelae; °ill. p. 85; °Charon.

occupátio. °ager publicus.

Octávia. 1. *Octávia* (Maior). Half-sister of °Augustus. **2.** *Octavia* (Minor). Daughter of C. Octavius and Atia (or Accía) (c. 65-11 BC), married to °Marcéllus and after his death (40 BC) to °Antony. In 37, she reconciled Antony and °Octavian (Treaty of Tarentum); °triumvirate. **3.** *Claúdia Octávia.* Daughter of °Claudius and °Messalina, born c. 42, married to °Nero, who repudiated her in 62, banished her to Pandateria and had her killed; °Julio-Claudian dynasty, p. 101.

Octávian, *Octaviánus.* Surname of the later °Augustus after °Caesar had adopted him.

Octávius, *C. Octávius.* Father of °Augustus. He died at °Nola in 59 BC.

Ocyrrhóë (Ὠκυρόη) (or Menalippe). Daughter of °Cheiron, who had the gift of prophecy. She was changed into

a mare (Ovid *Met.* 2, 632-675).

ódeum (ᾠδεῖον). A small °theatre as at °Pompeii. A well-known one is the Odeum at Athens, built by °Herodes Atticus c. 170 AD; there were 8000 seats.

Odóacer. A German prince who fled to Italy and became an officer of the bodyguard of the emperor. In 476 AD he dethroned °Rómulus Augústulus and reigned until 493.

Odýsseus (Ὀδυσσεύς, Ulíxes, = Úlysses). Son of Laertes, king of °Ithaca, whose adventures were described in the *Odyssey*; °Homer; °Penelope; °Telemachus; °ill. 115; °Odysseus' house; plan, p. 131.

Odyssey (Ὀδύσσεια). °Homer; °Odysseus.

Oécles (Οἰκλῆς). Father of °Amphiaraus.

Oédipus (Οἰδίπους). Son of °Laiüs, king of Thebes, and Jocasta. Warned that their son would kill his father and marry his mother, they abandoned him on Mt Cithaeron. He was found and adopted by Polybus, king of Corinth. Grown to manhood, he went to Delphi and was told by the °oracle of the prophecy. Therefore, not returning to Corinth, he went to Thebes, killing Laiüs, without knowing the latter was his true father, in a chance encounter on the way. At Thebes he saved the town from the °Sphinx by guessing her riddle and married queen Jocasta. They

115. Odysseus under the ram (Rome, Palazzo Doria).

130

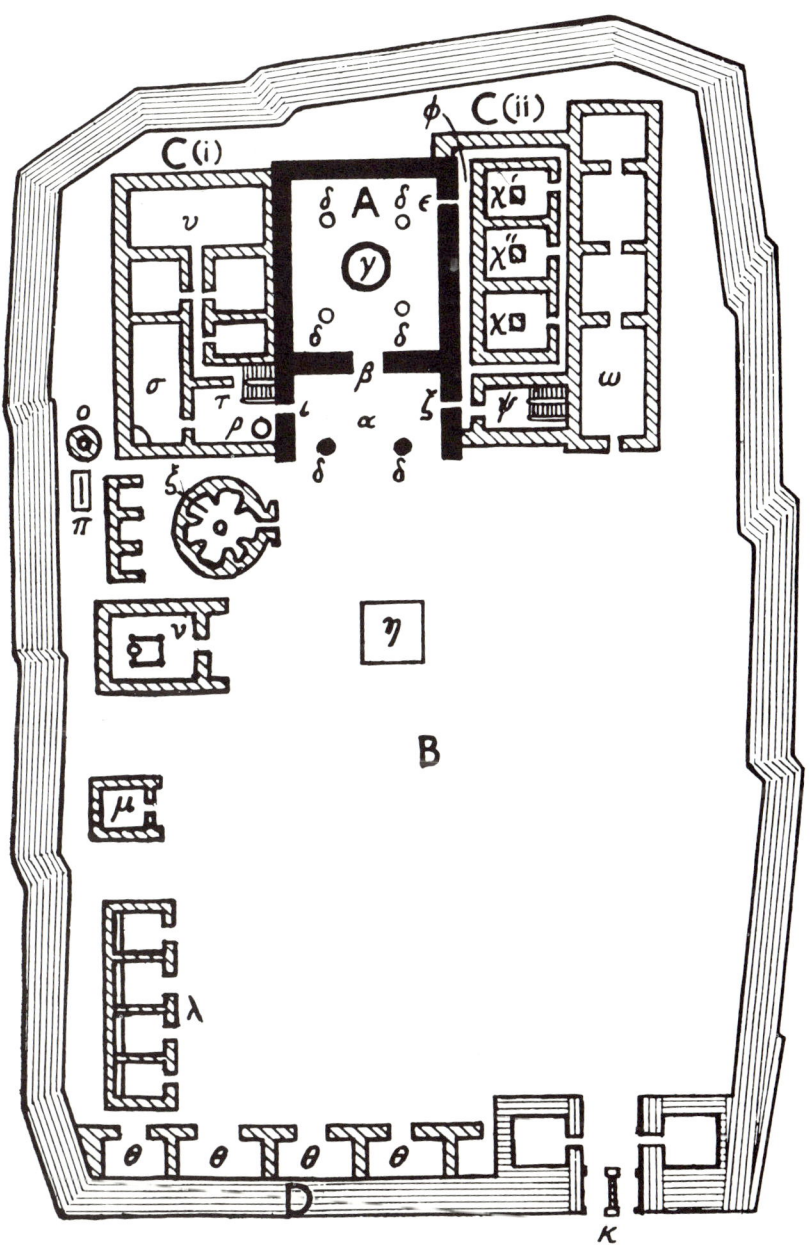

131

had four children °Eteocles, Polyneices, °Antigone and Ismene. The terrible secret of their relationship was revealed by °Teiresias. Jocasta hanged herself and Oedipus blinded himself; °Sophocles.

Oéneus (Oἰνεύς). King of °Calydon, husband of °Althaea, father of °Meleager.

Oenomáüs (Oἰνόμαος). King of Elis, father of °Hippodameia; °Tantalidae, p. 182.

Ogýgia ('Ωγυγία). °Calypso.

Oíleus (Oἰλεύς). King of the Locrians, one of the °Argonauts, father of °Ajax.

oinóchoë (oἰνόχοη). Greek wine-jug with one vertical handle and a round or trefoil mouth; °ill. 116.

olive. A slow-growing evergreen tree bearing small fruits which are harvested when unripe (when they are green) or ripe (black). For the Greeks the olive tree was sacred to °Athena who had given it to Athens. The 'original' olive tree stood, in Classical times, behind the °Erechtheum and twelve trees grown from it were planted in the garden of the °Academy (μορίαι). At the °Olympian Games a wreath of olive was given to the victor. The olive branch is a symbol of peace.

ólpe. A type of °oenochoe, tall and narrow with a circular mouth and vertical handle, hardly rising above the rim; °ill. 117.

117. Olpe.

116. Corinthian oinochoë from Selinus (c. 580 BC).

óligarchy (ὀλιγαρχία). The rule of a 'few', as opposed to democracy.

Olýmpia ('Ολυμπία). Sacred domain in Elis on the river Alpheüs.'The centre was the Altis, the sactuary of Olympian °Zeus, where in his temple stood the statue of Zeus by °Pheidias. Every four years the °Olympian Games were held in his honour (for the last time in 394 AD), with athletic, literary and musical competitions, chariot races, °pankration, and °pentathlon. Excavations at Olympia brought several important sculptures to light: the Hermes of °Praxiteles; the °Nike of °Paeonius; sculptures of the temple of °Zeus; °Pindar.

Olympian Games. °Olympia; °Nemean, °Isthmian, °Pythian Games.

Olýmpias (Ὀλυμπιάς). Mother of °Alexander the Great. After his death, she marched against his half-brother Philippus Aridaeus, but was defeated and killed by °Cassander.

Olýmpus (Ὄλυμπος). Mountain in northern Greece, the supposed home of the gods.

Olýnthiacs. Three speeches by °Demosthenes (352-348 BC) urging the Athenians to help Olynthus in Chalcidice, which was besieged by °Philip of Macedon.

Omphále (Ὀμφάλη). Queen of Lydia. °Heracles worked as a slave in her service.

ómphalos (ὀμφαλός) (=navel). Conical stone at °Delphi, supposed to be the centre of the earth; °ill. 118.

119. Ónager.

c. 200 AD, wrote a didactic poem on fishing ('Halieutica'), dedicated to °Caracalla who paid him one gold piece for each line. **2.** Of Apamea, wrote (about 215 AD) a didactic poem on hunting ('Cynegética'). (Possibly **1.** and **2.** are the same man.)

Optatiánus Porphýrius. Poet who, in the time of °Constantine the Great, wrote poems in an ingenious and elaborate manner, *e.g.* in the shape of an altar, water-organ, etc.

optimátes. A conservative group in the later Roman Republic, consisting of a small number of wealthy families, who favoured the interests of the Senate; °Catiline; °Clodius; °Gracchi; °Marius.

órdo, *ordines* = °centurion.

Óreads. °Nymphs.

Oreithýia (Ὠρείθυια). Legendary daughter of °Erechtheus (mother of °Calaïs and Zetes), carried off by °Boreas. Her story was told to girls as a warning against walking abroad unattended.

Oresteía. °Aeschylus.

118. The °omphalos in Delphi.

ónager. An engine of war, throwing stones to a height of 40m and over a distance of 30m; °ill. 119.

opisthódomus (ὀπισθόδομος). Recessed porch in the rear of a Greek temple, sometimes used as a treasure chamber.

Oppiánus (Ὀππιανός). **1.** Of Cilicia,

Oréstes ('Ορέστης). Son of °Agamemnon and °Clytaemnestra who avenged the death of his father. (°Aeschylus, *Choephori*; °Sophocles, *Electra*; °Euripides, *Electra*). Because of his matricide he was persecuted by the Furies (°Erinyes), (°Aeschylus, *Eumenides*; °Euripides, *Orestes*), until he was acquitted by the °Areopagus. He married °Hermione; °Pylades; °Tantalidae, p. 182.

Orígenes, of Alexandria (=Origen) (c. 184-253 AD). Author of theological and philosophical works. He dictated his work to a great number of °stenographic writers. His edition of the Bible in six languages is famous (°hexapla).

Oríon ('Ωρίων). Boeotian hunter, supposedly killed by °Artemis. He was turned into the constellation which still bears his name.

Orósius, *Paúlus Orósius.* A Spanish priest, who, at the request of °Augustine, wrote (414 AD) a history of the world in seven books, called 'Advérsus Pagános', which is also an apology.

Órpheus ('Ορφεύς). Traditionally, the earliest Greek lyric poet. He took part in the expedition of the °Argonauts. With his music and singing he attracted trees, wild beasts and even stones. When his wife Eurydice had died from a snake bite, he went down to the Underworld. He was allowed to bring her back, on the condition that he should not turn round and look at her before he had reached the Upper world. Since he did, Eurydice went back. Afterwards he wandered about, lamenting his loss (Ovid *Met.* 10, 1-77) until finally he was torn to pieces by the °Maenads (Ovid *Met.* 11, 1-66).

On vase and wall paintings, even in the °catacombs, he was often represented singing and surrounded by animals; °Orphism.

Órphism. A religious cult founded by Orpheus which spread from Thrace to Greece and the South of Italy. At the centre of the cult was °Dionysus, who had been devoured by the °Titans. From the ashes of the Titans mankind was born, a mixture of the divine Dionysus and the unholy Titans. The soul supposedly wandered through many reincarnations searching for purification. Orphic influence was great on °Pythagoras. We have the so-called Orphic °hymns dating from the 3rd century AD; °Mysteries.

Osíris. Egyptian god of the dead, husband of °Isis, father of °Horus.

Ossa (Όσσα). A mountain in Thessaly; °Giants.

Ostia. The port of Rome, fully excavated; °ill. 96.

óstracism (όστρακισμός). Instituted by the democrat °Cleisthenes in 507 BC. The Athenians could banish a man without disgrace or loss of citizen's rights for ten years (°Aristeides, °Themistocles; 6000 votes were necessary. The name is derived from °ostrakon, a potsherd, the writing material on which the name of the man to be 'ostracised' was scratched. Several hundred *ostraka* have been found; °ill. 120.

120. Two ostraka bearing the name of °Themistocles. On the round ostrakon the voter added "ἴτω" = "he must go".

óstrakon (ὄστρακον). A broken piece of pottery, much used in antiquity on which to scratch names, etc; °ostracism. Sometimes a literary work was written on an *ostrakon*; °Sappho; °ill. 121.

Óstrogoths. °Goths.

Ótho, *M. Sálvius Otho.* Roman emperor from Jan. 15th-April 16th 69 AD. He was a friend of °Nero, who took his wife °Poppaéa Sabína. He was proclaimed emperor by the soldiers and after his defeat near Bedriacum against °Vitellius, he killed himself.

ovátio. A minor °triumph; the 'triumphátor' rode on horseback or went on foot and wore a wreath of myrtle instead of laurel.

Óvid, *P. Ovídius Náso* (43 BC-c. 18 AD). A superficially brilliant poet whose work, though not profound, is technically perfect, excelling through refinement and irony. From his work it appears that in 8 AD he was banished by °Augustus to Tomi, where he died.

The following works of Ovid have come down to us:

Amóres. Love poems. *Heróides.* Fictional letters of legendary persons (*e.g.* °Penelope to °Odysseus). *Medi-*

cámina faciéi. About beauty-preparations. *Ars amándi.* A guide to love-making. *Remédia amóris.* A guide to escape from amorous entanglements. *Fásti.* An unfinished poem about Roman festivals. *Metamorphóses.* Mythological stories concerning changes of form. *Trístia* and *Epistulae ex Pónto.* Pathetic lamentations pleading for his return from exile. *Ibis.* A comprehensive curse, invoking disaster on an enemy. *Halieútica.* Didactic poem on fishing in the Euxine; °*Nux.*

oxymóron (ὀξύμωρον). A rhetorical figure by which contradictory terms are conjoined to give point to a statement or an expression, *e.g.* 'Seria ludere', 'μήτηρ ἀμήτωρ'.

Oxyrhýnchus. Town in Upper Egypt, which has proved to be the richest source of Roman and Byzantine °papyri yet discovered. Our knowledge of Greek literature depends to no small extent on these. The first scientific exploration of the site was by Grenfell and Hunt in 1895-96. In 1897 the first of the "Sayings of Jesus" ('Logia') were found there. The town is now only extensive mounds.

P

Pactólus (Πακτωλός). River in Lydia. Legend has it that °Midas bathed here to get rid of his 'golden touch'. °Agesilaus.

Pacúvius, *M. Pacúvius* (c. 220-c. 130 BC). Roman tragic poet and painter from Brundisium, related to °Ennius. His words are philosophical and the extant fragments suggest that he was a painstaking if slow worker, original in choice of subject, with pictorial power and command of metre. He was still admired

in the °Augustan Age.

paéon. A metrical foot: $\_ \smile \smile \smile$, or $\smile \_ \smile \smile$, or $\smile \smile \_ \smile$, or $\smile \smile \smile \_$.

Paeónius (Παιώνιος). Sculptor (c. 420 BC), mainly known for his °Nike at °Olympia.

Paéstum (Ποσειδωνία). Town in Lucania, which was abandoned under the Empire on account of malaria. It is well-known from the ruins of three large °Doric temples; °ill. 122.

Paétus, *Sex. Aélius Paétus.* Consul 198

εντυδωρψύχρο
κελατιδιδυσχωνμαλιαν
βροτοισοτεπεσοχωροσκισκι
ασταιθυσσομενων δεφυλλων
κωμακατιρρον

ἐν δ ὕδωρ ψῦχρον κελάδει δι ' ὔσδων,
μάλιαν βρόδοισι δὲ παῖς ὀ χῶρος
ἐσκίασται, θυσσομένων δὲ φύλλων
κῶμα κατ' ἴρρον.

136

122. Paestum. The temple of Hera in the foreground ('basilica'). Behind it the so-called 'temple of Poseidon', and far back where the road turns to the left the so-called 'temple of Demeter', probably sacred to Athena.

121 *(left)*. Ostrakon (17cm. high) on which (about 250 BC) was written an ode of °Sappho, from the sixth line:

BC. The first lawyer to publish a work, 'Tripártita', containing the law of the XII Tables with a commentary on the forms of legal action. Also attributed to him was the 'Iús Aeliánum'.

palaeógraphy. The study which concentrates on ancient writing.

Palaeolíthic Age. The Old Stone Age, when man lived by hunting, and on roots and berries, using primitive stone implements; °Neolithic, °Mesolithic Ages.

palaéstra (παλαίστρα). A building with central colonnaded court-yard covered with fine sand, where youths were taught the art (*e.g.*) of wrestling.

Palamédes (Παλαμήδης). Son of °Nauplius and °Clymene. When °Odysseus feigned madness to avoid going to Troy, Palamedes found him out. In revenge, Odysseus hid a sum of gold in his tent and accused him of treachery. Palamedes was found guilty and stoned to death. (Later he was thought to be the inventor of the alphabet, weights and measures and dice.)

Pálatine (Móns Palatínus). One of the °Seven hills on which °Rome was built. After Augustus' time it was the quarter of the imperial palaces (Palátium); plan, p. 165.

palimbácchius. A metrical foot: _ _ ◡.

pálimpsest (from 'πάλιν; ψηστός). A manuscript on which the original writing was scraped away in order to use the material again. Chemical and other technical processes have often made the original text legible. °Gaius' 'Institutiónes', the letters of °Fronto and °Cicero's 'De Republica' have survived in palimpsests only; °ill. 123.

pálindrome (παλίνδρομον). A word or text which reads the same backwards and forwards, *e.g.*: ΝΙΨΟΝ ΑΝΟΜΗΜΑ ΜΗ ΜΟΝΑΝ ΟΨΙΝ.

pálla. Cloak of Roman women, very much like the Greek °himation.

Palládium. Supposed image of the goddess °Athena in the citadel of Troy, on which the safety of the city depended. It was stolen by °Diomedes and

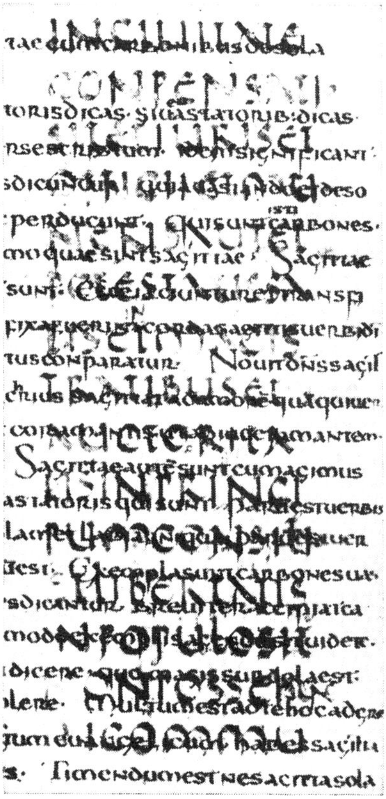

123. A palimpsest (19 cm. high). The original text (Cic. *De Rep.* 2, 57) begins as follows:

in civitate
conpensatio
sit et iuris et
officii et mu
neris aut et . . .

dating from the 4th or 5th cent. AD. On it was written in the 8th century (Augustine *In Psalms* 119, 5):

tae cum carbonibus desola
toris dicas siv(e v)astatorib: dicas.

°Odysseus. Eventually it was brought to Rome.

Pallánteum. Town built by °Evander on the °Palatine; °Virgil.

palmétte. A fan-shaped ornament divided as are palm leaves; used particularly on Greek pottery.

pálmus. °Weights and measures 2a.

Palmýra. Important city with an oasis, at the cross-roads of caravan routes in the Syrian desert. It flourished in the 3rd century AD under the empress °Zenobia. °Aurelian destroyed it in 273 AD, although Roman remains are still to be seen.

Pan (Πάν). Son of °Hermes and a nymph, god of shepherds and herds. He was amorous, with goat-like legs, ears and horns. He could induce 'panic' among men. He played the °syrinx; °Marsyas.

Panaétius, of Rhodes (c. 180-99 BC). °Stoic philosopher. In 144 he came to Rome, where he made himself outstanding in the circle of °Scipio Acmiliánus, whom he won over to his doctrines. He attempted to adapt Stoic ethics to the requirements of the Roman nobility. °Cicero used Panaetius' work in his 'De Officiis'.

Panathenáïc ámphora. This °amphora, with a broad body tapering sharply towards a small base, was given as a prize at the °Panathenáïc games and was decorated with °Athena on one side, and with the contest at which the prize was won on the other; °ill. 124.

Panathenáïc Games. The principal festival in Athens in honour of the goddess °Athena. It was held every fourth year with games and a procession, in which girls from the leading families carried an embroidered °peplos for the statue of the goddess. This scene was represented on the °Parthenon frieze; °Peisistratus.

Pandéctae (Πανδέκται) = °Digesta; °Corpus iuris civilis.

Pandíon (Πανδίων). °Philomela.

Pandóra (Πανδώρα). A girl created by °Hephaestus and gifted with beauty and talents by °Athena. Epimetheus married her in spite of the warnings of °Prometheus. Rashly, Pandora opened the box full of objects of desire, which could then play havoc among mankind;

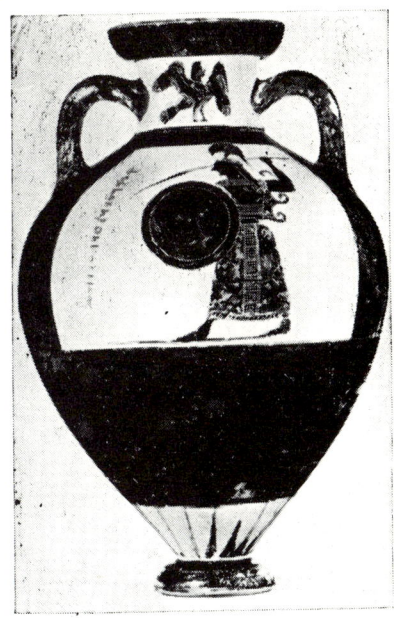

124. Panathenaic amphora *c.* 560 BC. The inscription (translated): 'I am one of the Athenian prizes'.

only Hope remained behind (°Hes. *Erga* 53-105).

panegýrics. Laudatory discourses written in the Imperial period, twelve extant, the oldest being that of °Pliny on °Trajan (100 AD). Others, dating from 289-389 AD, were by various authors in correct Latin, but full of base flattery.

Panegýricus ad °**Messállam.** Written by an unknown poet, found among the work of °Tibullus (4, 2 = 3, 7).

pankrátion (παγκράτιον). A combination of wrestling and boxing. Everything was fair to defeat the adversary, except biting; °Olympia.

Pánsa, *C. Víbius Pánsa.* Follower of °Caesar. He was killed when °consul (43 BC), fighting against °Antony near °Mutina.

Pántheon. A well-preserved temple rebuilt in °Rome by °Hadrian on the site of the temple (built by °Agrippa in 27 BC) which had been burned down. It is now used as a church. The famous dome has a diameter of 42 m.

lex Papía Poppaéa, *de maritándis ordínibus.* A law passed by the consuls of 9 AD at the instigation of °Augustus. It decreed, among other things, that the unmarried could not accept an inheritance.

Papiniánus, *Aemílius Papiniánus.* °Praefectus praetorio under °Septimius Severus. He was considered one of the greatest of all Roman lawyers. 595 quotations of his works have been included in the °Corpus iuris civilis.

Papínius. °Statius.

papyrólogy. The study of °papyri.

papýrus (πάπυρος). A reed of the sedge-family (Cýperus papýrus) which grew plentifully in ancient Egypt and is now extinct except in Sicily where it grows by the Anapos. The stems were split and opened out and by pasting them together in two layers at right angles, a cheap writing material was produced. Later it was superseded by °parchment (°Pergamum). Many papyri, dating from 2000 BC-8th cent. AD, have been preserved in the dry desert of Egypt. These consist largely of documents and letters. Literary works found on papyri are (*e.g.*) by °Aristotle, °Bacchylides; °Menander; ill. 9; °books.

parábasis (παράβασις). That part of the Old °Comedy when the chorus, after the first °epeisodion, came forward and addressed the audience on the poet's behalf.

Párcae. °Fates.

parchment. Invented, according to °Varro, at °Pergamum, when Ptolemy V (Epíphanes, 205-181 BC) had forbidden the export of °papyrus from Egypt, in order to prevent the growth of the library at Pergamum in competition with the library at °Alexandria.

Páris (Πάρις; Ἀλέξανδρος). Son of °Priam and °Hecuba Appointed by °Zeus to act as arbiter, he decided to award the apple of °Eris (°Peleus) to °Aphrodite as the most beautiful of the three goddesses. She gave him the promised reward, °Helen, °Menelaus' wife, whom he seduced. This was the (supposed) immediate cause of the °Trojan War. He was killed by a shot from °Philoctetes' bow.

párma. **1.** Small round buckler of the °velites. **2.** Light shield (after °Marius' time the oval shield of the *levis armatura*).

Parménides of Eléa (Παρμενίδης). (c. 500 BC). Pupil of °Xenophanes; the principal philosopher of the °Eleatic School.

Parménio (Παρμενίων). General of °Philip of Macedon and °Alexander the Great. When his son, Philotas, had conspired against Alexander and had been put to death, Alexander also had Parmenio killed as he, too, was supposed to be implicated in the plot (330 BC).

párodos (πάροδος). The first ode sung by the chorus after its entrance in Greek tragedy.

paronomásia (παρονομασία, adnominátio). Pun ('regum rex regalior'), also with words not etymologically related. Then it is called *parechésis* (παρήχησις) *e.g.* 'amor amarus'.

Páros (Πάρος). One of the °Cyclades, famous for its marble; Marmor Parium.

Parrhásius (Παρράσιος). Famous Athenian painter (c. 400 BC), rival of °Zeuxis. He excelled in depicting dramatic scenes.

Párthenon (ὁ Παρθενών). Temple of °Athena °Parthenos on the °Acropolis; °Elgin marbles; plan. p. 4

Párthenos, *Athéna Párthenos.* Statue by °Pheidias in the °Parthenon. The statue itself is lost, but later copies are extant; °ill. 130.

Pasipháë (Πασιφάη). Wife of °Minos; °Circe.

pássus. A pace, or Roman measure of length of outstretched arms; °Weights and measures 2a, p. 199.

páter patrátus. °Fetiales.

Patróclus (Πάτροκλος). Son of °Menoetius, dearest friend of °Achilles, wearing whose armour he died in the war against °Troy.

patronýmic. A name derived from one's father, in Greek times (*e.g.* 'Ατρείδης = son of Atreus); °names.

Paulínus of Nóla (353-431 AD), from Burdigala. Pupil of °Ausonius. He was baptized in 391 and became bishop of Nola in 409. Many of his poems and letters are extant.

Paúlus. 1. *Aemílius Paúlus.* °Aemilius. **2.** *Iúlius Paúlus,* °*praefectus praetorio* for °Alexander Severus; he wrote a number of legal works of which 2080 fragments are in the °Digesta.

Pausánias (Παυσανίας). **1.** King of Sparta, defeated the Persians near °Plataea in 479 BC and then centred his ambitions on Asia Minor. His boundless pride created many enemies. The Athenians broke away from the Greek coalition and founded the °Delian League. Pausanias was recalled by the Spartans and found guilty of treason for his illegal actions in Asia Minor. He fled for safety to a temple where he was starved out. **2.** King of Sparta (408-394 BC), was more moderate than °Lysander and facilitated the restoration of the democracy at Athens, after the fall of the °Thirty Tyrants. **3.** Greek geographer and traveller from Lydia; he wrote a 'Description of Greece', a guide-book concerning art, religion and architecture dating from before 150 BC; °explorers.

pédiment. The triangular end of a temple or other ridged roof, usually framed with a °cornice; °Doric order, etc.

Pégasus (Πήγασος). The legendary winged horse on which °Bellerophon fought the °Chimaera. Pegasus was said to have produced many famous springs out of the earth by a stamp of his hoof, *e.g.* on °Helicon, which was named °Hippocrene.

Peisístratus (Πεισίστρατος). Athenian nobleman, who three times was absolute ruler of Athens. Twice he was expelled from the city and in 528 BC his two sons °Hippias and °Hipparchus succeeded him. Peisistratus claims our admiration for his justice, liberality and moderation. He promoted the arts (building a temple of °Athena, and instituting the °Panathenaea and °Dionysia); he fostered relations with foreign rulers, thus establishing connections of future importance; °tyrant.

Péleus (Πηλεύς). Son of Aeacus, married to °Thetis and father of °Achilles. Eris, goddess of strife, who had not been invited to their wedding-party, threw a golden apple among the guests as a prize for the most beautiful. °Hera, °Athena and °Aphrodite were the candidates; °Zeus gave the decision to °Paris; °Aeacidae, p. 3.

Pélias (Πελίας). Uncle of °Jason; °Alcestis; °Medea.

pélike (πελίκη). Name given to a neckless °amphora; °ill. 125.

125. Pélike.

Pélion (Πήλιον). Mountain in Thessaly; °Cheiron; °Giants.

Peloponnésian War (431-404 BC). Waged between Sparta and Athens, which both aspired to °hegemony in Greece. The immediate cause was that the Athenians supported Corcyra against Corinth. The first part of the war was called the Archidamian war (431-421), which ended with the Peace of °Nicias. Then followed a time of comparative peace (421-413). The third period, the 'Decelean War' (413-404), began with the seizing of °Decelea by the Spartans. In 404 they occupied Athens and

°Lysander put it under the rule of the °Thirty Tyrants; °Pericles; °oligarchy; °Archidamus.

Pélops (Πέλοψ) Son of °Tantalus, butchered by his father to test the gods' power and served to them as a meal. °Zeus restored Pelops to life. Later he went to Elis, and married °Hippodameia after having overcome her father °Oenomaus in a race with the help of °Myrtilus. However, when Pelops then killed Myrtilus, the latter cursed the whole race of Tantalus; °Tantalidae p. 182.

pélta (πέλτη). A small light shield of leather without a rim, used by the °Amazons.

Penátes (Di Penátes). Roman tutelary deities of the house, originally of the store-room. They were worshipped at the hearth and received part of the meal; °Lares; °Vesta.

Penélope (Πηνελόπη). Daughter of Icarius, faithful wife of °Odysseus. She waited twenty years for him to return from °Troy.

pentámeter. Metrical line composed of two halves, each of $2\frac{1}{2}$ feet:

⏑⏑ ⏑⏑ ⏑ ⏑⏑ ⏑⏑⏑.

Chiefly used alternately with the °hexameter; °distichon.

pentáthlon (πέντα θλον). A combination of five athletic games: the long-jump, running, the discus, javelin-throwing and wrestling: "ἅλμα, ποδωκείην, δίσκον, ἄκοντα, πάλην", which shows also the use of the °pentameter; °Olympia.

Pentélicon (Πεντελικὸν ὄρος). Mountain in Attica with important marble-quarries; °Paros.

Penthesileía (Πενθεσίλεια). Queen of the °Amazons, killed when fighting °Achilles.

Péntheus (Πενθεύς). Grandson of °Cadmus, king of Thebes. He opposed the cult of °Dionysus and was devoured by the Bacchantes, among whom was his mother °Agave (°Euripides, *Bacchae*; Ovid *Met.* 3, 511-733).

péplos (πέπλος). Woollen garment for women made from a rectangular piece of cloth measuring about 2 by 3 m. The simplest way of wearing the peplos was with an overlap and pinned together on the shoulder so that the right-hand side fell open, but many variations were possible; °ills. 126-129.

126. Girl sacrificing (c. 450 BC, 1.43 m. high). She is wearing an open woollen °peplos without girdle, fastened on the shoulders.

127. Athena is wearing an open peplos (with long bosom fold and one girdle over it), fastened on the shoulders. Under the Corinthian helmet can be seen the leather lining.

128. Part of a metope of the temple of Zeus at Olympia. Athena is wearing a peplos without girdle.

Pérdiccas (Περδίκκας). **1.** King of Macedon (c. 440-413 BC), who alternately supported both parties during the °Peloponnesian War. **2.** General of °Alexander the Great, who gave him his signet-ring on his death-bed. He tried to keep the empire united, but was murdered in Egypt by his officers; °Diadochi.

Peregrinátio Aethériae. Travelogue of a distinguished lady to the Holy Land at the end of the 4th century AD. The name of the lady was not certain; sometimes she was called Egeria.

143

129. Open peplos with short bosom fold and one girdle underneath.

Pérgamum (Πέργαμον). Town in Mysia, which became the capital of the kingdom, founded in 283 BC by Philetaerus. After a flourishing period, °Attalus III bequeathed the wealthy kingdom to Rome. Excavations begun in 1878 brought to light a city which must once have been of great beauty, a splendid example of Hellenistic town-planning, with many palaces, theatres and public buildings laid out on a hill-side. There was a famous school of sculpture and a library, second only to that of Alexandria; an altar to °Zeus, famous for its frieze on which a fight between the Gods and the °Giants was found. °Hellenistic age.

Periánder (Περίανδρος). °Tyrant of Corinth, son of °Cypselus (early 6th cent. BC). The arts and crafts, industry and commerce flourished under him; the potters produced large amounts of work; °Arion came to his court. He was universally accepted as one of the °Seven Sages and his forceful character left a deep impression.

Periboéa (Περίβοια). Mother of °Ajax; °Aeacidae, p. 3.

Péricles (Περικλῆς). Son of Xanthippus and Agariste, Athenian statesman, general and orator. He was leader of the democratic party. Together with °Ephialtes in 462 BC he took away the power of the °Areopagus and gave it to the °Heliaea and the °Ecclesia. After Ephialtes' death in 461, Pericles became the most influential man in Athens, which he made more powerful and prosperous. During his lifetime the most famous buildings on the °Acropolis were constructed. Athens became the centre of the arts (°Herodotus; °Pheidias; °Sophocles; °Anaxagoras). He tried to suppress the imminent conflict with Sparta by a plan to abandon the countryside and bring the population together within the city walls. When, however, the plague broke out, his plan failed and he fell into disgrace, and he himself died of the plague in 429 BC; °Aspasia, °Thucydides, °Peloponnesian War.

Peripatétic School. The philosophic school of °Aristotle, so-called because of the walking-place (περίπατος) of the °Lyceum where Aristotle taught. The successors of Aristotle were °Theophrastus and °Strato. In course of time, the school split up and the several branches concentrated on different sciences: physics, anatomy, astronomy, biography, etc.

peristýlium (= péristyle). °domus.

Perséphone (= Prosérpina, Περσεφόνη). Daughter of °Demeter, carried off by °Hades (Ovid. *Met.* 5, 341-661). She became his wife and queen in the Underworld. Half of the year she spent with her mother on earth, and half with Hades.

Pérseus (Περσεύς). **1.** Son of °Zeus and °Danaë. He succeeded with the help of

°Athena and °Hermes in severing the head from °Medusa. From the blood which dropped from her head sprang the horse °Pegasus with whose aid Perseus delivered °Andromeda (Ovid *Met.* 4, 663-803); °Alcaeus; °Atlas. **2.** *Perseus, King of Macedon* (179-168 BC). He tried to free himself from Roman rule (in the Third Macedonian War), but was defeated in 168 by L. °Aemílius Paúlus near Pydna and died as prisoner of the Romans in 166.

Persian Wars (τὰ Μηδικά). The wars of the Greeks against the Persians began in 493 BC with the expedition of °Darius (°Athos) and ended in 448 with the peace of °Callias; °Salamis, °Thermopylae, etc.

Pérsius, *Aulus Pérsius Fláccus* (34-62 AD). A °satyric poet. His style was rugged but his indignation sincere.

Pértinax, *P. Hélvius Pértinax.* Roman Emperor (1st January-28th March, 193 AD), successor to °Commodus, tried to restore Augustan principles of government but was murdered.

Pervigílium Venéris. Bright and lively poem in honour of Venus (time and poet unknown) with the repetitive refrain 'cras amet qui numquam amavit, quique amavit cras amet'.

pes. °Weights and measures 2a, 2b.

Petíllius. °Ceriális.

Petrónius ('Árbiter'). 1. Courtier of °Nero, who fell into disgrace in 66 AD through the influence of Tigellinus, and was compelled to commit suicide in 66 (Tac. *Ann.* 16, 18: 'elegantiae arbiter'). **2.** Writer of a picaresque novel (°satire). Only fragments of his work have come down to us among which is one longer piece: the *Céna Trimalchiónis*, a witty description of a banquet at the house of Trimalchio, a freedman. This work is one of our best sources of vulgar Latin. *N.B.* Whether the courtier and the novelist are one and the same person is not certain.

Phaeácians (Φαίακες). Mythical people living on the island of Scheria, described by °Homer; °Alcinoüs; °Nausicaä.

Phaédon (Φαίδων). Pupil of °Socrates, after whom the dialogue 'Phaedon' by °Plato, in which Socrates' last hours were depicted, was named.

Phaédra (Φαίδρα). Daughter of °Minos, wife of °Theseus; °Euripides; °Hippolytus.

Phaédrus (Φαῖδρος). **1.** Freedman of °Augustus (c. 50 AD), who wrote a Latin book of fables based on the fables of °Aesop and some of his own. **2.** Athenian citizen after whom °Plato called one of his dialogues.

Phaenárete (Φαιναρέτη). Mother of °Socrates; she was a midwife by profession.

Phaéstos (Φαιστός). Site of an important Minoan town in southern °Crete, destroyed c. 1400 BC, later partially reinhabited; °disk of Phaestos; °Minoan civilisation.

Phaéthon (Φαέθων). Son of the sun-god Helios, who asked leave of his father to guide the solar chariot for one day, for which he had no experience. The horses bolted with him and Zeus killed Phaethon with a thunderbolt (Ovid *Met.* 1, 750-752, 328). His sisters, the °Heliades, mourning for him, were turned into poplar trees, their tears dropping as amber.

phálanx (φάλαγξ). Infantry in a set order of battle, particularly the form used by °Epaminondas, when its left flank was made strongest, and attacked. The right flank was more vulnerable and was for defence. This method was adopted by °Philip II of Macedon.

Phálaris (Φάλαρις). °Tyrant of Agrigentum (565-549 BC), who supposedly roasted his enemies in a hollow brazen bull.

Phárnaces (Φαρνάκης). King of the Cimmerian Bosphorus, who was defeated by °Caesar at Zela in Pontus in 47 BC. The latter announced his victory in the Senate with the famous words, 'Veni, vidi, vici'.

pháros (φᾶρος). Linen cloak.

Pháros (Φάρος). Island in front of the port of °Alexandria on which stood the famous light-house built in about 280 BC by Sostratus. It was considered one of the °Seven Wonders of the World.

Pharsálus (Φάρσαλος). Town in Thessaly, where °Caesar defeated °Pompey in 48 BC.

Pheídias (Φειδίας). Athenian sculptor, chiefly in bronze, at the time of °Pericles. He is said to have made: 1. The statue of °Zeus (= 'chryselephántine') at °Olympia, overlaid with gold and ivory; 2. Athena °Parthenos in the Parthenon on the °Acropolis, also overlaid with gold and ivory, 9m high; °ill. 130; 3. Athena °Promachos, a bronze statue on the Acropolis; 4. Athena °Lemnia.

pherecratéüs. A metrical line: ⌣⌣ ⌣ ⌣ ⌣ ⌣ ⌣ _. e.g. ἁ πάνδυρτος ἀηδών.

130. Late and inferior copy of the statue of Athena Parthenos made by Pheidias for the Parthenon.

phiále (φιάλη). Greek libation bowl, shallow, and sometimes used for drinking. It had no handle, but instead a central boss for inserting the fingers while pouring.

Philémon and Baúcis (Φιλήμων: Βαυκίς). An elderly couple who received two poor travellers hospitably. The travellers proved to be °Zeus and °Hermes. Their unusual piety was rewarded by being united in death as in life (Ovid *Met.* 8, 611-724).

Philétas (Φιλητᾶς). Elegiac poet of Cos, from Alexandria, teacher of °Theocritus. Fragments of his work are extant.

Philip (Φίλιππος). 1. *Philippus II.* King of Macedon and father of °Alexander (359-336 BC), who restored the power of his country and succeeded in obtaining a °hegemony in northern Greece (°phalanx). He was murdered in 336. 2. *Philippus VI.* King of Macedon (221-179), started a war against Rome in 217, which ended in an advantageous peace in 205, but in 201 the Romans declared war again and defeated him in 197 at °Cynoscephalae. 3. *Philippus Arabs* (M. Iúlius Philippus Arabs). Roman emperor 244-249 AD. During his reign Rome commemorated its thousandth anniversary.

Philippi (Φίλιπποι). Town in Macedon where, in 42 BC, °Brutus and °Cassius were defeated by °Octavian and °Antony. St Paul preached there.

Philíppics, °Demosthenes; °Cicero.

Phílo (Φίλων). 1. of Byzantium. Probably an architect (early 3rd cent. BC), pupil of °Ctesibius. He wrote about the military use of mechanics. 2. of Alexandria (Phílo Judaéus), Jewish philosopher (c. 20 BC-50 AD), wrote works on religion and law based on Greek philosophy.

Philoctétes (Φιλοκτήτης). Son of Poeas, one of the °Argonauts who inherited the bow and arrows of °Heracles. On his way to Troy he got an obnoxious infection from a snake-bite, so that the Greeks were compelled to leave him behind on Lemnos. After ten years he was wanted again, as an oracle had foretold that °Troy could only be taken be the arrows of Heracles. He recovered and killed °Paris (tragedy of °Sophocles).

146

Philodémus (Φιλόδημος). Greek poet (4th cent. BC) and °Epicurean from Gadara in Syria. He had a school of philosophy in Naples. In the house of his patron °Piso at °Herculaneum, works of his have been found, *e.g.* 'On Music' and 'On Death'.

Philoméla (Φιλομήλα). Legendary daughter of the Athenian king Pandion, raped by Tereus, king of Thrace, husband of her sister Procne. Tereus cut her tongue out to prevent her telling, but she worked her story into an embroidery which she sent to her sister. The sisters then killed Itys, Tereus' son, and served the boy as a meal to him. Tereus pursued the women, but Zeus turned him into a hoopoe, Procne into a swallow and Philomela into a nightingale (Ovid *Met.* 6, 412-674).

Philopoémen (Φιλοποίμην). Chief commander of the °Achaean League (253-183 BC) after °Aratus. In 183 he was captured by the Messenians and condemned to death.

Philóstratus. °Flavius 4.

Phíneus (Φινεύς). **1.** Legendary king of Thrace. For some offence he was blinded by °Zeus. The °Harpies stole his food, and he nearly starved but was released by °Calaïs and °Zetes. **2.** Betrothed of °Andromeda. He was turned into a stone by °Perseus with the help of the head of °Medusa (Ovid *Met.* 5, 1-235).

Phíntias (Φιντίας). °Damon.

Phlégyas (Φλεγύας). Father of °Ixion and °Coronis.

Phócion (Φωκίων). Athenian general (402-318 BC), political opponent of °Demosthenes. He promoted peace with °Philip. His eloquence was inferior to that of Demosthenes, but his integrity commanded constant respect.

Phocýlides (Φωκυλίδης), of Miletus (6th cent. BC). He wrote a book of aphorisms. Many began with the words: 'This again is by Phocylides' (Καὶ τόδε Φωκυλίδεω).

Phoébe. A Titan, mother of Leto, grandmother of °Artemis. In later poetry her name is often substituted for that of the moon: °Artemis (Diana).

Phoénix (Φοῖνιξ). **1.** Mythical bird, which every 500 years burned itself and rose from the ashes with renewed youth. **2.** Counsellor and friend of °Achilles. **3.** of Colophon (c. 300 BC). Satirical poet.

Phórcys (Φόρκυς). °Gorgons.

phórminx (φόρμιγξ). In Homer possibly the same instrument as the °cithara (cf. Hom. *Od.* I, 153 κίθαριν and 155 φορμίζων). It was plucked with the hand and gave a clear sound. According to some, it is identical with the later °lyre.

Phórmio. °Terence.

phrátry (φρατρία). Subdivision of the °phyle.

Phríxus (Φρίξος). Legendary son of Athamas; his mother Nephele was rejected by Athamas, who then married °Ino, daughter of °Cadmus. Phrixus and his sister Helle were threatened with death by Ino and they fled on a ram with a °golden fleece to Colchis. Helle fell into the sea, henceforth called °Hellespont. Phrixus reached Colchis where he married the daughter of °Aeëtes, to whom he gave the golden fleece: °Jason.

Phrýnichus (Φρύνιχος). **1.** Athenian tragic poet (c. 500 BC). Only fragments of his work survive. **2.** Athenian comic writer at the time of °Aristophanes. **3.** Attic lexicographer (c. 180 AD). Besides a lexicon of 'Attic' words in thirty-seven books, he wrote a textbook for orators, of which fragments are extant.

Phthiótis (Φθιῶτις). °Achaea 3.

phýle (φυλή). In Attica all citizens were organized according to their parentage in four *phylae*. °Cleisthenes changed this into a grouping of ten *phylae* according to residence. The *phylae* were subdivided in °phratryes and they formed the basis of state administration; °boule.

Pictor. °Fabius Pictor.

Pícus. Roman sylvan deity. His disdain for the love of °Circe made her

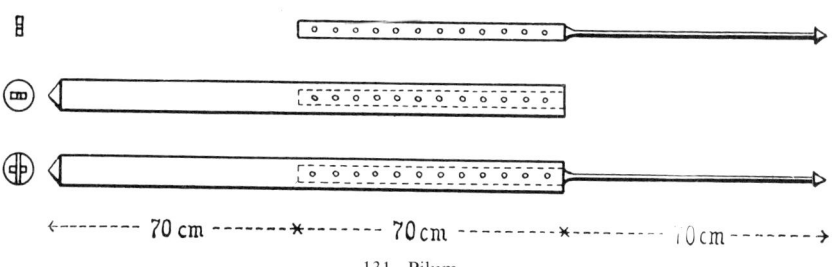

131. Pilum.

change him into a wood-pecker (Ovid *Met.* 14, 320-396).

pílum. Roman javelin with long iron point; °ill. 131.

Píndar (Πίνδαρος). Lyric poet from Thebes (c. 518-446 BC), whose forty-five odes have been arranged according to the festivals of the victors: °Olympian, °Pythian, °Nemean, °Isthmian Games. His language is an elaborate poetical creation (consisting of several dialects), at times of unparalleled sublimity.

Piraéus (Πειραιεύς). The main harbour of °Athens to which it was connected by the °Long Walls under the administration of °Pericles; finally destroyed in 56 BC.

Piríthoüs (Πειρίθοος). King of the °Lapiths, friend of °Theseus, with whom he tried to carry away °Persephone. They were caught and detained in the Underworld. Theseus was later set free by °Heracles..

Píso. 1. *C. Calpúrnius Píso*, was the envy of °Nero because of his wealth, noble birth and popularity. When his conspiracy was revealed, he killed himself as did °Seneca, °Lucan, and others (65 AD). 2. *Cn. Calpúrnius Píso*, appointed by °Tiberius as governor of Syria in 18 AD. He got into conflict with °Germanicus and was accused of poisoning him. In 20 AD he committed suicide. 3. *L. Calpúrnius Píso Caesonínus*. Consul in 58 BC, father-in-law of °Caesar. He sought the banishment of °Cicero, who had, very rightly, attacked him in his speeches.

Piso was the patron of °Philodemus. 4. *L. Calpúrnius Píso Frúgi*. Consul in 135 and 133 BC, adversary of C. °Gracchus. He wrote a contemporary history of Rome, fragments of which are extant.

Pistórium. Town in Etruria (Pistoia), north-west of Florence, where, in 62 BC, °Catiline was killed.

píthos (πίθος). A large Greek vessel for provisions, which varied in form from prehistoric times; °ill. 132.

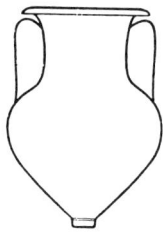

132. Pithos.

Píttacus (Πίττακος). One of the °Seven Sages, lawgiver in Mytilene (612-602 BC). His best remembered law doubled the penalty for all offences committed under the influence of drink.

Pityocámptes (Πιτυοκάμπτης). °Sinis.

Plánia. °Delia.

Plataéa (Πλαταιαί). Town in Boeotia, which sought close contact with Athens in order not to be overruled by Thebes. In 479 BC the town was destroyed by the Persians and in the same year the Greeks defeated the Persian army under °Mardonius in its vicinity.

Pláto (Πλάτων). The philosopher whose doctrines laid the foundation of all western philosophy and who has been recognized as such since the Renaissance; °ill. 133. He was the son of Ariston, lived in Athens (430-347 BC) where c. 408 he met °Socrates and turned from being a tragic poet into a philosopher. After Socrates' death (399) he travelled, and visited Megara and Syracuse, where he found °Dionysius an adversary, but his brother-in-law °Dio a friend. In c. 387 he returned to Athens and founded there his school, the °Academy. His principal works are:
1. The early dialogues:
a. Apology. °Socrates' defence against his judges.
b. Crito. Socrates' refusal to escape from prison, so as not to infringe the laws.
c. Ion. A rhapsodist in discussion with Socrates.
d. Hippias Minor. On deceit and injustice.
e. Laches. On courage.
f. Charmides. On moderation (σωφροσύνη).
g. Euthyphro. On reverence towards the gods.
h. Lysis. On the beauty of body and soul.
i. Protágoras. On whether virtue could be taught.
2. The dialogues after the journey to Sicily:
a. Gorgias. On education and its purpose.
b. Menexenus.
c. Meno. Defines memory and knowledge.
d. Euthydemus. Concerning dialectics and controversy.
e. Cratylus. On language.
f. Symposium. On the importance of love in the search for truth, the good and beauty.
g. Phaedo. Shortly before his death Socrates spoke about the immortality of the soul.
h. Politeia (Res Publica). On the ideal state which would be realised when

philosophers were kings, and kings philosophers.
i. Phaedrus. About the Platonic ideas.
3. Dialogues of the last period:
a. Parmenides.
b. Theaetetus. On knowledge.
c. Sophist.
d. Politicus. Sequel to the *Sophist*, on the statesman.
e. Philebus.
f. Timaeus. On creation.
g. Critias.
h. Nomoi (Leges). Laws.
Plato related the doctrine of °Heraclitus (of the continual change of all things) with the idea that virtue, the knowledge of what is good, was unchanging and everlasting, by accepting that there was a changing perceptible world which reflected another 'world' far away: the world of 'ideas'. The soul in a succession of re-incarnations, passing through many bodies, formed part of the world of ideas and still remembered

133. Plato.

it. By °Eros she was driven to search for the idea of the good. °Aristotle was the most famous of his pupils.

lex Plaútia Papíria. °Marsic War.

Plaútus, *T. Máccius Plaútus,* of Sarsina in Umbria. A writer of comedies. They were very free adaptations of Greek originals, lively and comic. The best-known plays are: *Menaechmi* (Comedy of Errors), *Bacchides* (The Sisters), *Aulularia* (The Miser), *Miles Gloriosus* (The Boastful Officer), *Captivi, Rudens* and *Amphitryo* (The Birth of Hercules).

plebisicítum. °concilium plebis.

plebs. Beside the old patrician families in Rome there were the 'plebs', the rest of the citizens. The original distinction later became a political one. Only the patricians could hold public office. As a result of many gradual changes, the distinction disappeared. In 445 BC °conubium between all citizens came into practice (*lex* °*Canuleía*). In 366 BC one °consul had to be a plebeian (°Sextius), and in 339 BC one of the °censors: (*lex* °*Publilia Philonis*). The army could no longer be recruited exclusively from the patricians, which made it necessary to grant more privileges to the plebs; °secessio plebis; °tribunus.

Pleíades. Seven daughters of °Atlas: Alcýone, Merope, Celaeno, Electra, Asterope, Taÿgete, °Maea. They were pursued by °Orion and out of pity Zeus changed them into pigeons. They were placed in the heavens as a constellation.

plemóchoë (πλημοχόη). A Greek perfume vase with high foot, turned-in rim, and knobbed lid.

pléonasm. Combination of two words, one of them repeating part of the meaning of the other: *e.g.* ʹἐκτόπιοι δόμων'; ʹpotius malunt'; ʹin ea opinione erat, ut putaret'. When two words express the same meaning, the phenomenon is called ʹtautólogy': *e.g.* ʹdeinde postea', ʹαὐτοῦ ταύτη'.

plinth. Literally a brick, or rectangular block of masonry, used particularly for the lower square member at the base of a column.

Plíny. 1. *C. Plínius Secúndus* the Elder (23-79 AD), procurator of °Germany, °Gaul and Africa, and author of an encyclopaedia 'Naturális História', a systematic compilation of an enormous amount of data on all sorts of subjects.

He died of asphyxiation during the eruption of Vesuvius (Plin. *Epist.* 6, 12; 6, 60); °Pompeii. **2.** *C. Plínius Secúndus* the Younger (61-c. 113). Nephew and adopted son of **1**, governor of Bithynia. We have a collection of his letters to his friends and to the emperor °Trajan, and a °panegyric on Trajan.

Plotínus (205-270 AD). Philosopher, founder of °Neo-Platonism. His pupil °Porphyrius classified his philosophical essays into six 'Enneades'.

plurális maiestátis. °Diocletian.

Plútarch (Πλούταρχος), of Chaeronea (c. 46-c. 120 AD). Philosopher and historian. He was a friend of °Trajan and °Hadrian, and travelled extensively, his work testifying to a familiarity with the entirety of Greek knowledge. He wrote *a.* several pairs of biographies, comparing a Greek with a Roman (twenty-three such pairs survive), and *b.* philosophical works, 'Moralia', about ethics, religion, literature, politics, physics, etc.

Plúto (Πλούτων). °Hades.

Pnyx (Πνύξ). Meeting-place of the people on a low hill to the west of the °Acropolis in Athens; there were seats arranged in a semi-circle round the speakers' platform (βῆμα).

Póllio. °Asínius.

Póllux (Πολυδεύκης). **1.** °Castor. **2.** *Iúlius Póllux,* of Naucratis in Egypt. Teacher of rhetoric in Athens after 178 AD. His 'Lexicon' in ten books is extant.

Polýbius (Πολύβιος), of Megalopolis (c. 201-120 BC). He was (166-150) a hostage in Rome, where he became a friend of °Scipio. He travelled to Spain in 151, and even further, so that he could have been an eye-witness of the destruction of Carthage and Numantia, and later Corinth. He wrote a history of the world in forty books. Books 1-5 are extant as are extensive excerpts of the rest.

Pólycarp (Πολύκαρπος). Bishop of Smyrna and martyr (c. 155 AD). We have his letters to the Philippians.

Polycleítus (Πολύκλειτος), of Sicyon (c. 450 BC). Sculptor, who later lived in Argos, made statues, especially of athletes. °Pliny (*Nat.* 34, 55) called his work an example for other sculptors. He was immensely popular during his lifetime and after. Numerous Roman copies survive: his famous 'Doryphorus', his 'Diadumenus' (now in Athens), the statue of °Hera for the temple at Argos (overlaid with gold and ivory?) and an °Amazon (New York); °ill. 106.

Polýcrates (Πολυκράτης). °Tyrant of Samos (c. 537-522 BC), known for his riches. He built many public works (aqueduct, harbour, temple, bazaar) and was a patron of scholars and poets (°Anacreon).

Polydeúces. °Pollux.

Polydórus (Πολύδωρος). Youngest son of °Priam and °Hecuba. When the °Trojan war was raging Priam sent him with much gold to Polymnestor of Thrace, who, filled with greed, killed him; °Euripides, 'Hecuba'.

Polygnótus (Πολύγνωτος), of Thasos (c. 450 BC). Painter in Athens. He is best remembered by his 'Fall of Troy' in the °Stoa Poikile.

Polyhýmnia (Πολύμνια). °Muses.

Polyneíces (Πολυνείκης). Twin-brother of °Eteocles.

Polypérchon (Πολυπέρχων). °Antipater.

Polyphémus (Πολύφημος). The °Cyclops who was blinded by °Odysseus (Hom. *Od.* IX); °Euripides, 'Cyclops'.

Polýxena (Πολυξένη). Daughter of Priam, sacrificed by °Pyrrhus on °Achilles' grave; °Euripides 'Hecuba'.

Pomóna. Italian goddess who especially presided over fruit-trees.

Pompéii. Town in Campania, partially destroyed by an earthquake (63 AD). In 79 it was buried under a 5 m deep layer of volcanic ash and lava, when Vesuvius erupted. Systematic excavations began in 1806. The remains uncovered, of both public and private buildings, together with their attendant furniture, wall-paintings, inscriptions and *graffiti*, etc, present a unique example of Roman life; °Herculaneum.

Pompey. **1.** *Cn. Pompeíus* (106-48 BC). Fought under °Sulla. From his soldiers he got the cognomen 'Mágnus' (= the Great). After Sulla's death he fought on the side of the °optimates. The *lex* °Gabina (67) made him commander-in-chief against the pirates, the *lex* °Manilia (66) against °Mithridates. When, in 61, the Senate would not sanction his measures in Asia, he concluded the first °triumvirate with °Caesar and °Crassus. He married Caesar's daughter Julia. After the death of Julia and Crassus the differences of opinion became greater and led to the Second Civil War in 49, when Pompey was the leader of the *optimates*. After his defeat near °Pharsalus he fled to Egypt, where he was murdered. **2.** *Cn. Pompeíus Mágnus.* Eldest son of **1**, killed (45) in the battle of °Munda. **3.** *Sext. Pompeíus.* Dominated the sea after Caesar's death and settled in Sicily. °Agrippa defeated him near Mylae in 36. **4.** *Pompeíus Trógus.* Historian who wrote a history of the world 'Históriae Philíppicae'. The work is only known through an abstract by °Justinus. **5.** °Festus.

Pompónius. **1.** *Sex. Pompónius.* Lawyer (2nd cent. AD). His 'History of Law' is included in the °Digesta. **2.** *Pompónius Méla* (1st cent. AD?). Wrote a handbook on geography, the oldest we have in Latin.

pons sublícius. Wooden bridge across the °Tiber, built by °Ancus Marcius; °plan p. 165.

póntifex. A member of the high college of priests in Rome. They led religious ceremonies and saw to the observance of the State cult in general. They supervised the °fasti. Originally there were three *pontifices*, after Caesar's time sixteen. The head of the college, °Pontifex Maximus, had his seat in the

°regia.

Póntius Herénnius. °Caudium.

Poppaéa Sabína. °Tacitus said of her: 'huic feminae cuncta alia fuere praeter honestum animum' (this woman had everything except decency). She was first married to a Roman °knight, then to °Otho and in 62 AD to °Nero. In 65 she died from the effects of a kick Nero gave her in a fit of passion.

Porchester (Portus Adurni). Roman fortress built at the head of Portsmouth harbour. The wall remains; °Britain.

Pórcius. °Cato.

Porphýrius (232-304 AD). °Neo-Platonist. He wrote many commentaries on °Plato and °Aristotle; °Plotinus.

Porsénna. King of the °Etruscans from Clusium. He besieged Rome, according to legend, in 507 BC; °Cloelia; °Horatius Cocles; °Mucius.

Pórticus Deórum Conséntium. A colonnade on the °Capitoline, where twelve gilded statues of the °Di Consentes stood.

Portland Vase. Vase of blue and white glass dating from the beginning of the Roman Empire; now in the British Museum; °ill. 134. Frequently copied by the English Wedgwood factory.

Pórtus Adúrni. °Porchester.

Poseídon (Ποσειδῶν). God of the sea and earthquakes. He was always represented as a mature man holding a trident. The °Isthmian games were held in his honour; °Amphitrite; °Kronos; °Neptune.

Posidónius, of Apamea in Syria (c. 135-51 BC). °Stoic philosopher, pupil of °Panaetius. He lived chiefly in Rhodes, where °Cicero and °Pompey visited him. Only fragments of his works are extant.

posséssor. °ager publicus.

Postúmius, *A. Postúmius Albínus* (c. 150 BC). °Annalist, who wrote a history of Rome in Greek.

potéstas. °imperium.

potsherd. °ostracism; °ostrakon.

praeféct Cápuam Cúmas, °praefecti iure dicundo.

praefecti iure dicundo. Officials charged

134. The Portland vase.

with the jurisdiction in the cities in Italy, which had no independent jurisdiction: the *praefecturae*. After 90 BC the office was no longer necessary because all towns in Italy gained civil rights.

praeféctus praetório. Commander of the 'cohortes praetoriae' (°praetorium), most powerful adviser to an emperor.

praerogatíva. °comitia centuriata.

praetextátae, *fábulae praetextátae*. Historical tragedies in which the chief characters were Roman heroes and accordingly wore the Roman °toga praetexta; °Accius; °Ennius; °Naevius; °Pacuvius.

praétor. Originally one of the two chief commanders of the Romans; after 367 BC, legal civil officers after the consuls in rank (six °lictors). The *praétor urbánus* dealt with lawsuits between citizens, the *praétor peregrínus* when one or both parties were not Roman citizens. Later there were more praetors who could become governors of provinces.

praetórium. Military headquarters in a fortress or military camp; later, especially of the imperial bodyguard. In 2 BC °Augustus organized them into nine cohorts ('cohortes praetoriae') under the command of two 'praefecti praetorio'; three were encamped in Rome. In 23 AD all nine cohorts came to Rome.

Pratínas (Πρατίνας). Poet in Athens (c. 500 BC). He wrote tragedies and °satyric plays.

Praxíteles (Πραξιτέλης). Athenian sculptor, 4th cent. BC, probably son of °Cephisodotus. His best-known works are: 1. *Aphrodite of Cnidus*, of which we have some Roman copies; 2. *Hermes with the Infant Dionysus*, of which the original is said to have been found at °Olympia in the °Heraion; others say it is a copy; °ill. 135. 3. *Apollo Sauróctonus* (= 'lizard-killer').

Príam (Πρίαμος). Legendary king of Troy, son of °Laomedon, married to °Hecuba. He was killed when °Troy fell; °Dardanidae, p. 60.

Priápus (Πρίαπος). Roman god of fertility, of doubtful origin, whose statue was often erected in gardens.

Priéne (Πριήνη). Town in Ionia, east of Samos, destroyed by the Persians but rebuilt in 350 BC. It has been completely excavated, revealing the 'chess-board' street system later copied by the Romans. The architect was probably Hippodamus.

prínceps senátus. °censor.

Prisciánus, of Caesaréa in Mauretania. Grammarian (c. 500 AD), who wrote an extensive Latin grammar, making full use of his predecessors' work, and including quotations from works now lost.

Próbus. 1. *M. Aurélius Próbus.* Emperor 276-282 AD. **2.** *Valérius Próbus.* Roman linguist, 1st century AD; °Appendix Probi.

Prócas. Father of °Numitor and

135. The head of Hermes by Praxiteles.

Amulius; °Dardanidae, p. 60.

proceleusmáticus. A metrical foot: ⌣ ⌣ ⌣ ⌣.

Próclus (Πρόκλος). °Neo-Platonist (410-485 AD), who wrote commentaries on °Plato, °Aristotle and °Euclid, and many other works, e.g. °hymns.

Prócne (Πρόκνη). °Philomela.

procónsul (originally *pro consule*). Governor of a senatorial province (°provincia). This office was reserved for ex-°consuls and ex-°praetors.

Procópius (Προκόπιος), of Caesaréa in Palestine (527-565 AD). Secretary to °Belisarius and historian of °Justinian.

Prócris (Πρόκρις). Daughter of °Erechtheus, married to °Cephalus.

Procrústes (Προκρούσιης). Legendary robber in Attica, who fitted his victims to his bed by stretching them out or mutilating them. °Theseus killed him in the same way.

Próculus. Jurist (1st cent. AD), after whom the school of °Labeo was called 'Proculiani'.

Pródicus (Πρόδικος). °Sophist, a contemporary of °Socrates. His special subject was °synonymics.

Proétus (Προῖτος). Legendary king of Tiryns; °Bellerophon.

Prómachos, *Athéna Prómachos.* Statue by °Pheidias on the °Acropolis; ills. 136, 137.

Prométheus (Προμηθεύς). Legendary son of °Iapetus, stole the fire, which °Zeus had hidden, for men and thus became their benefactor and founder of 'civilisation'. Zeus punished him by chaining him to a rock and sending an eagle to eat his liver; °Heracles released him (°Aeschylus, 'Prometheus').

pronáos (πρόναος). Space or hall in a Greek temple, enclosed by the portico and the projecting side walls; °Doric order.

Propértius, *Sex. Propértius* (c. 49-15 BC), born at Assisi. Elegiac poet famous for his poems addressed to °Cynthia. His poems expressed genuine feelings, sometimes deeply moving, sometimes humorous.

propraetor (originally *pro praetore*). °provincia.

Propylaéa (Προπύλαια). Roofed entrance to and one of the best-known buildings on the °Acropolis, built by °Mnesicles in 437-433 BC; ill. 138.

proscríptio (= proscription). In 82 BC, °Sulla drew up a list of his political opponents, who were declared outlaws and whose property was confiscated. In 43 BC, °Antony and °Octavian used the same method; °Cicero was one of the victims.

Prosérpina. °Persephone.

Protágoras (Πρωταγόρας), of Abdera (c. 485-416 BC). °Sophist in Athens. He denied all objective truth. Well-known are his sayings: 'I know nothing about the gods, whether they do or do not exist' and 'Man is the measure of all things'. °Plato attacked him in his 'Protagoras' and 'Theaetetus'.

Protesiläus (Πρωτεσίλαος). Supposedly, the first Greek to set foot on land near °Troy, where he died.

Protéus (Πρωτεύς). Sea-god, who had the power of sooth-saying, but to avoid answering questions took all manner of shapes (Hom. *Od.* IV, 364 ff.).

Protógenes (Πρωτόγενης). Painter in Rhodes, contemporary of °Alexander the Great. His works were not appreciated until °Apelles offered to buy them.

província (= province). A territory outside Italy under Roman dominion and administered by a governor from Rome. The first province was Sicily (241 BC). In the course of the 2nd and 1st centuries BC their number grew, till at the end of the republic there were thirty. They were governed by a °praetor, a °proconsul or °propraetor. In 27 BC °Augustus entrusted most of the provinces to the senate, but kept some under his own control, especially those which were important for the defence of the empire. The senatorial provinces were governed by proconsuls, who also had that title when they had not been consuls. The imperial provinces were governed by a °*legátus Augústi pro praetóre,* who could be either an ex-consul or an ex-praetor.

provocátio. The right to appeal to the people ('ad populum'). This was a common right of the Roman citizen against a decision of any official except a °dictator (300 BC). The *provocatio* was introduced in 509 BC (*lex °Valéria*).

Prudéntius, *Aurélius Prudéntius Clémens,* born 348 AD. The greatest Christian Latin poet. In 405 he published his complete poetical works: 1. *Kathemérinon libri IV.* Songs for the canonical hours, and hymns. 2. *Peristéphanon.* On martyrs. 3. *Apotheósis.* Epic poem on the divine origin of Christ. 4. *Hamartigénia.* On the origin of sin. 5. *Psychomáchia.* An allegory on the struggle of good and evil for the human soul. 6. *Cóntra °Sýmmachum.*

Prúsias (Προυσίας). 1. *Prusias I.* King of Bithynia (c. 237-192 BC), to whom °Hannibal fled. 2. *Prúsias II,* his son

136. Athena °Promachos.

137. *(left)*. Athena Promachos. Reverse of a coin of °Ptolemaeus I Soter. In the field, left: ΑΛΕΞΑΝΔΡΟΥ (as on the coins of °Alexander the Great), on the right: a Corinthian helmet, an eagle on a thunderbolt (the mark of the Ptolemies) and the moneyer's(?) mark Δ Φ.

138. Reconstruction of the °Acropolis at Athens (°plan, p. 4), showing the Propylaea.

(237-192), was prepared to extradite Hannibal.

Prýtanes (Πρυτάνεις). °Boule.

'Pseudo-Longínus'. An obscure author (c. 25 AD) of a work 'De Sublimitate' (περὶ ὕψους) on literary criticism.

psýkter (ψυκτήρ). A Greek vessel with a high foot, used for cooling wine; ill. 139.

Ptólemy. **1.** *Claúdius Ptolemaéus* c. 100-178 AD). Mathematician, geographer and astronomer. Part of his work is extant (Almagest). He had great influence on scientific thought until the time of Copernicus. **2.** *Ptolemaéus I Sóter* (c. 327-283 BC). Son of Lagos, general of °Alexander the Great,

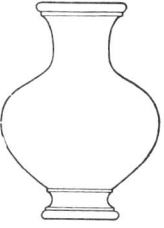

139. Psykter.

after whose death he became °satrap of Egypt. He made °Alexandria the cultural centre of the Hellenistic world. After him twelve more Ptolemaéi ruled over Egypt, until the Roman conquest.

lex Publília Philónis. 339 BC, of the dictator Q. Pubílius Phílo (°secessio plebis). It consisted of three parts: 1. 'ut plebiscita omnes cives tenerent.' 2. 'ut legum quae comitiis centuriatis ferrentur ante initum suffragium patres auctores fierent.' 3. 'ut alter utique censor ex plebe crearetur.'

Publílius Sýrus. Mimic poet, contemporary of °Cicero. Only a collection of his aphorisms is extant; °mime.

púgio. The Roman dagger, a pointed weapon, 20-25 cm long and worn on the left side after the *gladius Ibericus* came into use.

Púnic Wars. Three wars waged between Rome and Carthage: 1. (264-241 BC) ended in favour of the Romans with the battle off the °Aegatic Isles. 2. (218-201) started with the capture of °Saguntum by °Hannibal and ended in the battle of °Zama in 202. 3. (149-146) started by the Roman landowners because of the economic power of Carthage and ended with the destruction of Carthage.

purple. The dye which the Romans valued so highly. It was first made in Phoenicia from several species of shellfish: purpura, buccinum and murex. Later vegetable juices were used instead. The colour was not red, but varied from red to dark violet. Reddish violet was the most usual.

Pýdna (Πύδνα). Port in Macedon, where °Aemílius Paulus defeated °Perseus in 168 BC.

Pygmálion (Πυγμαλίων). King of Cyprus, who fell in love with the statue of a girl he had made. °Aphrodite gave it life (Ovid *Met.* 10, 242-297).

Pýlades (Πυλάδης). The faithful friend of °Orestes.

Pýlos (Πύλος). **1.** Town in Elis on the river Peneüs. **2.** Town in Messenia, north of the island of Sphacteria. Excavations, begun in 1939 (°linear B), revealed a palace which may have been that of Nestor; they still continue.

pýramid. Egyptian structure of stone with square base and sloping sides; °Giza; °step-pyramid; °ill. 140.

Pýramus. A young man in Babylon who loved a girl who lived next door, Thisbe. They promised to meet outside the town, but owing to misunderstandings they were both killed (Ovid *Met.* 4, 55-166).

Pýrrha (Πύρρα). °Deucalion.

Pýrrhic victory. °Asculum; °Pyrrhus.

pyrrhíchius. A metrical foot: ◡ ◡.

Pýrrho (Πύρρων), of Elis. The first recognised °Sceptic philosopher, who died c. 270 BC.

Pýrrhus (Πύρρος). **1.** °Neoptolemus. **2.** King of Epirus (319-272 BC), who claimed descent from °Alexander the Great. He assisted Tarentum against the Romans and, driven by ambition, he crossed to Italy and defeated the Romans at °Heraclea and °Asculum (280, 279) at the cost of great losses to his army. In 275 he was defeated at Beneventum and returned to Greece; °Fabrícius.

Pythágoras (Πυθαγόρας). Greek philosopher (6th cent. BC), who founded a religious and philosophic society in Croton, with very strict rules. He had absolute authority among his pupils and the words 'αὐτὸς ἔφα' (= he said so himself) settled any argument. His doctrine sought the origin of all things in numbers. He studied mathematics (Pythagorean theorem), music (the intervals of the musical scale) and astronomy. He also taught °metempsychosis, being influenced by the °Orphic mysteries, and pretended that he himself was a reincarnation of °Euphorbus.

Pýthia (Πυθία). The priestess of the oracle of Apollo at °Delphi, who, according to legend, sat over a ravine from which sulphurous vapour rose; °tripod.

Pýthian Games. Held at °Delphi; °Pindar; °Isthmian, °Nemean, °Olympian Games.

pýxis (πυξίς). A cylindrical box for toilet articles, with a knobbed lid; °ill. 141.

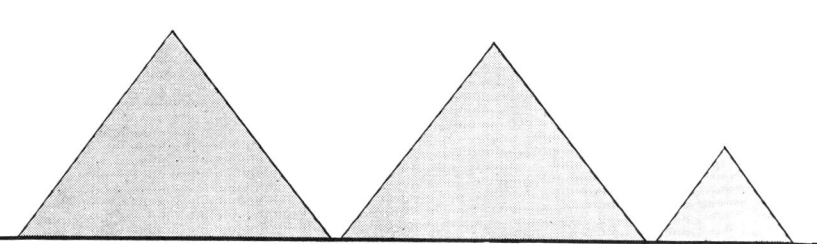

140. The three great pyramids, the °Parthenon, the °Colosseum.

Q

141. Pyxis.

Quadrigárius. °Annalists.
quadrívium. °Seven liberal arts.
quaéstor. Roman official. In early times
the quaestors helped the king or
°consuls judically. After 447 BC they
were independent, elected in the
°comitia tributa. The two *quaestóres
urbáni* were responsible for the State
Archives and the treasury (°aerarium)
and it was their duty to trace capital
crimes. The two *quaestores consulares*
(after 421) were attached to the consuls
and were in charge of the military
chest. In 267 BC the *quaestores clássici*
(or *Italici*), were appointed to control
the contributions of the allied states.
The number of quaestors rose and
after the time of °Sulla there were thirty.
These were attached to generals in the
field and to provincial governors.
quartárius. °Weights and measures 2c.,

the Eiffel Tower and the tower of Utrecht on the same scale.

quattuórviri viárum curandárum (or **víis in úrbe purgándis**). Officials in charge of cleaning the streets of Rome, under the supervision of the °aediles.

Quínctius. °Cincinnatus.

Quintílian, *M. Fábius Quintiliánus.* Professor of rhetoric, of Spanish origin, in Rome (c. 35-100 AD). He wrote a text-book '*Institútio Oratória*', in which he described the education of an orator and gave a short survey of Greek and Roman literature. It was written in a lucid and vigorous style.

Quíntus Smyrnaéus (4th cent. AD). He attempted to continue the *Iliad* of °Homer in an epic poem, showing a thorough knowledge of his subject.

Quirínal. One of the °Seven Hills on which Rome was built.

Quirínus. An ancient Roman war-god, worshipped on the °Quirinal. Later he was identified with the deified °Romulus. The cult of Quirinus was led by the °flámen Quirinális.

R

Ra (or Re). The Egyptian sun-god; °Anubis.

Rámses (Ramesses etc). Name of eleven Egyptian pharaohs of the 19th and 20th dynasties (c. 1320-1100 BC). *Ramses II* (1298-1232 BC) built many temples; °Abu Simbel.

Ras Shámra (Ugarit). Phoenician port, famous for the excavations which give evidence for the extent of prehistoric trade. Mycenaean pottery finds indicate that there was close commercial contact with the Aegean; °Helladic civilisation.

reading. In antiquity people used to read aloud. Augustine relates as a peculiarity how the church-father Ambrosius could not be heard when he was reading and °Acontius must have been sure that Cydippe would in fact read the words on the apple aloud.

reaping machine. A relief (°ills. 142, 143) found in south-east Belgium (near Buzenol) in 1958 clearly shows the type of reaping machine mentioned by °Pliny. With the help of a relief found earlier, we can form an idea of what it looked like and how it was worked.

The bin was driven into the corn-field and kept in position by the man on the right. The ears were cut between the pointed ends and fell into the bin.

Red-figured pottery. °Black-figured pottery.

régia. The traditional home of King

142. A relief showing a reaping machine found at Buzenol.

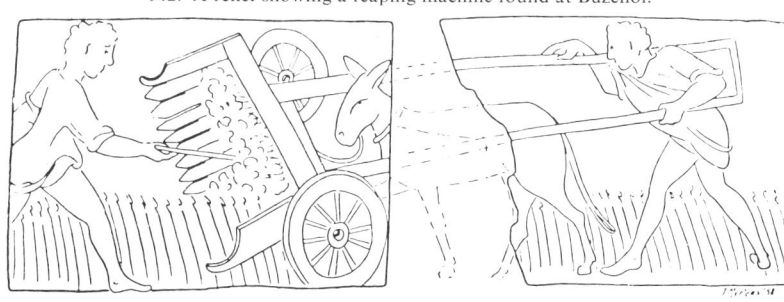

143. The two reliefs assembled.

°Numa Pompilius, later the official residence of the °Pontifex Maximus. The °fasti were affixed to the walls;

°plan p. 80.

Régulus, *M. Atilius Régulus*. He defeated the Carthaginians in 256 BC near

160

Ecnomus (Southern Sicily) and was taken prisoner by them in 255 (°Xanthippus). He was set free on parole to negotiate peace terms at Rome. Regulus, however, advised the Romans not to make peace and returned to Carthage, where according to tradition he was tortured and put to death.

Reiziánum. A metrical foot: ⌣ ‒́ ⌣ ⌣ ‒́ ⌣̄, or ⌣ ‒́ ⌣ ‒́ ‒, named after F. W. Reiz (1733-1790).

Rémus. °Romulus; °Dardanidae, p. 60.

rescrípta. °constitutiones.

restitútor impérii. °Aurelian.

ópus reticulátum. Form of construction, consisting of lozenge-shaped bricks set diagonally, resembling a net in effect; °ill. 96.

Rhadamánthus (‘Ραδάμανθus). Legendary son of °Zeus and °Europa, brother of °Minos. He was a just king of Crete and after his death became one of the three judges in the Underworld; °Aeacus.

Rhéa. Daughter of °Uranus (Heaven) and °Gaea (Earth), wife of °Kronos. She was especially worshipped in Crete (where °Zeus was born) by the °Curetes. At Rome her cult (as ‘Magna Mater’), was introduced as a result of a consultation of the °Sibylline books in 204 BC. Her statue, a black meteoric stone, was shipped from Pessinus (in Phrygia) to Rome and a temple was built on the °Palatine hill.

Rhéa Sílvia. Mother of °Romulus and Remus; Dardanidae, p. 60.

Rhiánus. (‘Ριανός). A poet from Crete (c. 225 BC), of whose works only epigrams survive.

Rhodes (‘Ρόδος). Island in the Mediterranean, south of Asia-Minor, with extensive trade-relations, for which reason it always tried to remain neutral. °Alexander the Great conquered Rhodes, but in 305-304 it beat off the attack of °Demetrius Poliorcetes. To commemorate this victory the °‘Colossus of Rhodes’ was erected (290), one of the °Seven Wonders of the World. It was a bronze statue of °Helios, 30 m high, by the sculptor Chares, a pupil of °Lysippus. It fell during an earthquake in 222. In later times Rhodes became a centre of higher education: °Panaetius, °Posidonius and the rhetor Molon had many pupils in Rhodes: e.g. Ti. °Gracchus, °Cicero, °Pompey, °Caesar, °Tiberius.

rhýton (ρυτόν). Drinking-horn, often formed in the shape of the head of an animal; °ill. 144.

Richborough (Rutupiae). Roman port separating the island of Thanet from the rest of Kent; °Britain.

Roman Emperors

27 BC-14 AD	Augustus
14-37	Tiberius
37-41	Gaius (Calígula)
41-54	Claudius
54-68	Nero
68-69	Galba
69	Otho
69	Vitellius
69-79	Vespasian
79-81	Titus
81-96	Domitian
96-98	Nerva
98-117	Trajan
117-138	Hadrian
138-161	Antoninus Pius
161-180	Marcus Aurelius
161-169	Lucius Verus
180-192	Commodus
193	Pertinax (1 Jan-28 March)
193	Didius Iulianus
193-211	Septimius Severus
211-217	Caracalla
211-212	Geta
217-218	Macrinus
218-222	Heliogabalus
222-235	Alexander Severus
235-238	Maximinus Thrax
238	Gordianus I
238	Gordianus II
238	Balbinus
238	Papienus Maximus
238-244	Gordianus III
244-249	Philippus Arabs
249-251	Decius
251-253	Trebonianus
253	Aemilianus
253-260	Valerianus

Roman emperors

144. A rhyton (*c.* 425 BC).

253-268	Gallienus	
268-270	Claudius II Gothicus	
270-275	Aurelian	
275-276	Tacitus	
276-282	Probus	
282-283	Carus	
283-285	Carinus	
283-284	Numerianus	
284-305	Diocletian	
286-305	Maximianus Herculius	
305-306	Constantius I Chlorus	
305-311	Galerius (east)	
306-308	Maximianus Herculius	
306-312	Maxentius	
306-337	Constantinus Magnus	
308-324	Licinius (east)	
311-313	Maximinus Daia (east)	
309-310	Maximianus Herculius	
337-340	Constantínus II	
337-350	Constans (west)	
337-361	Constantius II	
361-363	Iulianus Apostata	
363-364	Iovianus	
364-375	Valentinianus I (west)	

364-378	Valens (east)	
375-392	Valentinianus II	
375-383	Gratianus	
379-395	Theodosius I	

west

395-423	Honorius	
425-455	Valentinianus III	
455-456	Avitus	
457-461	Maiorianus	
461-465	Libius Severus III	
467-472	Anthemius	
472	Olybrius	
475-476	Romulus Augustulus	

east

395-408	Arcadius	
408-450	Theodosius II	
450-457	Marcianus	
457-474	Leo I	
474	Leo II	
474-491	Zeno	
491-518	Anastasius I	
518-527	Justinus I	
527-565	Justinian I	

Rome. It is generally accepted that Rome was founded c. 754 BC, a date supported by excavations. The first settlement (by the Latins) was on the °Palatine; later the Sabines settled on the °Quirinal hill. Between c. 700 and 500 BC the °Etruscans ruled there, and the settlements were united, forming a township which then extended as far as the °Capitol and the place of the later °forum. In 378 BC it was encircled by a wall, the so-called wall of °Servius. Under °Augustus the building material, mud-bricks, was replaced by marble, which greatly changed the aspect of the city. Other important changes were brought about by the great fires in the reign of Nero and in 80 AD. In 330, Constantinople became the major capital and the decline of Rome set in; plans pp. 80, 81, 165, 166.

Rómulus. Son of °Mars and °Rhea Silvia, legendary founder and first king of Rome. He killed his brother Remus after a quarrel, and died after twenty-four years of rule. °Quirinus; °Dardanidae, p. 60.

Rómulus Augústulus. The last emperor of the western Roman Empire. In 476 AD he was dethroned by °Odoacer.

Rosétta (Rashid). Village in Egypt in the Nile delta where, in 1799, a French engineer officer found a basalt slab, on which are three inscriptions in °hieroglyphics, demotic and Greek. It provided Champollion with the key to the decipherment of the hieroglyphics.

róstra. In 338 BC the consul C. Maenius seized the town of Antium. The speaker's platform in the °forum at Rome was adorned with the beaks (°rostra) of enemy ships captured in this battle (° plan, p. 81) and thereafter was given that name.

róstrum (= beak). Bronze projection below the prow of war-galleys, at the water-line, used to ram the enemy's ships.

Roxána ('Ρωξάνη). Wife of °Alexander the Great; °Cassander.

Rubéllius, *C. Rubéllius Blándus.* Married °Julia, the grand-daughter of °Tiberius in 33 AD. Their son was Rubéllius Plautus; °Julio-Claudian dynasty, p. 101.

Rúbicon. Unidentified stream north of Ariminum. Caesar crossed it on 10th January, 49 BC, thus illegally leaving his province and attacking °Pompey. The present Rubicon only got its name in 1902.

Rústicus. 1. (*Q.?*) *Iúnius Rústicus Arulénus* (*L. Arulénus Rústicus*). °Tribune of the °plebs in 66 AD, °Stoic philosopher. He tried to help Paetus Thrasea by °'intercessio'. **2.** *Q. Iúnius Rústicus.* °Stoic philosopher, teacher of °Marcus Aurelius. (These two may represent the same man.)

Rutílius Namatiánus. °*Praefectus urbis* in 414 AD. He wrote an elaborate itinerary from Rome to Gaul in graceful elegiacs.

Rutúpiae. °Richborough; °Britain.

(overleaf) Roman coins (13-25) all original size: 13. bronze °as, about 160 BC; *obv.* head of Janus. – 14. and 15. °denarius of Caesar, 56-49 BC; *obv.* elephant trampling a serpent; this commemorates Caesar's victory over °Ariovistus, 58 BC; *rev.* sacrificial implements, from left to right: °simpulum, °aspergillum, securis, °apex, because Caesar was °*pontifex maximus* after 63 BC. – 16. and 17. °victoriatus, 240-197 BC; *obv.* laureate head of Jupiter; *rev.* the goddess Victoria crowns a °trophy, helmet, lance and cuirass. – 18. and 19. °aureus; *obv.* head of Augustus; *rev.* heifer ('vitula'), an allusion to the derivation of the word Italia from *vitula*, *vitulari* 'to celebrate a victory', the appointment of °Agrippa in 14 BC as king of the Cimmerian Bosphorus, where Io once passed when she had been transformed into a cow. – 20. bronze °sestertius of °Gaius; *obv.* AGRIPPINA M(arci) F(ilia) MAT(er) CAESARIS AVGVSTI and a portrait of Agrippina. Her hair is parted down in the middle and combed out in waves with a cluster of ringlets over either ear and a heavy chignon behind. – 21. bronze °dupondius of °Trajan, 106-111; *obv.* IMP(eratori) CAES(ari) NERVAE TRAIANO AVG(usto) GER(manico) DAC(ico) P(ontifico) M(aximo) TR(ibuno) P(lebis) COS (= *consuli*) V (= *quintum*) P(atri) P(atriae) and radiate head of Trajan. – 22. °antoninianus of Gallienus; *obv.* radiate head of the emperor and GALLIENVS AVG(ustus). – 23. bronze °follis of

14

13

16

15

17

18

20

21

19

24

22

23

25

°Diocletian; *obv.* laureate head and IMP(erator) C(aius) DIOCLETIANVS P(ius) F(elix). –
24. and 25. golden °solidus; *obv.* laureate head of °Constantine the Great and CONSTANTINVS
P(ius) F(elix) AVG(ustus); *rev.* Mars in flowing robe, holding spear and °trophy, with two seated
captives and VIRTVS EXERCITVS GALL(ici) TR (= minted at Treves).

164

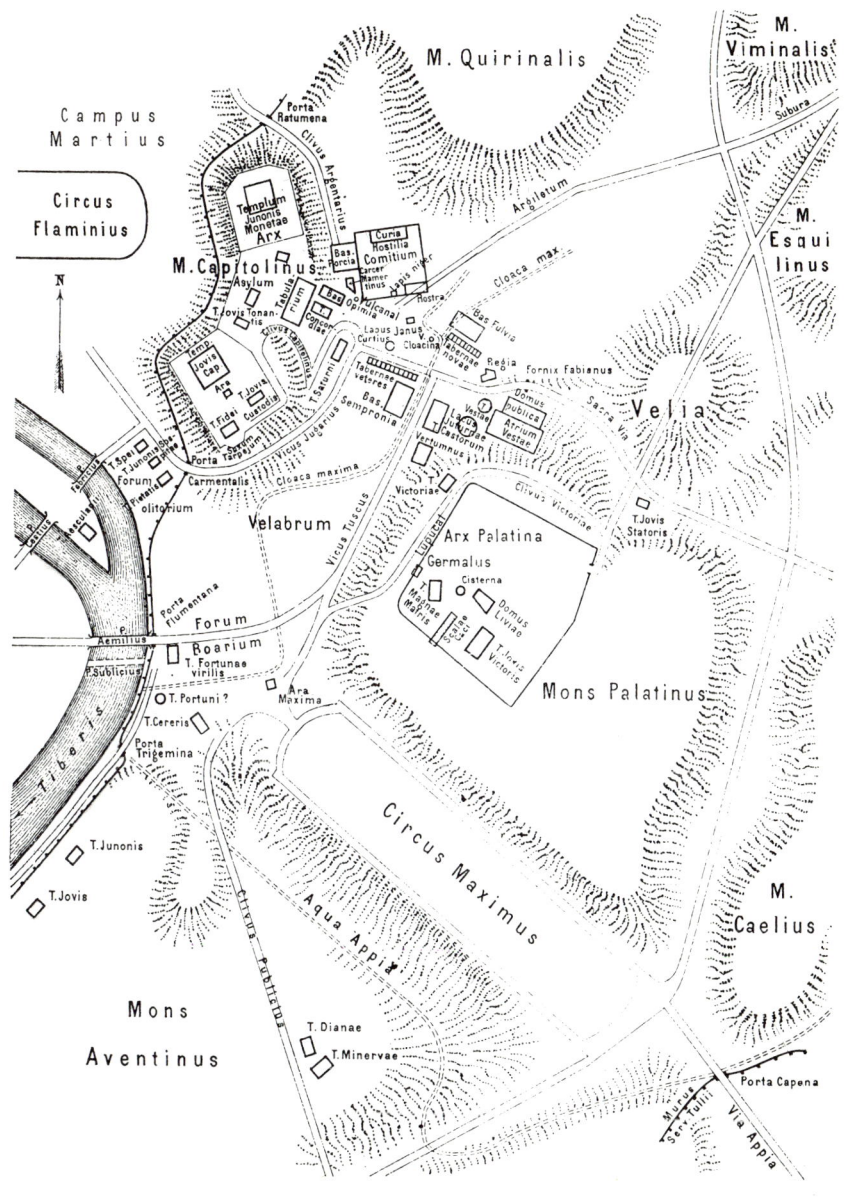

The centre of Rome.

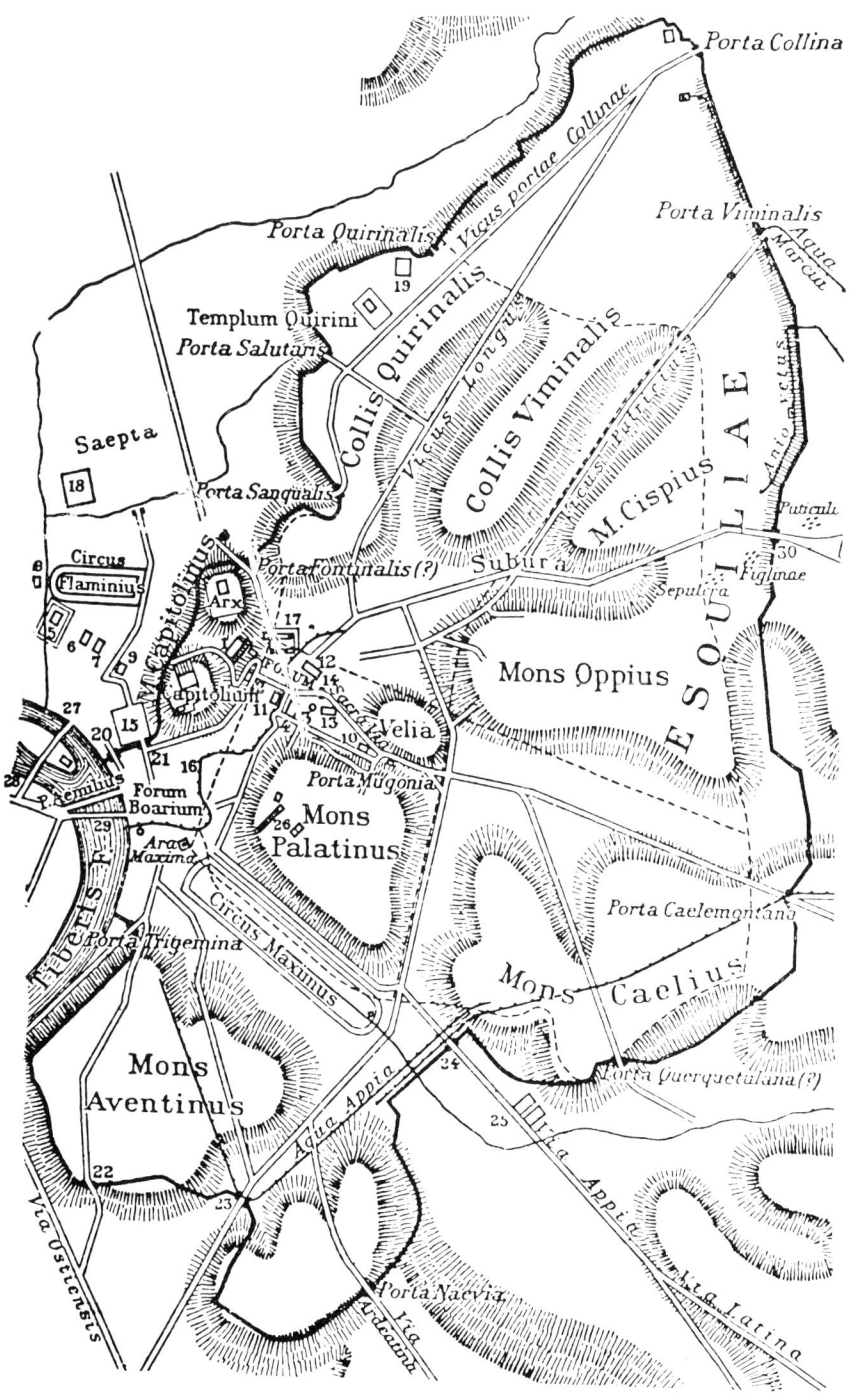

Rome in Republican times.

S

Sabína. 1. °Poppaea. **2.** *Vibia Sabína.*
Wife of the emperor °Hadrian.
Sabínus. 1. *Flávius Sábinus.* Father of
the emperor °Vespasian. **2.** *Flávius
Sabínus.* Brother of °Vespasian. He was
°praefectus urbis (56-69 AD) and was
put to death by °Vitellius (20th December, 69). **3.** *T. Flávius Sabínus.* Consul
(69 and 72 AD). He was probably no
relation of Vespasian.
via Sácra. The oldest street in Rome,
running across the °forum; plan pp. 80,
81.
Sagúntum. Town on the east coast of
Spain, taken and destroyed by
°Hannibal in 219. This led to the 2nd
Punic War.
Sálamis (Σαλαμίς). **1.** Island on the
coast of Attica, near which the Greeks
defeated the Persian fleet of °Xerxes in
480 BC. **2.** Town on the east coast of
Cyprus, where °Cimon defeated the
Persians in 449 BC.
via Salária. A road which ran from Rome
through the country of the Sabines to
Reate.
St. Albans. °Verulamium; °Britain.
Sálii. A college of priests in Rome, to
conduct the worship of °Mars and
°Quirinus. There were twenty-four
priests. On festival days they went in
procession through the city carrying
the °ancilia with them and singing a
song ('carmen Saliare'), the text of
which was not wholly intelligible from
republican times onwards.
Sállust. 1. *C. Sallústius Críspus* (86-
34 BC). In 50 he was expelled from the
senate, being a partisan of the democrats. In the °Civil War he fought on
the side of °Caesar and was made
governor of Numidia in 46 where he
became rich. He laid out beautiful
gardens in Rome, the famous 'Horti
Sallustiáni'. After Caesar's death he
turned to the writing of books on

history: 1. *Coniurátio* °*Catilínae.*
2. *Bellum Iugurthínum.* 3. *Históriae,* describing the events of 78-67 AD, of which
only fragments are extant. The contents of his works are biased by his
political ideas. He developed a very
personal style: dignified, to the point,
but somewhat archaic. He had a great
influence on °Tacitus. **2.** °Crispus.
Sálmacis (Σαλμακίς). A spring in Caria.
°Hermaphroditus.
Salmóneus (Σαλμωνεύς). King of Elis,
brother of °Sisyphus. Pretending to be
°Zeus, he imitated thunder and lightning.
Zeus smote him with a real thunderbolt
and threw him into Tartarus.
sálpinx (σάλπιγξ). A trumpet, 1-1.20 m
long, used in the army; °ill. 145 (a).
Salviánus (c. 400-470 AD). He wrote
'De gubernatióne Dei', in which he
wanted to prove to the Romans that
the Goths were sent by God to punish
the world and establish a new one.
Sálvius. °Julian.
Sammónicus. °Serenus.
Sámnites. Tribe in Samnium, conquered
by the Romans in three wars (343-340
BC; 326-304; 298-290). In the °Civil
War they revolted again and were
defeated (in 82) by °Sulla.
Sámothrace (Σαμοθράκη). Island off the
coast of Thrace, where the famous
statue of °Nike was found; this is now
in the Louvre.
sandálium. °solea.
Sápphic verse: ‿ ‿ ¯ ‿ ¯ ‿ ‿ ¯ ‿ ¯ ‿;
The Sapphic stanza consists of three of
these followed by an °Adonic verse.
Sáppho (Σαπφώ). Lyric poetess in
°Lesbos (c. 600 BC), who may be ranked
among the greatest. Two complete
poems and some fragments are extant.
Saqqára (Sakkara). Village in Egypt,
west of Memphis, where the °Step-
Pyramid of °Djoser is situated.
sarcóphagus (σαρκοφάγος). A stone

145A. Salpinx.

145B *(below)*. Roman sarcophagus, *c*. 260 AD, showing relief decoration.

coffin, in Roman times often embellished with sculptures or bearing inscriptions. The name 'flesh-eater' perhaps comes from the kind of stone, supposed to have the property of consuming the flesh of corpses, being so porous as to admit 'flesh flies'; °ill. 145(b).

Sardanápalus (Σαρδανάπαλος). Legendary last king of °Assyria, who met his death in debauchery at the fall of °Nineveh (612 BC). In reality the last king was called Sin-shar-ishkun, whose character was unlike that of Sardanapalus. Perhaps °Ashurbanipal is meant (668-626).

Sárgon. 1. c. 2350-2300 BC. Founder of the dynasty of °Akkad. **2.** *Sargon I* of °Assyria (c. 752-739 BC). **3.** *Sargon II* of Assyria (721-705), founder of the last Assyrian dynasty.

Sarpédon (Σαρπηδών). Legendary son of °Zeus and °Europa, commander of the Lycians, who fought in the Trojan

War. He was killed by °Patroclus.

Sassánidae. Ruling dynasty of the neo-Persian Empire founded by Ardahir I or Artaxerxes (c. 229 AD) after the expulsion of the Parthians (°Arsacidae). The most important kings were Shapur I (241-273), who took °Valerian prisoner at Edessa and marched into Asia-Minor (a trilingual inscription about this expedition was found at Persepolis) and Shapur II (310-379). The empire lasted until the reign of Vesdejird III (632), but was then over-run by the Arabs (637-651 AD).

sátire (*satura*). A poem in which contemporary vices or follies are held up to ridicule. The genre was first used by °Ennius, then by °Lucilius, who made it more biting and sarcastic. Lucilius' influence made this kind of satire popular (°Horace, °Juvenal, °Persius). °Varro introduced the *Saturae Menippeae* (°Menippus) in Rome, which consisted of a mixture of prose and poetry (°Seneca, 'Apocolocyntósis'; °Petronius).

sátrap (σατράπης). Governor of a province in the Persian empire and in that of °Alexander the Great.

Sáturae Meníppeae. °satire.

Sáturn (= Satúrnus). Ancient Italian deity of agriculture, later identified with °Kronos. The 'Saturnalia' were held in December in his honour. Slaves were allowed liberties with their masters, presents were exchanged and Rome was full of festivity. In the temple of Saturn at the foot of the °Capitol was the °aerarium; plan, p. 80.

Saturnália. °Saturn.

Satúrnian metre. A metrical line in Roman poetry:

⏑ ‒́ ⏑ ‒́ ⏑ ‒́ ‒ ‒́ ⏑ ‒́ ⏑ ‒́ ‒ ("malúm dabúnt Metélli Naévió poétae"); °Livy, I.

satýrical play. In the Athenian theatre after the three tragedies there followed a satyrical play, in which the chorus were disguised as °satyrs, and the play presented parts of ancient legend, in grotesque fashion. The only complete satyrical play extant is the 'Cyclops' of °Euripides, and we have about 400 verses of °Sophocles' 'Ichneutai'.

sátyrs (σάτυρος). Companions of °Dionysus, bestial in their desires and behaviour with horned heads, horse-tails and goats' legs.

Scaévola. °Mucius Scaevola.

scápus. °shaft.

scárab (*scarabaéus*). **1.** The scarab beetle (dung beetle) 'Ateuchus sacer', held sacred by the ancient Egyptians. **2.** A gem stone cut in the form of a beetle, having on the flat under-side a design in *intaglio*.

Sceptics. Philosophers who doubted the trustworthiness of 'knowledge' ; °Pyrrho; °Arcesilaus.

Schéria (Σχερία). Island of the °Phaeacians; °Nausicaä.

Schliemann, H. Schliemann (1822-1890). Started (1870) digging at Hissarlik to find the site of ancient Troy. At °Mycenae and °Tiryns he found remains of palaces and graves belonging to the °Helladic civilisation.

Scípio. 1. *P. Cornélius Scípio.* Consul 218 BC., defeated by °Hannibal near the river Ticinus and killed in 211 in Spain; father of Scipio 2. **2.** *P. Cornélius Scípio Africánus maior*, became commander-in-chief in Spain when his father was killed. He landed in Africa in 204 and defeated Hannibal at °Zama in 202, was awarded a triumph and the °cognomen Africánus. **3.** *P. Cornélius Scípio Aemiliánus Africánus minor.* Son of L. °Aemílius Paulus, adopted by the oldest son of Scipio 2. He fought at °Pydna and in 147 became consul. In 146, he destroyed Carthage (end of the 3rd °Punic War) and in 133, he conquered Numantia. He gathered around him poets and scholars: °Polybius, °Panaetius, °Laelius, °Lucilius, °Terence.

Scíron (Σκίρων). A brigand near Megara in Attica, who threw his victims into the sea; °Theseus.

Scópas (Σκόπας). Sculptor of Paros, 4th cent. BC. Surviving works are of the temple of °Athena at Tegea and reliefs in the °Mausoleum of Halicarnassus.

Scribónia. Married in 40 BC to the (later) emperor°Augustus. Shortly after giving birth to Julia in 39 she was rejected by him;°Julio-Claudian dynasty p. 101.
script. °alphabet;°hieroglyphics.
scriptúra. Grazing-fee;°ager publicus.
scrípulum. °Weights and measures 2d.
scútum. **1.** Oval Roman shield with a central boss;°ill. 146. **2.** A second form provided better protection for the body;°ill. 147.

146. A Roman soldier, holding his 'scutum'.

147. A Roman infantryman (c. 25 BC), showing the larger form of 'scutum'.

Scýlla (Σκύλλα). **1.** Daughter of°Nisus. **2.** Sea-nymph, who was changed into a monster by °Circe, later becoming a dangerous rock (in the Straits of Messina?), opposite just as dangerous a whirlpool, °Charybdis; °Odysseus.
secéssio plébis. In 494 BC the dissatisfied plebs withdrew to the °Mons Sacer beyond the Anio on the via Nomentana. °Menenius persuaded them to return, while by way of concession the offices of °tribunus plebis and °aedilis plebis were created and the °concilium plebis instituted. In 449 BC the second *secessio* resulted in a new law, the *léges Valériae Horátiae* of which the most important provisions were: *a.* that no magistrate should be elected without °provocatio; *b.* that the *tribuni plebis* should be sacrosanct; *c.* legislation become the task of the *comitia tributa* (Liv. 3, 55). This last provision was so often violated that two more laws were necessary stating: 'Ut quod plebs tributim iussisset populum teneret' (*lex* °*Publília Philónis* in 339 and *lex* °*Horténsia* 287).
Sedúlius, c. 450 AD. He wrote an epic poem 'Carmen Paschále', on the miracles of Christ.
Seisachthéia (Σεισάχθεια). °Solon.
Sejánus, *L. Aelius Seiánus.* °Praefectus praetorio (26-31 AD), favourite of °Tiberius. He tried to persuade °Livilla to poison°Drusus by promising to marry her, thus hoping to become emperor. However, Tiberius was warned, and had him executed (31).
Seleúcids. A dynasty of rulers to the east of the realm of °Alexander the Great, founded by °Seleucus. Their domination east of the Euphrates ended c. 250 BC, when they suffered a defeat against°Arsaces, the rest of the Seleucid Empire being conquered by the °Maccabees.
Seleúcus (Σέλευκος). *Seleúcus I Nicátor.* General of °Alexander the Great; 321 BC °satrap of Babylonia; °Seleucids.
sélla curúlis. An ivory embellished folding chair without back or arms, official seat of all higher Roman officials;

148. Sella curúlis.

°curule magistratus; °ill. 148.

semántics. That branch of philology which deals with the meaning of words.

Sémele (Σεμέλη). Daughter of °Cadmus, mother of °Dionysus.

Semirámis (Σεμίραμις). In Greek legend the wife of °Ninus, king of Assyria. After his death, she ruled for many years. She founded °Babylon and her armies invaded Libya. (The original Semiramis was undoubtedly Sammuramat, dominant after the death of her husband Shamshi-Adad V (824-810 BC).)

Semprónia. Sister of Ti. and C. °Gracchus, married to °Scipio Africanus Minor.

Semprónius. °Gracchus.

semúncia. °abacus.

senárius. Most commonly used Latin verse of six feet in Roman Comedy: ◡́◡◡◡́ ◡◡́◡◡́ ◡◡́◡◡́; °trimeter.

senátus (= senate). Originally the council of all patricians (*patres*) who were 'senes' (aged sixty and over). Later their number was limited to 600. The office of °quaestor assured a seat in the Senate. Once a plebeian could become a senator, the official term *patres*

conscripti came into use.

The power of the Senate was based on tradition, not on laws, and although the king and later the consuls did not need the approval of the Senate, they used to consult the Senate on all important matters.

Séneca. 1. *L. Annaéus Séneca* wrote 'Controvérsiae' (imaginary trials) c. 37 AD, and 'Suasóriae' (speeches which gave advice). (Possibly he has been confused with **2.**) **2.** *L. Annaéus Séneca* (c. 4 BC-65 AD). Philosopher. He was banished to Corsica by °Claudius (41-48 AD). °Agrippina allowed him to come back and entrusted him with the education of °Nero. His influence on the emperor decreased and in 62 he had to retire. Because of his participation in the conspiracy of °Piso, he had to commit suicide (Tac. *Ann.* 15, 60-63). Many of Seneca's works are extant: 1. Fourteen philosophical works on ethical, mostly °Stoic, problems. 2. 124 letters to °Lucilius. 3. *Naturáles Quaestiónes.* An exposition of atmospheric and terrestrial phenomena with moralizing speculations. 4. A °satire on the Emperor °Claudius: *Apocolocyntósis.* 5. Tragedies, *e.g. Oedipus.* 6. a *fabula* °*praetextata*: *Octavia*, possibly.

Sennácherib. Assyrian king (705-681 BC), son of °Sargon II, founder of °Nincvch.

septenárius. The trochaic septinarius: ◡́◡◡◡́ ◡◡◡́ ◡◡◡́ ◡◡◡́ ◡◡.

Septímius Sevérus, *L. Septímius Sevérus.* Emperor 193-211 AD, successor to Pertinax. With the support of the army he succeeded in maintaining the unity of the empire. During his reign the °*praefectus praetorio* gradually became the most powerful man of the realm. In Rome, Septimius built the °'Septizonium' and a triumphal arch (°arcus); °Sevéri, p. 172.

Septimóntium. °Seven Hills.

Septizónium. A °nymphaeum built by °Septimius Severus.

Séptuagint. Greek version of the Old Testament made, in the 3rd century BC, for the Alexandrian Jews, who only knew Greek, according to legend by seventy-two translators.

Serápis (Σέραπις). Graeco-Egyptian deity, introduced in Egypt by °Ptolemy I as part of the religious policy he inaugurated. °Ptolemy also built a rich temple at Alexandria, the Serapeum. Serapis was represented with the bearded countenance of °Zeus, a bushel (grain measure, indicative of fruitfulness) on his head.

Q. Serénus Sammónicus. 3rd cent. AD. He wrote a poem in 1107 hexameters, containing sixty-three medical prescriptions full of magical formulae and charms.

Sérgius. °Catiline.

Sertórius, *Q. Sertórius* (123-72 BC). Moderate partisan of °Marius, who became governor of Spain in 82, where he was popular, establishing schools and promoting the arts and literature of Greece and Rome. He had to flee from the partisans of °Sulla, but the Lusitanians called him back in 80. Until 72, the Roman armies, under Q. °Metellus and Cn. Pompeius (°Pompey), tried to crush him, but with very little success. An officer, jealous of his fame, killed him at a banquet.

Servília. Half-sister of °Cato, mother of °Brutus.

Sérvius. Grammarian, c. 400 AD, wrote a commentary on °Virgil.

Sérvius Túllius. Legendary sixth king of Rome. He is said to have built the first wall around the city (°Rome) and to have divided the Roman people into tribes; °centuriae.

sestértius. Roman silver coin, worth $2\frac{1}{2}$ °asses; p. 164.

Set. Brother of °Osiris.

Seven against Thebes: °Adrastus, °Polyneices, °Tydeus, °Capaneus, Hippomedon, °Amphiaraus, Parthenopaeus (according to others instead of Tydeus and Polyneices, °Eteocles and Mecistheus); °Statius, °Euripides; °Aeschylus.

Seven Hills of Rome, °Aventine, °Caelian, °Capitoline, °Esquiline, °Palatine, °Quirinal, °Viminal.

Seven Liberal Arts. A classification of Classical learning: the three lower subjects, grammar, rhetoric and dialectic (*trivium*), and the four higher subjects, music, geometry, arithmetic and astronomy (*quadrivium*); °Martianus Capella; °Cassiodorus.

'Seven Sages': °Bias, °Cheilon, °Cleoboulus, °Periander, °Pittacus, °Solon, °Thales.

Seven Wonders of the World. The °pyramids, the hanging gardens of °Babylon, the temple of °Artemis at °Ephesus, the statue of °Zeus at °Olympia, the °Mausoleum of Halicarnassus, the Colossus of °Rhodes, the lighthouse on the island of °Pharos (Egypt).

Severi. Two Roman emperors who were related to each other; °Severi p. 173.

sextárius. °weights and measures 2c.

Séxtius, *L. Séxtius Laterános.* Tribune 376-367 BC (*lex °Licinia Sextia*), first plebeian consul in 366 BC.

shaft (*scapus*). In architecture, the main body of a column between the °capital and the °base.

Shápur. °Sassanidae.

shera (*schwa*). The neutral vowel sound ə; °alphabet.

shield. °weapons.

Síbyl (Sibylla). Prophetess. Sibyls became very old, the one at Cumae was reputed to be well over a thousand. She offered °Tarquin nine books of wisdom (the 'Sibylline books'). When he found the price too high, she offered six books at twice the original price, then three at four times the price, having burned the rest. Tarquin bought them in the end. They were put into the charge of a special college of priests, to be consulted in times of crisis. In 83 BC they were destroyed in the burning of the °Capitol.

Sibylline Books. °Sibyl; °decemviri; °Rhea.

sicílicus. °abacus.

Sidónius Apollináris, *C. Sóllius Apollónius Sidónius.* A Gallo-Roman nobleman born at Lugdunum (c. 430-483 AD), son-in-law of the emperor °Avitus,

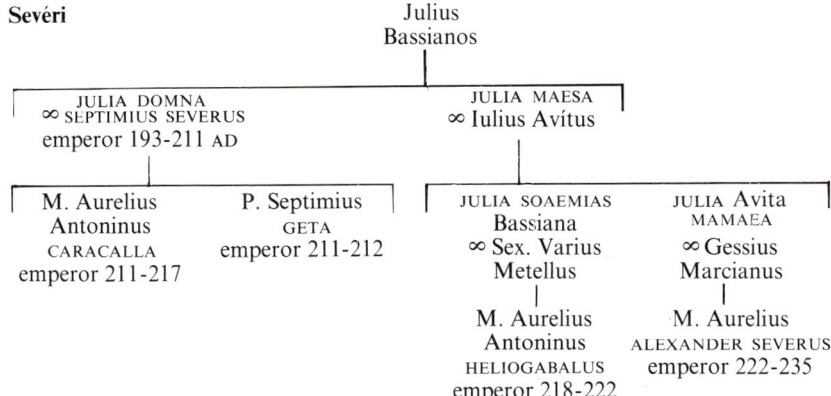

Sevéri

Julius
Bassianos

JULIA DOMNA ∞ SEPTIMIUS SEVERUS emperor 193-211 AD		JULIA MAESA ∞ Iulius Avítus	
M. Aurelius Antoninus CARACALLA emperor 211-217	P. Septimius GETA emperor 211-212	JULIA SOAEMIAS Bassiana ∞ Sex. Varius Metellus	JULIA Avita MAMAEA ∞ Gessius Marcianus
		M. Aurelius Antoninus HELIOGABALUS emperor 218-222	M. Aurelius ALEXANDER SEVERUS emperor 222-235

bishop of Arverni in 470. A collection of letters and three long °panegyrics are extant.

sígnum. The standard of a °manipulus; °ill. 149.

Sílchester (Calléva Atrebátum). Roman town near Reading. The grid street plan can, in the right season, still be observed by air photography in the corn fields, because the cereal has grown shorter and ripens earlier over buried wall foundations or road surfaces ('vegetation marks'); °Britain, °Priene.

Silénus (Σειληνός). Companion of °Dionysus. He was a °satyr in all general attributes and was drunk most of the time.

síliqua. °Weights and measures 2d.

Silius Itálicus, *Ti. Cátius Sílius Itálicus.* Consul in 68 AD. An art-lover, he was a connoisseur of books and pictures, and possessed many country-houses. He wrote an epic, 'Púnica', on the 2nd Punic War. He died from voluntary starvation to shorten an incurable ailment when he was 75.

Sílvius. Son of °Ascanius (or of °Aeneas and Lavinia); °Dardanidae p. 60.

Simónides (Σιμωνίδης). **1.** Of Amorgos, c. 6th-5th cent. BC, satiric poet. We have some °iambic fragments, and a °satire on women. **2.** Of Keos (c. 556-468 BC), lyric poet. Only fragments of his work are left. Well-known is the lament of °Danaë, tossed about at sea.

símpulum. A sort of ladle, looking very much like a °kyathos; used at libations. It was the attribute of the °Pontifex Maximus; °ill. p. 164.

Sínis (Σίνις). Brigand on the °Isthmus of Corinth, who bent two pines together (Pityocamptes), tied his victim to them and then tore him into pieces by untying the trees; °Theseus.

Sírens (Σειρῆνες). Half women, half birds, who enticed passing sailors with their bewitching songs (Hom. *Od.* XIV, 39-54).

sístrum (σεῖστρον). Egyptian musical instrument consisting of a thin oval metal frame furnished with transverse metal rods loosely fixed in it, and a handle by which it was shaken. It was used in the worship of °Isis.

Sisyphus (Σίσυφος). Legendary first king of Corinth, the most cunning and grasping of men. He was condemned in °Hades to roll a rock up a hill, down which it continually rolled again.

skýphos (σκύφος). Deep drinking cup with two horizontal handles on the rim.

Smérdis (Σμέρδις). Brother of °Cambyses, murdered by the latter.

149. Standards ('signa') on Trajan's column.

150. Soccus.

When Cambyses was later in Egypt, the Persian priests (Magi) conspired against him, one of whom was said to be Smerdis (Pseudo-Smerdis). This priest was killed by seven Persian noblemen, among whom was °Dareios Hystaspes (Hdt. 3, 61-87).

sóccus. A slipper, originally worn by women, later also by men; °ill. 150.

Social War. The war (90-88 BC) fought by Rome against the Marsi, Paeligni, °Samnites, Lucani and others, who thought their fidelity to Rome in the 2nd Punic War had not been sufficiently rewarded, for they were still denied Roman °citizenship. The insurgents were defeated and parts of Italy were laid waste, but Italy south of the Po was given citizenship by the *lex Iúlia* (90) and the *lex Plaútia Papíria* (89).

Sócrates (Σωράτης). Philosopher in Athens (469-399 BC). We know him from the descriptions of °Plato and °Xenophon and the caricature of °Aristophanes. Contrary to the °sophists, who only taught rich students, Socrates good-humouredly cross-questioned every Athenian, whether rich (°Alcibiades) or poor, with whom he came into contact. His questions were directed towards truth and the pursuit of moral conduct in life. He tried to define 'virtue' by pointing out the nature of separate virtues in concrete cases. His method of questioning first disproved the intellectual errors of his opponent. This caused much opposition, and the accusations of °Anytus and °Meletus ('corruption of the Athenian youth'

and 'undermining the state cults') cost
him his life; °dialogue, °Plato.
sólea. Also called *sandalium* or
crepid(ul)a. It was not worn in the
street, but only at home, and was
attached to the foot by straps; °ill. 151.

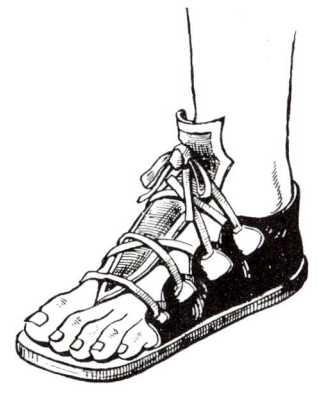

151. Sólea.

sólidus. A gold coin, introduced by
°Constantine the Great, 312 AD. Its
weight was 1/72 libra; °ill. p. 164.
Solínus, *C. Iúlius Solínus,* 3rd cent. AD.
He wrote, using the work of °Pliny,
a collection of historical and geographical remarks on various parts of
the then known world full of curious
inaccuracies.
Sólon (Σόλων). Athenian legislator (639-
559 BC), one of the °Seven Sages who
modified the severe laws of °Draco.
He cancelled all existing debts and
mortgages (°'seisachtheía'), thereby
freeing many peasants and citizens.
Yet the rich remained the most
privileged. The citizens were now
divided into four classes:
1. *pentakosiomedímni*, with an annual
income of at least 500 bushels of corn,
wine or oil; could be elected °archons;
compelled to undertake a °liturgy.
2. *híppeis*, with 300 bushels, should
enlist with their own horses.

3. *zeugítae*, with 200 bushels, served as
hoplites (heavy-armed infantry), pro-
viding their own arms.
4. *thétes*, with less than 200 bushels;
could not hold office, served as rowers,
marines,etc.
Further, Solon strengthened the power
of the °ecclesia and extended the
authority of the °Areopagus.
'Sómnium Scipiónis'. Part of the sixth
book of °Cicero's 'De Republica',
elaborating on the idea that those who
died in the service of their country
should also be rewarded after death.
Sophists (σοφισταί). Professional
'teachers of wisdom', who travelled all
over Greece and beyond (c. 5th cent.
BC) using philosophy and rhetoric, and
laying particular stress on the latter
which was taught as one of the roads
to success. They asked fees and some
amassed fortunes. After some time
their teaching deteriorated, since they
encouraged a cynical disbelief in moral
restraints; °Protagoras; °Gorgias;
°Hippias; °Prodicus.
There was a revival in the 2nd cent.
AD. The most important of these
sophists were °Herodes Atticus, °Aelius
Aristides, °Dio Chrysostom, °Flavius
Philostratus, °Lucian, °Athenaeus.
Sóphocles (Σοφοκλῆς). The great tragic
poet, together with °Aeschylus and
°Euripides, in Athens (495-406 BC).
He was the first to use three actors
and a choir of fifteen. Only seven
tragedies are extant: 1. *Ajax*. The madness and remorse of °Ajax and the
quarrel over his burial. 2. *Antígone*.
In spite of the order of °Creon,
°Antigone buried the body of her
brother °Polyneices. 3. *Oedipus Rex*.
°Oedipus discovered his terrible deed
and put out his eyes. 4. *Eléctra*.°Orestes
returned and killed the murderers of
his father°Agamemnon. 5. *Philóctetes*.
°Neoptolemus used a ruse to make
Philoctetes give him the bow and
arrows of Heracles, but driven by
remorse returned them; only the
appearance of °Heracles himself as
°'deus ex machina' induced °Philoctetes

to help capture Troy. 6. *Oedipus Coloneüs*. The sequel to *Oedipus Rex*; the blind Oedipus, taken care of by his daughters Antigone and Ismene, arrived at Colonus, where he was to die. 7. *Trachíniae*. Death of °Heracles and °Deianeira. Note also 8. Fragment of a °satyric drama *Ichneutai*.

Soránus. He came from Ephesus; c. 125 AD, he wrote about gynaecology, of which work only fragments exist. His other medical book is known from the translation by °Caelius Aurelianus.

Sosígenes (Σωσιγένης). Mathematician and astronomer in Alexandria, who was °Caesar's expert in his introduction of the Julian °calendar in 47 BC.

Sósii. Publishers of °Horace who lived on the °vicus Tuscus.

Sóstratus (Σώστρατος), of Cnidus. Architect of the lighthouse of Alexandria; °Pharos.

Spártacus. Leader of the revolt of the slaves in Italy (73-71 BC), who after many victories was defeated by °Crassus.

spátha. In the 3rd century AD the *gladius* was replaced by the spatha, a long, flat double-edged sword, worn on the left side; °ill. 152.

sphinx (σφῖγξ). **1.** In Greece a mythical creature of Eastern origin, 'introduced' in the prehistoric period, which killed, at Thebes, any man who could not solve her riddle, °Oedipus; °ill. 153. **2.** In Egypt a statue of a recumbent lion with a human head, often used to line avenues.

Spína. Town in the Po delta, trade-centre of the °Etruscans from the 6th century onwards. Excavations have revealed many important graves.

spinning. The spinning-wheel became known in Europe during the Middle Ages. In antiquity, women used to spin by hand on a 'ἠλακάτη', *colus*, on which the wool was placed; °ill. 154.

spira. The °base of a column.

spóndee (spondaeus). A metrical foot: ‿ —.

spondíacus, *versus spondíacus*. A °hexa-

152. Spatha.

153. Sphinx on a tomb at Xanthus (Lycia) c. 480 BC (63 cm. high).

meter of which the fifth foot is a °spondee.

stádium. °Weights and measures 2a.

stámnos (στάμνος). A Greek vessel with two horizontal handles, which served as a container for wine; °ill. 155.

stásimon (στάσιμον). Choral ode between two °epeisodia, accompanied by a flute-player.

154. Spinning.

155. Attic stamnos (*c*. 435 BC). A soldier bidding farewell.

Státius. 1. °Caecílius. **2.** *P. Papínius Státius*. Epic poet (c. 40-96 AD). His epic *Thebaïs* described the campaign of the °Seven against Thebes. The *Achilleïs* is unfinished and told of °Achilles and the daughters of °Lycomedes. Further, we have a collection of occasional poems: *Silvae*.

stéle (στήλη). **1.** Greek monument over a grave, sometimes an upright marble slab with a relief, sometimes a more elaborate structure with sculpture; °ill. 20. **2.** Upright marble slab bearing an inscription containing the text of a law or decree.

stenógraphy (=shorthand). Invented by M. Túllus Tíro, an ex-slave of °Cicero, hence the name 'nótae Tironiánae'. The first shorthand speech recorded in history is that by °Cato (not Cicero) against °Catiline in 63 BC.

Sténtor (Στέντωρ). Greek herald at Troy. He could call as loudly as fifty men together. Hence the English word 'stentorian'.

step-pyramid. A stage in the development of the °mastaba to the °pyramid. The best known step-pyramid, built by the architect °Imhotep, is at °Saqqara; °ill. 156; °Djoser.

156. Step-pyramid.

státer (στατήρ). A Greek standard coin; =°didrachm; °ill. p. 85.

Stesíchorus (Στησίχορος). Choral poet in Sicily, c. 640-555 BC. His subject-matter was based on Greek epic poetry.

Stheneboéa (Σθενέβοια). °Bellerophon.
Sthéno (Σθεινώ). °Gorgons.
stichomýthia. Dialogue in Greek plays.
Stílicho, *Flávius Stílicho.* A Vandal who
ruled in the place of the emperor
°Honorius in the West after the schism
of the Roman empire. In 408 he was
disgraced and was killed.
Stílpo (Στίλπων). Philosopher of the
°Megarian school (c. 380-300 BC), tutor
of °Zeno of Cition.
stímulus. 1. A pointed stake, concealed
beneath the surface of the ground, to
repel hostile troops, used (*e.g.*) by
°Caesar at the siege of Alesia; °ill. 157.
2. (κέντρον). A goad or whip for
driving horses, etc.; °pp. 13, 85.
stóa (στοά). Colonnade. Well-known is
the *Stoa Poikile* at Athens, named after
its paintings by °Polygnotus. The stoa
at Athens built by °Attalus II on the
east side of the °agora was laid bare
and reconstructed in 1953-1956. It is
now a museum; °ills. 158, 159.

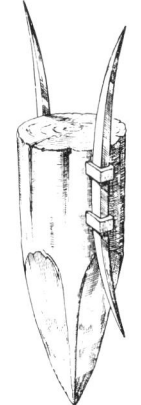

157. Stimulus.

158. The Stoa of °Attalus in Athens, as rebuilt.

159. The rebuilt Stoa of °Attalus in Athens. The interior.

Stóics. °Zeno of Cition taught in the °Stoa Poikile at Athens, c. 310 BC. His doctrines were therefore called 'Stoic'. Zeno and his successors (°Cleanthes, °Chrysippus) considered only one thing good—virtue; and only one thing evil—not to be virtuous. The rest was neither good nor evil, therefore irrelevant (τὰ ἀδιάφορα). The world was pervaded by the 'λόγος', absolute knowledge, the universe was periodically consumed by fire (ἐκπύρωσις). The soul was material and part of the universal fire. The 'Middle Stoa' (2nd and 1st cent. BC) was represented by °Panaetius and °Posidonius, who greatly influenced °Cato, °Cicero and °Pompey. During the latest period outstanding among Stoic philosophers were °Seneca, °Musonius, °Epictetus and °Marcus Aurelius.

stóla. °tunica.

Stólo. °Licinius.

Stone Age. The earliest technological period of human culture, which was marked by the exclusive or predominant use of stone, obsidian (Greece), or flint, as a material for weapons and tools; °Palaeolithic; °Mesolithic; °Neolithic Ages.

Strábo (Στράβων). Historian and geographer of Pontus, c. 66 BC-21 AD. He travelled widely in Greece, Asia Minor, Italy and Egypt, and wrote a *Geography* in seventeen books; °ill. 160.

Stráto (Στράτων), of Lampsacus. Physicist and leader of the °Peripatetic school (287-269 BC).

stría. °fluting.

stróphe (στροφή). A series of verses in Greek drama, the metrical structure of which was repeated in a following system, called antístrophe: °epode.

179

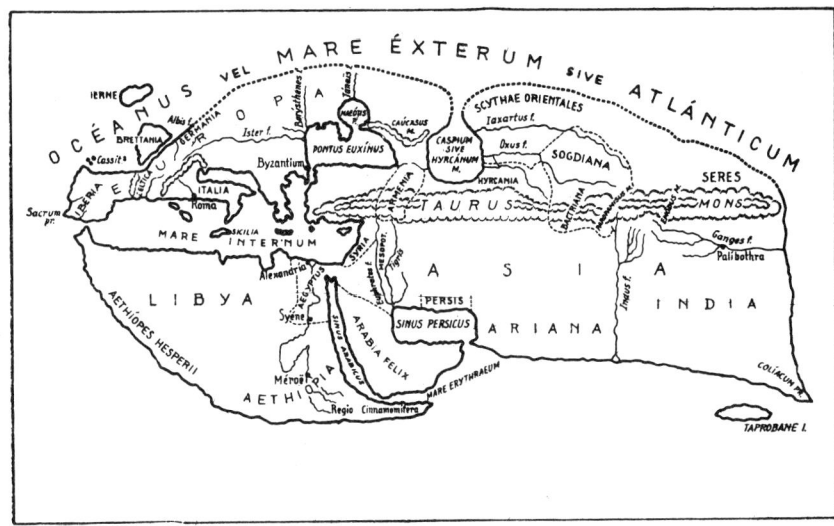

160. The world according to °Strabo.

Stróphius (Στροφίος). Father of °Pylades.

stýlobate (στυλοβάτης). A continuous °base upon which a row of columns was supported.

Stýmphalus (Στύμφαλος). Town and lake in Arcadia, inhabited by mythical birds with metal attributes that they used as arrows, which were killed by °Heracles.

Styx (Στύξ). One of the rivers of °Hades.

subúcula. °tunica.

Subúrra. A busy shopping street in Rome, running from the Porta °Esquilina to the °Argiletum and the °forum; plan p. 166.

Suetónius, *C. Suetónius Tranquíllus,* c. 75-150 AD. Secretary ('ab epistulis') to °Hadrian. In the imperial archives he found the subject-matter for his biographies of the emperors from °Caesar to °Domitian.

Súidas. Author of a Greek lexicon, c. 1000 AD. The name of the author is due to a mistake. The title of the work was 'de Suda', which means 'stronghold'.

Súlla, *L. Cornélius Súlla* (138-78 BC). He distinguished himself in the war against °Jugurtha and in the °Social War. In 88, he became °consul and, assigned by lot, commander-in-chief in the war against °Mithridates. However, °Marius arranged to take over this task by the interference of the people against the wishes of the Senate. Sulla defeated the supporters of Marius and left for Asia. After a hasty peace treaty, he returned in 83 to put an end to Marius' reign of terror. The °proscriptions ensued, which cost the lives of 4,700 citizens. He divided land among 120,000 veterans, became °dictator and gave the administration of the state to the Senate together with the judicial powers. The power of the °tribunes was limited. Then he retired from political life (79 BC).

Sulpícia. Niece of °Tibullus. Her poems have been incorporated in his work (4, 7-12).

Sulpícius Sevérus (c. 400 AD). Orator from Gaul, who became a Christian, and wrote a concise history 'Chrónica'. The first book deals with Old Testament times, the second with ancient history up to the time of °Stilicho. He also wrote a biography of St Martin.

Súmer. Prehistoric kingdom between the lower courses of the Euphrates and the Tigris, with the capital at Lagash; °Ur, °Lagash.

suovetaurília. The Roman offering of a pig (*sus*), sheep (*ovis*) and bull (*taurus*); °ill. 161.

161. Suovetaurilia.

Súsa. Town in south-west Persia, after the time of °Cyrus winter-residence of the °Achaemenids. Excavations brought the laws of °Hammurabi to light.

suspensúra. °hypocaust.

sýcophant (συκοφάντης) (='delator'). Professional prosecutor who received the proceeds of half the fines and the forfeited goods. This led to disastrous practices.

Sýmmachus. 1. Translated the Old Testament, at the time of °Septimius Severus. He tried to follow the Greek as closely as possible; Hieronymus greatly praised the translation; °hexapla. **2.** *Q. Aurélius Sýmmachus* (c. 345-402 AD). Orator and politician. He defended Paganism and was an opponent of °Ambrosius. Fragments of some of his speeches are extant.

Symplégades (Συμπληγάδες). In legend, 'Clashing Rocks', two rocks at the entrance of the Black Sea, which intermittently clashed against each other. When the °Argonauts had safely passed them, they remained fixed.

synálepha (συναλοιφή). °elision.

sýncope (συγκοπή). Omission of a vowel in the middle of a word (*e.g.* vinclum = vinculum).

synízesis (συνίξησις). Contraction of two vowels for the sake of the metre, as in °Homer.

synonýmics. The study of the different shades of meaning in synonyms.

sýrinx (σῦριγξ). **1.** Pan-pipe, made of seven or nine reeds of different lengths. **2.** River-nymph pursued by °Pan and changed into a reed, out of which Pan made a pipe (Ovid *Met.* 1, 690-712).

Sýrus. °Publilius Syrus.

T

tablínum. °domus; °plan p. 66.

tabulárium. The record-office of Rome, built after the fire on the °Capitoline in 83 BC; °plan p. 80.

Tácitus. 1. *P. Cornélius Tácitus* (c. 55-120 AD). Roman historian. He wrote first a dialogue on the causes of the decline of the art of oratory: *Dialógus de oratóribus*; then a biography of his father-in-law °Agricola. His greater works are *Históriae*, a history of Rome from 69 AD (four and a half books are left, covering the years 69 and 70) and the *Annáles* ('Ab excéssu dívi Augústi'), of which we have most of I-VI (14-37 AD) and XI-XVI (47-66 AD). Tacitus was a senator and looked at historical events from the point of view of a nobleman, but he made use of every dramatic situation. His work excels in sharp characterization, deep understanding of human motives and bitter pessimism. **2.** *M. Claudius Tácitus.*

Roman emperor (275-276 AD), elected by the Senate, murdered by his soldiers.

taénia. In the °Doric order the projecting small fillet which crowned the °architrave and joined it to the °frieze.

tálent (τάλαντον). Greek unit of weight and money (26 kg, 6000 °drachmae). A talent was divided into 60 minae; °Weights and measures 1e.

Tanágra (Τάναγρα). Town in Boeotia where in 457 BC the Athenians were defeated by the Spartans and Thebans. It is famous for its °terracotta figurines, found in great numbers since 1873. They date from c. 335-200 BC, and mostly represent women. Their height varied from 5-30 cm.

Tántalus (Τάνταλος). Legendary king of Asia Minor, whose riches were proverbial. He was condemned to suffer eternal hunger and thirst because of his crime against his son °Pelops; °Niobe; °Tantalidae.

Tantálidae

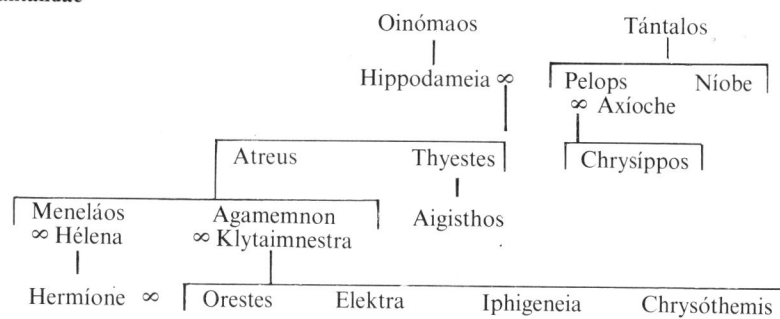

Tarpeía. Daughter of Sp. Tarpéius, who defended the °Capitol at the time of °Romulus against the Sabines. Desiring their gold bracelets, Tarpeia promised to betray the citadel, provided she got 'what the Sabines wore on their left arms'. To punish her perfidy the king of the Sabines and his followers crushed her under their shields when they entered the city.

Tarpeían Rock. Steep hill in Rome, south-east of the °Capitol, whence the Romans threw down their condemned criminals.

Tarquín. 1. *L. Tarquínius Collatínus*, °Lucretia. **2.** *L. Tarquínius Príscus.* Fifth king of Rome. He built the °Cloaca Maxima, the °Circus Maximus and the temple of °Jupiter Capitolinus. He was the first Etruscan. **3.** *L. Tarquínius Supérbus.* Last king of Rome, °tyrant, married to Tullia, daughter of °Servius Tullius. In 510 BC he was expelled. His son was Sex. Tarquínius (°Lucretia).

tautólogy. Repetition in the immediate context of the same idea or statement in other words; °pleonasm.

taxámeter (ὁδόμετρον). Machine described by °Heron to measure distances; °ill. 162.

tégula. °tiles.

Teirésias (Τειρεσίας). Blind sooth-sayer of Thebes, who pointed °Oedipus out as the murderer of °Laius. He kept his powers of prophecy in °Hades; °Sophocles; °Homer, *Od.* XI, 90-151.

Télamon (Τελαμών). Son of °Aeacus, who took part in the expedition of the °Argonauts and the °Calydonion hunt; °Aeacidae p. 3.

Telémachus (Τηλέμαχος). Son of °Odysseus and °Penelope.

Télephus (Τήλεφος). Legendary son of °Heracles and a priestess of °Athena, Auge, married to one of °Príam's daughters. When the Greeks landed in Mysia on their way to Troy, Telephus was wounded by °Achilles. The infected wound did not heal and only when rust from the lance was put on the wound did Telephus recover, after which he fought on the Greek side. °Euripides wrote a tragedy on the subject, which has been lost.

Tell-el-Amárna. °Amarna.

ténsa. A Roman chariot used in religious processions; °ill. 163.

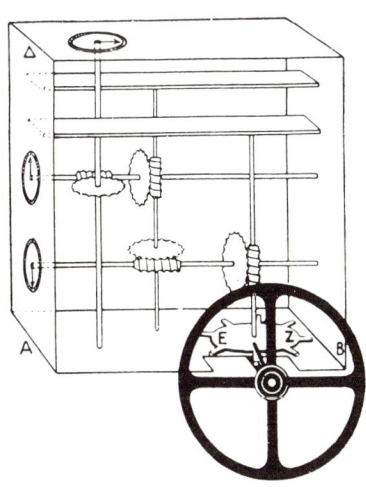

162. Taxameter.

163. A tensa.

Térence. 1. *P. Teréntius Áfer.* Roman writer of comedies (195-159 BC). He was a slave from Africa in the service of a senator Teréntius Lucánus, hence the name. As a freedman he belonged to the circle of °Scipio. Six of his comedies are extant. They were more subtle in humour than those of °Plautus. 1. *Andria* (the girl of Andros). 2. *Heautontimoroúmenos* (the self-tormentor). 3. *Eunuchus.* 4. *Phormio.* 5. *Adelphi.* 6. *Hecyra* (the mother-in-law); °Menander. **2.** °Varro.

Terentiánus Maúrus (3rd cent. AD). Wrote a handbook on metres.

Téreus (Τηρεύς). °Philomela.

Terpánder (Τέρπανδρος). Musician in °Lesbos. He is said to have invented the °lyre with seven strings.

Terpsíchore (Τερψιχόρη). °Muses.

terracótta. A hard red unglazed pottery of a fine quality, from which tiles, bricks, architectural decorations, figurines, etc., were made; °Tanagra.

térra sigilláta (Samian Ware). Common household ware of Roman times, with relief decoration. First made in Arretium ('Arretine' ware), later on in Gaul and Germany, etc.

Tertúllian, *Q. Septímius Flórens Tertulliánus* (c. 155-220 AD). Jurist in Carthage. He became a Christian (c. 193) and wrote, both in Latin and Greek, a great number of works (thirty-one are extant) in defence of Christianity, in a passionate and incisive style. Some works of his first period are: *Apologéticum* (defence of Christianity), *De praescriptióne haereticórum, Ad mártyras, De spectáculis, De baptísmo, De paeniténtia, De patiéntia, Ad uxórem, De testimónio ánimae, De cúltu feminárum, De oratióne.* When he had become a follower of the Montanistic sect and had openly broken with the church in 211, he wrote *De pállio, De ánima, De fúga in persecutióne.*

testúdo (= tortoise). A protective covering formed by the shields of the soldiers held over their heads during an assault on an enemy stronghold; °ill. 164.

164. A testudo (from °Trajan's column).

Téthys (Τηθύς). Wife of °Oceanus, mother of all rivers.

tétradrachm. Greek coin, worth four °drachmae; °ill. p. 85.

tetrámeter. °septenarius.

tétrarchy (τετραρχία). Country under the protection of Rome, governed by a 'tetrarch' (lower in rank than a king).

Teúcer (Τεῦκρος). **1.** Son of °Telamon, half-brother of °Ajax; °Aeacidae, p. 3. **2.** King of Troy, so that the Trojans were also called 'Teucri'; °Dardanidae p. 60.

Teutónes. °Cimbri.

Tháles (Θαλῆς), of Miletus. One of the °Seven Sages (c. 624-546 BC), famous for his posing: 'What is difficult? To know oneself. What is easy? To give advice.' He was the founder of Greek mathematics and astronomy and the first to prophesy an eclipse of the sun (28th May, 585 BC; °Alyattes). In his philosophy water was considered to be the origin of all things.

Thália (Θάλεια). **1.** °Graces (Hes. *Theog.* 909). **2.** °Muses.

Thámyris (Θάμυρις). A supposed Thracian singer, who dared to challenge the °Muses on the °cithara and lost.

Thápsus (Θάψος). Town on the coast of Africa, where °Caesar defeated the Pompeians in 46 BC.

Theáno (Θεανώ). Priestess of °Athena in Troy, married to °Antenor.

theatre (θέατρον). The theatre in its classical form originated in Athens in the 6th cent. BC, but was later modified. Round the circular 'orchestra' or chorus space rose the semi-circular *auditorium*, opposite to which was often the stage (σκηνή), the background, as at °Epidaurus, °Athens. Later a curtain ('aulaeum'), was used to cover the stage from the auditorium during the intervals. It was lowered into the ground at the beginning of the performance and raised at the end; °ill. 165. The first permanent theatre in Rome was built by °Pompey in 55 BC. Until then Rome had wooden structures, which had to be erected at every festival; °ill. 166. In an amphitheatre the auditorium surrounded a circular or oval arena, used for gladiatorial combats; °Colosseum.

Thémis (Θέμις). **1.** Legendary daughter of °Uranus and °Gaea, goddess of Justice, law and order. She possessed the oracle of °Delphi before °Apollo. **2.** Mother of °Anchises; °Dardanidae p. 60.

Themístocles (Θεμιστοκλῆς). Athenian politician (c. 524-459 BC), and, after the banishment of °Aristeides in 483, leader of Athenian politics. He per-

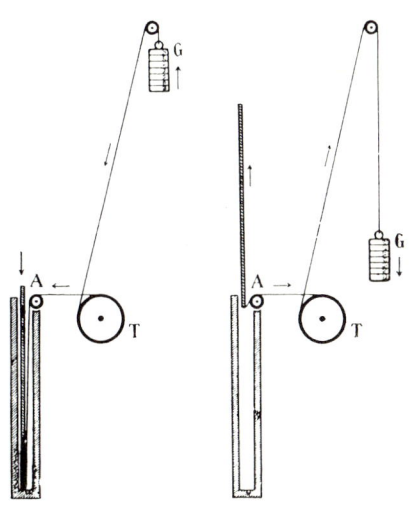

165. Moving the 'aulaeum'. When the weight (G) comes down the 'aulaeum' is raised from the slot and *vice versa*.

suaded the Athenians to build a fleet with the proceeds from the silver-mines of °Laurium, defeated the Persians at °Salamis in 480, reconstructed the walls of Athens and reinforced the °Piraeus. He made many enemies, and in c. 471 he was banished by °ostracism.

Theócritus (Θεόκριτος), of Syracuse (c. 300 BC). Composer of °bucolic idylls. °Virgil.

Theódoric the Great. King of the Ostrogoths (455-526 AD), succeeded °Odoacer in Italy in 493; °Boëthius; °Goths.

Theodósius. 1. *Theodósius I the Great.* Roman emperor (379-395 AD), who fought Paganism and prohibited all pagan sacrifices and the °Olympian games. After his death his empire was divided between °Arcadius and °Honorius. **2.** *Theodósius II.* Grandson of **1.**, emperor 408-450. During his reign the °Codex Theodosiánus was published (438).

166. The Roman theatre of Orange.

Theodótion. He published an edition of the °Septuagint corrected from the original text; °hexapla.

Theógnis (Θέογνις), of Megara (c. 6th cent. BC). °Gnomic poet, with a strong aristocratic bias.

Theógony. °Hesiod.

Theophrástus (Θεόφραστος), of Lesbos (c. 372-287 BC). Pupil of °Aristotle, after whose death he became leader of the °Peripatetic school, which then attained its most complete development. Of his enormous output only the 'Characters of Men' and two horticultural works are extant.

Theopómpus (Θεόπομπος), of Chios, born c. 378 BC. Historian and orator. Only fragments of his Greek history have come down to us.

Therámenes (Θηραμένης). Athenian statesman, who was one of the °Thirty Tyrants, but soon afterwards quarrelled with the extremists, especially °Critias, who had him executed.

thérmae (= Baths) **of Caracálla.** °Caracalla.

Thermópylae (Θερμοπύλαι). Pass in the valley of the Spercheius, between the sea and the mountains. Here °Leonidas was killed with 300 men in 480 BC and here the Romans defeated °Antiochus in 191 BC.

Thersítes (Θερσίτης). The most ugly and despised of the Greeks at Troy (Hom. *Il.* II, 211-277).

Theséum (Θησεῖον). Externally the best preserved °Doric Greek temple standing to the west of the °agora in Athens. Probably the name is incorrect and the temple may have been sacred to °Athena and °Hephaestus. It was built in 449-444 BC.

Théseus (Θησεύς). Legendary hero, son of °Aegeus, educated by his grandfather, returned to Athens when grown up. On the way home he killed the following: °Procrustes, °Sinis, °Sciron, and later in Crete, the °Minotaur. On returning to Athens he forgot the prearranged signal, and Aegeus, thinking his son had failed, threw himself into the sea, hence the name 'Aegean'. In

186

the expedition against the °Amazons he won their queen °Hippolyta and married her. Their son was °Hippolytus.

Théspis (Θέσπις). The 'first' tragic poet and actor. He is said to have taken his plays about on wagons.

Thétis (Θέτις). One of the °Nereids, wife of °Peleus, mother of °Achilles; °Tethys.

Thirty Tyrants (οἱ τριάκοντα). Thirty prominent Athenians, elected on °Theramenes' proposal to revise the laws after the victory of Sparta (404 BC; °Lysander). They held a reign of terror in Athens for eight months; °Critias; °Thrasybulus; °oligarchy.

Thísbe (Θίσβη). °Pyramus.

Thrasýbulus (Θρασύβουλος). Athenian statesman, who defeated the °Thirty Tyrants and restored the democracy.

thrónos. °chairs.

Thucýdides (Θουκυδίδης). Outstanding Athenian historian (c. 455-396 BC), who wrote the history of the °Peloponnesian War to 411. He told the facts objectively, alternating events with speeches in which he characterized the speakers in a masterly way. He approached his subject logically, thus raising the standard of historical writing from that of the more gullible °Herodotus.

Thyéstes (Θυέστης). Son of °Pelops and °Hippodameia; °Tantalidae p. 182.

thýrsus (θύρσος). A staff terminating in an ornament like a pine-cone, and sometimes wreathed with ivy or vine-branches, borne by °Dionysus and his followers; °Maenad.

Tibérius, *Ti. Iulius Caesar Augústus.* The emperor Tiberius. Before his adoption he was called Ti. Claudius Néro, born 42 BC, son of Ti. °Claudius Nero and °Livia Drusilla, and adopted by °Augustus in 4 AD. In several campaigns he defeated the Vindelici (15 BC), the Pannonii (12-10 and 6-9), the °Germans (8 BC-5 AD). Augustus disliked him and so did not want him as a successor, but when all other possible successors were dead, he appointed him as his successor together with °Livia. At the age of fifty-six, he became emperor. He reigned

with difficulty, thus justifying Augustus' fears; Roman historians usually portrayed him as a cruel and licentious despot. His continual fear of assassination caused him to leave Rome for Capri from 26 till his death in 37; °Julio-Claudian dynasty p. 101.

Tibérius Geméllus, *Ti. Iulius Caesar.* Son of °Drusus and °Livilla, born 19 AD, murdered by °Gaius in 37; °Julio-Claudian dynasty p. 101.

tíbia. °aulos.

Tibúllus, *Albius Tibúllus.* Elegiac poet (c. 50-19 BC). There were four books of poems to his name. The third book, however, was by °Lygdamus, and the fourth contained the °*Panegýricus ad Messállam,* which was not by Tibullus. 7-12 were by °Sulpicia. He did not belong to the circle of Maecenas.

Ticínus. Tributary river of the Po, where in 218 BC. °Hannibal defeated the Romans.

tiles. The Romans used two sorts of tiles: the flat roof-tiles (*tégulae*) and the hollow tiles (*ímbrices*) covering the rims of two adjacent tiles; °ill. 167.

167. Roofing-tiles.

Timaéus (Τίμαιος). **1.** Philosopher from Locri, follower of °Pythagoras. A dialogue by °Plato is named after him. **2.** From Taormina in Sicily, c. 346-c. 250 BC, wrote a history of Sicily, of which some fragments are extant.

Tímgad. City founded in Numidia in 100 AD at the command of °Trajan. Excavations have revealed, among many other buildings, four public baths, since 1881.

Timóleon (Τιμολέων), of Corinth, renowned for his moderation. He freed Syracuse in 343 BC from the tyrant °Dionysius II, and in 339 BC the whole of Sicily from the Carthaginians, whom he defeated in a battle on the river Crimisus.

Tímon (Τίμων). **1.** Famous misanthropist at Athens at the time of °Pericles. **2.** of Phlius. °Sceptic philosopher and poet (c. 320-230 BC).

Timothéüs (Τιμόθεος). **1.** Son of Conon, elected general in 378 BC when the Second °Athenian Confederacy was founded. **2.** Composer of °dithyrambs from Miletus (c. 450-360). We have one of his works, a lyric named 'The Persians' on a °papyrus of the 4th century BC.

Tíro. °stenography.

Tíryns (Τίρυνς). Citadel in Argolis, one of the oldest in Greece; °Mycenae. It was first excavated by °Schliemann in 1884-5, who found °Cyclopean masonry and a megaron (= hall) decorated with frescoes after the style of the °Minoans; °Helladic civilisation.

Tisíphone (Τισιφόνη). One of the °Erinyes.

Tissáphernes (Τισσαφέρνης). °Satrap in Sardis, who helped °Artaxerxes to defeat his brother °Cyrus.

Títans (Τιτᾶνες). An older generation of gods before the °Olympians: °Kronos, °Iapetus, Oceanus, °Mnemosyne, °Themis, °Rhea, °Pheobe. They were overcome by °Zeus and the younger generation.

lex Títia. °triumvirate.

Títus, *T. Flávius Vespasiánus.* Emperor (79-81 AD), succeeded his father °Vespasian. In 70 he destroyed Jerusalem and then became °praefectus praetorio. On the whole he ruled justly.

tmésis (τμῆσις). The separation of the elements of a compound word by the interpolation of another word or words: *e.g.* : 'quo res cumque cadent'.

toga. The woollen dress which distinguished the Roman citizen. They thought the toga uncomfortable and impractical, so they never wore it while working, only on public occasions. Originally the toga was worn by men and women, but after the beginning of the Empire respectable women no longer did so; °stola.

The oldest form known is that of a bronze statue (the °'Arringatore' = Orator) in Florence, 3rd cent. BC. This toga was draped as follows: Placed on the left shoulder, it fell in front of the left side of the body and, resting on the left arm, reached the middle of the shin. The border along the neck, bunched into thick folds forming a roll (°ill. 168: A), passed diagonally across the back, coming forward under the right arm and across the breast again, and thrown back over the left shoulder, so that the end hung down on the back (°ill. 168: B-D).

The second form of the toga is to be seen on many statues of the 3rd and 2nd century BC (°ills. 169; 170). The piece of material used was longer and wider, the material itself more supple, and both ends reached the floor. This toga covered the right shoulder and arm up to the wrist ('bracchium veste continebatur' Quint. *Inst.* 11, 3, 138); °ill. 168: I-IV.

In the last years of the Republic appeared a third form. Now the toga was draped from the left shoulder directly over the right shoulder in a wide fold (*sinus*), so that the right arm could be inside or outside, and even the head could be covered (°ill. 168: 1-5). *Cínctus Gabínus,* a special way to drape the toga. The head was covered and the end hanging over the left shoulder was now wound round the waist, pulled under the right arm and inserted in the *sinus* (°ill. 168: 6, 7).

Tóga cándida, worn by those who stood for an office ('candidates').

Tóga pícta, dyed °purple and embroidered, worn by a 'triumphator'; °triumph.

Tóga praetéxta, with a purple border for °curule magistrates and for youths till they reached manhood. The °flamen wore a double *toga praetexta*.

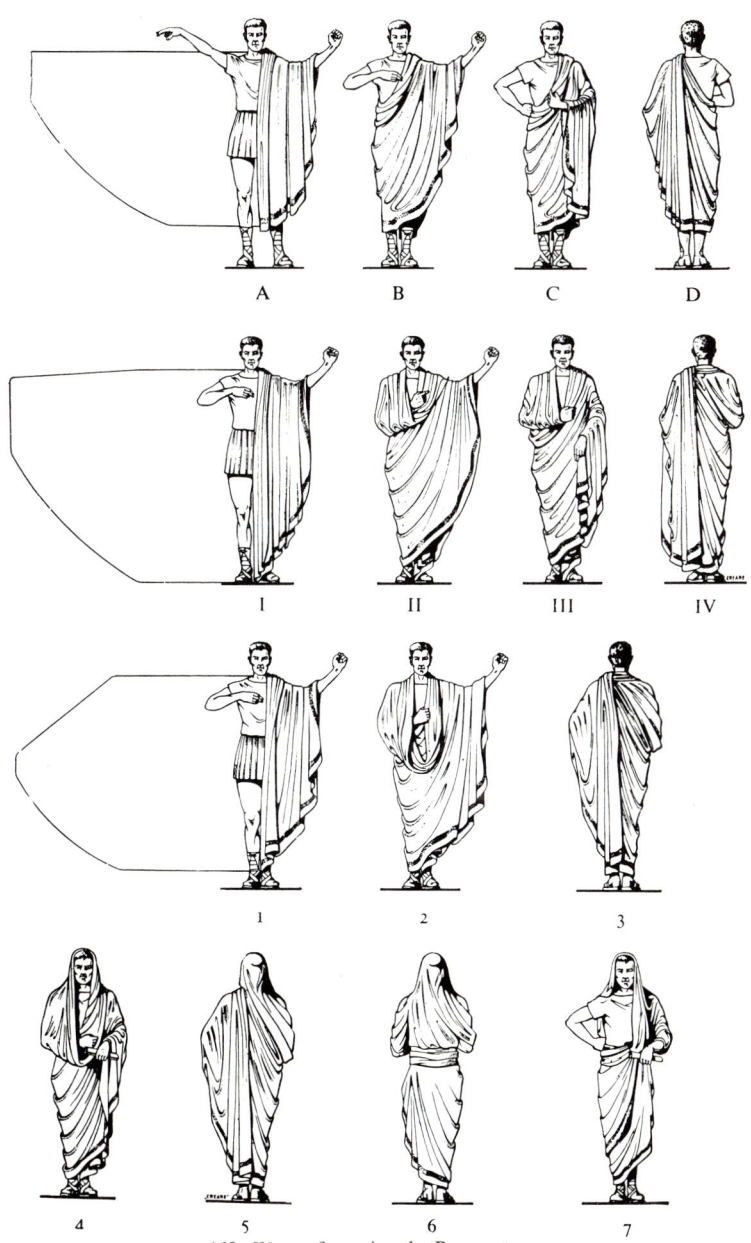

168. Ways of wearing the Roman toga.

169. A Roman wearing the toga.

170. A Roman wearing the toga.

Tóga púlla, dark brown or grey, worn as a sign of mourning.

Tóga púra or *Tóga virílis*, worn by adults (from the sixteenth year).

Tómyris (Τόμυρις). Queen of the Massagetae who after defeating °Cyrus, cut off his head and threw it into a vessel of human blood, because he had killed her son.

trábea. Probably a °toga with a purple border, worn by kings and augurs.

Trachíniae. Tragedy by °Sophocles.

Trájan, *M. Ulpius Traiánus* (53-117 AD). Roman emperor (98-117), adopted by °Nerva in 97. Trajan reinforced the German frontier by building the °limes and founding colonies, *e.g.* Ulpia Noviomágus (Nijmegen). He fought the °Dacians and defeated them. This campaign is depicted magnificently on Trajan's Column in Rome. He also expanded the Empire on the eastern frontiers. At home he won the respect of °senate and °equites, and enriched the city with new buildings. A born leader, he did not abuse his powers.

Trasuménnus lácus (= Lake Trasimene). Lake west of Perugia, where °Hannibal destroyed the army of °Flaminius in 217 BC.

'Treasury of °Atreus.' One of the beehive-tombs (or 'tholoi') found at °Mycenae. The dome was corbelled. °Helladic civilisation.

Trébia. A tributary of the Po, where °Hannibal defeated the Romans in 218 BC.

tresvíri. °triumviri.

tríbon (τριβων). Spartan cloak worn by philosophers.

tríbrach. A metrical foot: ◡ ◡ ◡.

tribúnus plébis. An officer of the °plebs first appointed in c. 500-450 BC, °secessio plebis. The tribunes were charged with the defence of the lives and property of the plebeians. Originally there were two. They had the right of veto (*intercessio*) against any act by the magistrates. They were sacrosanct and could address a meeting (*ius agendi cum populo*). Each tribune could stop the action of his colleagues by veto. Thus the importance of the office

decreased when their number increased.

tríbus (= tribe). Originally there were three: Rámnes, Titiénses (or Títies), Lúceres, subdivided into ten °curiae. In 495 BC all Roman citizens were divided into twenty-one *tribus* (seventeen *rusticae*, four *urbanae*). This number increased gradually up to thirty-five in 241 BC. The *tribus* were the units for °census, and after 400 BC for the military levy; °comitia tributa.

triclínium (from τρι–(3); κλίνη (bed). The dining-room in a Roman house with an arrangement of three couches round the table on three of its four sides. Each couch held several guests, reclining upon their left elbow. °ill. 171; °domus.

tríerarchy (τριηραρχία). One of the

171. A triclinium in °Pompeii (Casa del Moralista).

°liturgies in Athens, the duty to bear the expense of the maintenance of a °trireme.

tríglyph (τρίγλυφος). A feature of the °frieze of the °Doric order, consisting of a rectangular grooved member separating the °metopes.

trímeter. A verse consisting of three feet, especially the acatalectic iambic trimeter: ⏐⏑⏐⏑⏐⏑⏐; °senarius.

trípod (τρίπους). A three-legged vessel of any kind. Mostly, however, the Greeks meant a pot or cauldron (°lebes), resting on three legs, which could be placed over the fire. These were ordinary domestic utensils, but they were also elaborated as works of art and as a

origin of this custom is unknown. According to legend, °Heracles stole the Tripod from the temple, when the Pythia refused to answer his question; °ills. 172, 173.

173. A stater of **Croton**. To the left of the °tripod is ϙqO (= K R O), to the right a crab.

172. The fight of °Heracles and °Apollo for the Delphic °tripod (Roman copy of an archaic Greek relief, 76 cm. high).

reward. Thus °Homer mentioned tripods as prizes given to the victors in several contests. The Tripod in °Delphi was used as a seat by the °Pythia. The

Triptólemus (Τριπτόλεμος). Favourite of °Demeter, who sent him on an expedition to teach mortals agriculture (Ovid *Met.* 5, 642-661).

tríreme (τριήρης). Warship with possibly three rowers on each bench, each rower pulling an individual oar. The exact arrangement is not known; °ills. 174; 175.

Trístia. °Ovid.

Tríton (Τρίτων). Son of °Poseidon and °Amphitrite, a sea god, represented with the body of a fish and the forelegs of a horse. He blew on a shell trumpet.

triumph. The solemn procession of a victorious commander with his army and spoils into Rome. He entered the city in a chariot drawn by four white horses, dressed in °purple, a golden wreath on his head; °ovatio. In the time of the emperors the triumphal procession was abandoned and 'insignia triumphália' were awarded instead.

triumphal arch. °arcus 2.

triúmvirate. An association of three joint rulers. The first triumvirate in Rome was a political alliance (60 BC) between Julius °Caesar, °Crassus and °Pompey; the second triumvirate of °Octavian, °Antony and °Lepidus in 43 BC, was made official by the *lex Titia*.

174. Probable position of rowers in a trireme.

175. Reconstruction of a trireme.

triumvíri. **1.** *t. aére argénto aúro flándo feriúndo.* Officials of the mint in the temple of °Juno Moneta. **2.** *t. capitáles.* Police officials, instituted c. 290 BC. **3.** *t. monetáles* = **1.** **4.** *t. noctúrni* = **2.** **5.** *t. réi públicae constituéndae.* Official name of the members of the second °triumvirate.

Trívia. °Hecate.

trívium. °Seven Liberal Arts.

tróchee. A metrical foot: ∠ ⌣.

Trojan War. According to tradition, Troy was taken by the Greeks after a siege of ten years and destroyed by fire. The immediate cause of the expedition was °Helen's abduction by °Paris from Sparta. °Homer. °Schliemann found Troy in 1871 when he excavated the mound of °Hissarlik. His, and subsequent excavations have revealed seven 'cities' on the site; Troy VII is regarded as being the °Homeric settlement.

tropaéum (τρόπαιον). A trophy, a memorial of victory, first used by the Greeks. It was a tree or pole driven into the ground on which were fixed arms, shields, helmets etc. taken from the enemy, the whole arranged to resemble a human form; ills. 176; °p. 164.

176. Tropaeum (= trophy).

Trophónius (Τροφώνιος). Legendary architect. With his brother Agamedes he built a temple to °Apollo at °Delphi. Later he was honoured as a god (Jupiter Trophonius) and had a temple at Lebadea, which became a celebrated oracular shrine.

Trós (Τρως). °Dardanidae; p. 60.

trúllo. Houses in the shape of a cone, made of rough stone, found in Apulia.

túba. °salpinx.

Túllia. Beloved daughter of °Cicero (79-45 BC), married to L. C. Píso, secondly to Fúrius Crássipes, later to P. Cornélius Dolabélla, who was notorious for his dissipation.

Tulliánum. Ancient subterranean prison in Rome, where criminals were executed.

Túllius. °Cicero: °Servius Tullius.

Túllus Hostílius. Third king of Rome, who destroyed Alba Longa and built the °Curia Hostilia.

túnica. Roman dress corresponding to the Greek °chiton. Roman women often wore two tunics ('indumenta'), the first called 'subucula' or 'interula', and over it the °stola, resembling the Ionic chiton.
The tunic for men corresponded to the shorter °chiton.

Túrnus. King of the Rutuli, engaged to Lavinia, daughter of °Latinus, who became the wife of °Aeneas. Turnus was killed by him.

Tutankhamún. Pharaoh of the 18th dynasty (c. 1358-1349 BC), son-in-law(?)

of °Amenhotep IV. He was compelled to discontinue the reforms of the latter. His tomb was found, with its contents almost intact (by Howard Carter), in 1922; °Ur.

Týche (Τύχη). **1.** Goddess of luck and chance. **2.** North-western part of Syracuse.

Týdeus (Τυδεύς). Father of °Diomedes.

týmpanum. The vertical recess of the °pediment, usually filled with sculpture, as at °Aegina, °Athens, °Olympia.

Tyndáreüs (Τυνδάρεος). °Leda.

Týphon (Τυφών). Son of °Gaea, a monster with a hundred fire-breathing dragon-like heads. According to legend, it was killed by °Zeus' thunderbolt and crushed under mount Etna in Sicily (Ovid *Met.* 5, 315-334).

týrant (τύραννος). An absolute ruler who seized power in a Greek state, °*e.g.* Dionysius, etc. In ancient times the word had a more favourable meaning than nowadays.

Tyrtaéus (Τύρταιος). Elegiac poet from Miletus, who later went from Athens to inspire the Spartans in the 2nd Messenian War c. 620-600 BC. Some fragments are extant.

U

Úlpian, *Domítius Ulpiánus.* Roman jurist, °praefectus praetorio of °Alexander Severus, killed in 228 AD by his soldiers. Many of his writings are represented in the °Digesta, 2462 fragments in all.

Úlysses. °Odysseus.

umbílicus Rómae. The symbolic centre of Rome, erected by °Constantine the Great c. 325 AD.

úmbo. Oval or round metal knob in the middle of a shield; °scutum; °weapons.

úncia. °Weights and measures 2d.

Unitárians. °Homer.

Ur. Town south of the Euphrates, which

was excavated by Woolley 1922-29. Six layers of habitation were found and such a wealth of buildings and valuables as to make the site second only in fame to that of °Tutankhamun's tomb.

Uránia (Οὐρανία). °Muses.

Uránus (Οὐρανός). Oldest god in the myth of creation, father of °Kronos.

Urgulanílla, *Plaútia Urgulanílla.* Married to °Claudius. Her children were °Drusus and °Claudia; °Julio-Claudian dynasty p. 101.

úrna. °Weights and measures 2c.

V

Válens, *Flávius Válens.* Emperor of the East Roman Empire (364-378 AD), was killed at Adrianopolis fighting against the °Goths.

Valéntian, *Flávius Valentiánus.* **1.** Roman Emperor (364-375 AD). He ruled over the Western Empire and left the Eastern Empire to °Valens. **2.** *Valentiánus III.* Emperor 425-455.

léges Valériae Horátiae. °secessio plebis.

lex Valéria, 509 BC. 'Ne quis magistratus civem Romanum adversus provocationem necaret neve verberaret' (= 'that no magistrate should kill or flog a Roman citizen against the °"provocatio" ').

Valerian, *P. Licínius Valeriánus.* Roman Emperor (253-260 AD), ruled with his son °Gallienus. He fought against the °Parthians and died in captivity. During his reign °Cyprianus died.

Valérius. 1. *Valérius Antias.* °Annalists. **2.** °Cato. **3.** °Catullus. **4.** *Valérius Fláccus* (*C. Valérius Fláccus Setínus Bálbus*) wrote an °epic 'Argonautica' of which the last part is lost. **5.** °Martial. **6.** *Valérius Máximus* wrote (c. 31 AD) anecdotes on the deeds and sayings of great men. **7.** °Messalla. **8.** °Probus.

Vandals. A Germanic race which invaded Gaul in 406 AD, overran Spain, crossed to Africa (429) and seized Carthage (439). Their king Gaiseric founded an empire and attacked Sicily, etc, and sacked Rome in 455. °Belisarius destroyed the empire in 534.

Vapheío (Βαφιόν). Prehistoric site near Sparta, where two magnificent gold prehistoric cups were found, possibly imported from Crete. °Helladic civilisation, °Minoan civilisation.

Várro. 1. *C. Teréntius Várro.* The first of his family to hold °curule office; consul in 216 BC, in which year he was defeated by °Hannibal at °Cannae. **2.** *M. Teréntius Várro.* He was born at Reate in the country of the Sabines, learned as well as active (c. 116-27 BC). Works: 'Rérum rusticárum libri III', on agriculture and cattle-breeding, etc, of which books 5-10 are partly extant; 'De língua Latína'. By 39 BC he had written approximately 500 books.

Várus, *P. Quintílius Várus.* When governor in Germany his army was destroyed in the Teutoburgian Forest by °Arminius in 9 AD. He took his own life.

vases. °Geometrie; °Red-figured; °Black-figured: °Lecythus.

véctigal. ager publicus.

Vegétius, *Flávius Vegétius Renátus.* He wrote a handbook on strategy (c. 400 AD), 'Epitome rei militaris', and possibly on veterinary medicine, 'Mulomedicina'.

Véii. Southern °Etruscan city, nine miles north of Rome. After a ten-year siege, it was taken and destroyed by °Camillus (396 BC). A terracotta statue of °Apollo was found there in 1916; °ill. 15.

Velábrum. A quarter in Rome between the °Capitol and the °Palatine, originally a swamp. The °Cloáca Máxima passed through it. Later it was drained and became one of the busiest city centres with a market-place for food; °plan p. 165.

vélites. °centuria.

Velléius Patérculus, *C. Velléius Patérculus.* °Legate of °Tiberius, who wrote a short history of Rome in two books up to 30 AD, in which Tiberius was favourably mentioned.

Venántius Fortunátus. Bishop of Poitiers (567-c. 610 AD). Two of his hymns are still sung: 'Vexilla regis prodeunt', and 'Pange, lingua, gloriosi'.

Ventris. °Linear B.

Vénus. Roman goddess identified with the Greek °Aphrodite.

Vénus and °Rome. A temple was built in honour of both by °Hadrian, between the temple of Jupiter Stator and the

Vercéllae

Colosseum; plan p. 165.
Vercéllae. °Cimbri.
Vercingétorix. Gallic king of the °Arverni, raised the revolt against °Caesar (52 BC). He was defeated near Alesia and was killed in prison in Rome.
Vergínia (= Virgínia). Daughter of the plebeian L. Verginius. She was killed by her own father to keep her out of the hands of the °decemvir App. °Claudius whose slave she had become by law (450 BC). This led to the fall of the *decemviri* (Liv. 3, 44-49).
Vérres, C. *Vérres.* A notorious governor of Sicily (73-71 BC) who made use of his office to benefit himself by taking Greek antiquities. °Cicero accused him at the request of the Sicilians. Cicero's five speeches have survived.
Vérrius Fláccus. Grammarian at the time of °Augustus. He wrote a dictionary, which is only known to us from an abstract of °Festus.
ver sácrum. In times of crisis, the Romans would make sacrifices of animals born in the spring. Children as soon as they were grown-up were driven out of the country.
Vertúmnus. °Etruscan god. His statue stood in the °vicus Tuscus, where tradesmen made frequent offerings to him.
Verulámium (St. Albans). Excavations on this site have given a great deal of information on town life in Roman °Britain.
verútum. Javelin with long metal head, used by soldiers of the fourth class according to the classification of Servius; (*veru* = broach).
Vérus, L. *Aurélius Vérus.* Co-emperor with °Marcus Aurelius (161-169 AD); °Aurélii. p. 31.
Vespásia Pólla. The mother of the Emperor °Vespasian.
Vespásian, T. *Flávius Vespasiánus* (69-79 AD). Successor to °Vitellius. Born in 9 AD, he was appointed °legatus in Palestine in 67 and conquered Jerusalem. Through the intrigues of °Mucianus he was proclaimed emperor by the soldiers in 69. In 70, he went to

Rome, restored the state finances, rebuilt the Capitoline Temple, and built the °Colosseum. Rome then enjoyed a period of peace and prosperity.
Vésta. The Roman hearth-goddess, the equivalent of the Greek °Hestia. In the round temple in Rome, a sacred fire was kept burning by the °Vestal Virgins; °plan p. 81.
Véstal Virgins. Four, later six, priestesses of °Vesta who lived in the 'Atrium Vestae'. They had to keep the sacred fire of Vesta burning and were not to marry, if at all, before they were 40. For offences they were entombed alive. They were greatly honoured, being always preceded by a °lictor; a criminal who came across them was set free.
vía. A Roman road; °name of road.
Víctor. °Aurelius.
victoriátus. Roman silver coin, in value $\frac{3}{4}$ of a °denarius; used from c. 209 BC; °ill. p. 164, no. 17.
vícus Iugárius. Street in Rome, leading from the forum past the temple of °Saturn to the south; plan p. 81.
vícus Túscus. Street in Rome connecting the °Velabrum with the forum. The book-shop of the °Sosii, publishers for °Horace, was here.
vigintiséx víri. Twenty-six officials in the time of the Republic, *i.e.* °tresviri capitáles, °tresviri monetáles, °decemviri stlítibus iudicándis, °quattuorviri viárum curandárum, °duumviri viis extra urbem purgéndis, four °praefecti iure dicúndo. The two latter offices were abolished by °Augustus. Afterwards these magistrates were called *viginti viri.*
vigínti viri. °vigintisex viri.
Víminal. One of the °Seven Hills on which Rome was built.
Vipsánia. °Agrippina.
Vipsánius, M. *Vipsánius Agríppa* (c. 63-12 BC). Consul in 37, defeated °Pompey at °Mylae. In 31 °Octavian owed his victory at sea, near Actium, mainly to him. He married a daughter of °Augustus, °Julia, and became his counsellor and friend. He built the °Pantheon in Rome; °Julio-Claudian

dynasty p. 101.

Vírgil, *P. Vergílius Máro* (c. 70-19 ḃc). Born in Andes near Mantua. Most notable of all Roman poets. Works: **1.** *Bucólica* (Bucolics), later called *Éclogae* (Eclogues), pastoral poetry modelled on °Theocritus, describing an idyllic country life. He praised his patrons °Octavian, °Maecenas, °Asinius Pollio and others. To Asinius he dedicated the fourth Eclogue, which foretold the birth of a 'wonder-child'. **2.** *Geórgica* (Georgics), a didactic poem dedicated to Maecenas, dealt with agriculture, the cultivation of fruit trees, cattle-breeding and bee-keeping. **3.** *Aenéïs* (Aeneid), an °epic poem, the story of °Aeneas, in which he also glorified °Augustus and the origins of °Rome. **4.** Some lesser poems were possibly in the collection °Catalepton. °Aetna, °Ciris, °Copa, °Culex, °Moretum were probably not by Virgil.

Virocónium. °Wroxeter; °Britain.

Vísigoths. °Goths.

Vitéllius, *A. Vitéllius.* Proclaimed emperor in 69 AD by his soldiers in Germany, but soon after he had overcome °Otho at Bedriacum, his troops were defeated by °Vespasian. Vitellius was murdered in Rome.

Vitrúvius, *M. Vitrúvius Póllio.* A Roman architect, inspector of public buildings for °Augustus, who wrote his famous (extant) treatise 'De Architectúra' (c. 25 BC).

Vix. (North-east of Châtillon-sur-Seine.) In 1953 a Celtic grave was found there, dating from c. 500 BC. It was the grave of a princess, who had been buried with great splendour. A magnificent bronze °krater was brought to light, 1.64 m. high and weighing 208 kg, probably

°Etruscan in origin, it has been hammered out of one piece to a thickness of one millimeter all over.

Vólsci. Tribe in Central Italy. Together with the °Aequi they were often at war with Rome. By 338 BC all Volsci became subject to Rome; °Coriolanus.

vólute. The spiral or scroll ornament which occurs in the °capitals of the °Ionic and °Corinthian orders.

vólute kráter. °Krater with handles in the form of volutes rising above the rim; °François vase; °ill. 177.

177. Attic °volute-krater (c. 450 BC). On the body is a battle scene with °Amazons. On the neck a Dionysiac procession.

Vúlcan (Vulcánus). Roman god of fire and metal-working identified with the Greek °Hephaestus.

Vúlgate. Latin version of the Bible, translated by °Hieronymus.

W

wax tablet. A pair (or more) of pieces of wood hinged together and covered with wax on both sides. It could be written upon with a pointed instrument (stylus) and was largely used for correspondence, or preparatory work; °ill. 178.

weapons. For spears: °gaesum, °pilum,

178. In the University library of Leyden are seven wax-tablets ('Tabulae ceratae Assendelf-tianae') of the 3rd cent. AD found in °Palmyra, and made of birch wood. On them a schoolboy having little Greek wrote some fables of °Babrius. Here are the first four lines:

τονδοιποδεσμενοιστ
οπροσθενηθυμειδιεσωζον
ωσδηλθενεισμεσασυλασοζοισ
ταχερατασυνπλαχεισεθηρευθη

°verutum; for shields: °aspis, °clipeus, °parma, °scutum; for helmets: °helmet; for swords: gladius, pugio, °spatha; for arrows: arrow; also bow, °catapult, °onager.

weaving. A skill mentioned by °Homer. The loom was vertical and so was the warp which had weights attached to the bottom to make it hang straight. Two horizontal rods attached to alternate threads facilitated the passing through of the woof; °ill. 179.

179. Weaving: Penelope and Telemachus at the loom.

Weights and measuresı
1. Greek:
a. Measures of length (Attic)

δάκτυλος	1.85 cm
παλαιστή = 4 δάκτυλοι	7.4 cm
πούς = 4 παλαίσται	29.6 cm
πῆχυς = 1½ πόδες	44.4 cm
ὀργυιά = 4 πήχεις	1.77 m
πλέθρον = 100 πόδες	29.6 m
στάδιον (Attic) = 100 ὀργ.	177.6 m
στάδιον (Olympia)	192.27 m

b. Square measure

πλέθρον	876 m²

c. Liquid measures

κύαθος	4.5 cl
κοτύλη = 6 κύαθοι	27 cl
χοῦς = 12 κοτύλαι	3.24 l
μετρητής = 12 χόες	38.88 l

d. Dry measures

κοτύλη	27 cl
χοῖνιξ = 4 κοτύλαι	1.08 l
μέδιμνος = 192 κοτύλαι	51.84 l

e. Weights

χαλκοῦς	0.09 g
ὀβολός = 8 χαλκοῖ	0.727 g
δραχμή = 6 ὀβολοί	4.36 g
μνᾶ = 100 δραχμαί	436.6 g
τάλαντον = 60 μναῖ	26.196 kg

2. Roman:
a. Measures of length

dígitus	1.85 cm
palmus = 4 dígiti	7.4 cm
pes = 4 palmi	29.6 cm
cúbitus = 1½ pedes	44.4 cm
°passus = 5 pedes	1.479 m
actus = 120 pedes	35.489 m
mille passus = 1000 passus	1479 m
stadium	185 m

b. Square measures

pes quadrátus	0.087 m²
iugerum	2523.3 m²

c. Liquid and dry measures

cýathus	4.5 cl
quartarius = 3 cýathi	13.5 cl
hemína = 6 cýathi	27 cl
sextarius = 12 cýathi	54.6 cl
(liquid measure only)	
congius = 6 sextarii	3.24 l
urna = 24 sextarii	13 l
amphora = 2 urnae	26.2 l
(dry measure only)	
modius	8.73 l

d. Weights

síliqua	0.189 g
óbolus = 3 síliquae	0.568 g
scrípulum = 6 síliquae	1.137 g
drachma = 3 scrípula	3.411 g
uncia = 8 drachmae	27.288 g
libra = 12 unciae	327.453 g

Works and Days. °Hesiod.

Wroxeter (Viroconium). Site of a Roman town near Shrewsbury, founded in the 1st century AD. A street-plan and many houses have been revealed by air photography and excavations; °Britain.

X

Xanthíppe (Ξανθίππη). Wife of °Socrates. The nagging reputation of Xanthippe was based on the statements of later °Cynic philosophers.

Xanthíppus (Ξανθίππος). **1.** Father of °Pericles. **2.** Spartan general in the service of the Carthaginians, who defeated °Regulus (255 BC).

Xenócrates (Ξενοκράτης). °Academy.

Xenóphanes (Ξενοφάνης), of Colophon. He lived in Elea in southern Italy in the 6th century BC. He denied the existence of anthropomorphic gods and had strange ideas on astronomy. According to him there was one god, invisible, spherical, not finite and not infinite.

Xénophon (Ξενοφῶν). **1.** Athenian aristocrat, pupil of °Socrates. Invited by a friend, he joined the Greek mercenaries of °Cyrus, and was an interested spectator at the battle of °Cunaxa and afterwards became commander of the Greeks. His writings have survived. The most important of them are: 1. About Socrates: a. *Apológia Socrátis.* b. *Memorabília.* c. *Sympósium.* 2. *Cyropaedía* (Κύρου παιδεία), the education of a prince. 3. *Anábasis,* the expedition of the Greeks through Asia Minor. 4. *Hellénica,* sequel to the work of °Thucydides to 362 BC. 5. *On Horsemanship.* **2.** *Xénophon of Ephesus* (2nd-3rd cent. AD). Wrote a novel 'Ephesíaca'.

Xérxes (Ξέρξης). King of Persia (485-465 BC), son of °Darius I and Atossa. His expedition against Greece ended in defeat at °Salamis (480).

Z

Záma. Town in North Africa on the frontier of Numidia and Carthaginian territory. °Hannibal's camp was pitched here on the eve of the so-called 'battle of Zama', which was actually fought at some distance from the town.

Zéno (Ζήνων). **1.** Of Elea (5th cent. BC). Pupil of °Parmenides. He defended Parmenides' theory of the indivisible unity of all being by a 'reductio ad absurdum' of the normal idea about divisibility: Achilles and the tortoise. **2.** Of Citium in Cyprus (c. 336-264 BC), founder of the °Stoic doctrine.

Zenóbia (Ζηνοβία). Queen of °Palmyra (267-273 AD).

Zenodotus (Ζηνόδοτος), of Ephesus. A scholar, and first head of the °library at Alexandria (c. 285 BC). He published the first critical text of °Homer; °library at Alexandria.

Zéphyrus (Ζέφυρος). God of the West wind, husband of °Chloris.

Zétes (Ζήτης). °Calaïs.

zeúgma. Two subjects used with the same predicate so that one of the applications is forced: 'pacem an bellum gerens'.

Zeús (Ζεύς). Son of °Kronos, lord of °Olympus, supreme god of the Greeks, represented with beard and wavy hair. His most important temples were at °Dodona and °Olympia. His attributes were a thunderbolt, oak-wreath, aegis and eagle; °Hera. °Jupiter.

Zeúxis (Ζεῦξις). Painter at Athens at the time of °Socrates.

Zoílus (Ζωίλος). °Homeromástix.

zóphorus. °frieze.